Reforming Capitalism, Going Digital and Green

The book describes Japan's efforts since 2015 to exit the deflationary 'lost decades' and chart a new economic course through digital and green transformation, as well as 'new/sustainable capitalism.'

Japan is attempting to revitalize and reorient its economy through digital and green transformation. At the same time it is seeking to make a more equitable and sustainable transition through 'new/sustainable capitalism.' These twin efforts face strong headwinds, not least from a declining and ageing population, and social divisions from earlier neo-liberal policies. There are also contradictions, which are highlighted by corporate governance and labour market reforms, as well as technology push and competitiveness versus social needs-oriented innovation. The chapters in this volume, by Japanese and non-Japanese experts, highlight the emerging path of change towards Society 5.0, the quest to combine green and growth, and continued obstacles for full participation of women. They especially highlight the need for Japan to invest in people again, matching 'human-centred' rhetoric with concrete policy commitments and implementation. Only then will Japan truly emerge from its 'lost decades.'

This book is relevant for students, researchers, and policymakers in the fields of economics, sustainable development, environmental studies, public policy, and social sciences.

The chapters in this book were originally published as a special issue of *Asia Pacific Business Review*.

D. Hugh Whittaker is Professor in the Economy and Business of Japan at the Nissan Institute of Japanese Studies, University of Oxford, and author of the recent book *Building a New Economy: Japan's Digital and Green Transformation*.

Yoshifumi Nakata is Professor of Strategic Human Resource Management and Director of the Research Institute of STEM at Doshisha University. His research focuses on the relation between work environment and engineers' performance.

Reforming Capitalism, Going Digital and Green
Japan's Approach

Edited by
D. Hugh Whittaker and Yoshifumi Nakata

LONDON AND NEW YORK

First published 2025
by Routledge
4 Park Square, Milton Park, Abingdon, Oxon OX14 4RN

and by Routledge
605 Third Avenue, New York, NY 10158

Routledge is an imprint of the Taylor & Francis Group, an informa business

Preface © 2025 D. Hugh Whittaker and Yoshifumi Nakata.
Introduction, Chapters 3–7, 9 and 11 © 2025 Taylor & Francis
Chapter 1 © 2024 John Buchanan and Simon Deakin. Originally published as Open Access.
Chapter 2 © 2024 D. Hugh Whittaker. Originally published as Open Access.
Chapter 8 © 2024 Hiromi M. Yokoyama, Yuko Ikkatai, Euan McKay, Atsushi Inoue, Azusa Minamizaki and Kei Kano. Originally published as Open Access.
Chapter 10 © 2024 Fangmiao Zou. Originally published as Open Access.

With the exception of Chapters 1, 2, 8 and 10, no part of this book may be reprinted or reproduced or utilised in any form or by any electronic, mechanical, or other means, now known or hereafter invented, including photocopying and recording, or in any information storage or retrieval system, without permission in writing from the publishers. For details on the rights for Chapters 1, 2, 8 and 10, please see the chapters' Open Access footnotes.

Trademark notice: Product or corporate names may be trademarks or registered trademarks, and are used only for identification and explanation without intent to infringe.

British Library Cataloguing in Publication Data
A catalogue record for this book is available from the British Library

ISBN13: 978-1-032-98615-9 (hbk)
ISBN13: 978-1-032-98617-3 (pbk)
ISBN13: 978-1-003-59962-3 (ebk)

DOI: 10.4324/9781003599623

Typeset in Myriad Pro

by Newgen Publishing UK

Publisher's Note
The publisher accepts responsibility for any inconsistencies that may have arisen during the conversion of this book from journal articles to book chapters, namely the inclusion of journal terminology.

Disclaimer
Every effort has been made to contact copyright holders for their permission to reprint material in this book. The publishers would be grateful to hear from any copyright holder who is not here acknowledged and will undertake to rectify any errors or omissions in future editions of this book.

Contents

Citation Information	vii
Notes on Contributors	ix
Preface	xii
D. Hugh Whittaker and Yoshifumi Nakata	

Introduction: reforming Japanese capitalism   1
D. Hugh Whittaker and Yoshifumi Nakata

1   Has Japan's corporate governance reform reached a turning point? Some cautionary notes   13
John Buchanan and Simon Deakin

2   Japan's quest for a sustainable, virtuous circle of growth and distribution   31
D. Hugh Whittaker

3   Society 5.0 and new capitalism: complementarities and contradictions   47
Sébastien Lechevalier

4   The transformation of science, technology and innovation (STI) policy in Japan   65
Tateo Arimoto

5   Japan's triple sustainability challenge   79
Tokutaro Nakai

6   Evidence-based policy making in Japan's public expenditure: compatibility of fiscal health and investing for the future   94
Nobuo Akai

7   Much to be done in Japan's family and gender equality policies   108
Nobuko Nagase

8 Can affirmative action overcome STEM gender inequality in Japan? Expectations and concerns 123
Hiromi M. Yokoyama, Yuko Ikkatai, Euan McKay, Atsushi Inoue, Azusa Minamizaki and Kei Kano

9 Remedying Japan's deficient investment in people 139
Yoshifumi Nakata

10 The 'new trinity' reform of labour markets in Japan 156
Fangmiao Zou

11 Japan's 'consensual' variety of digital capitalism and its global relevance 175
Harald Kümmerle and Franz Waldenberger

Index 192

Citation Information

The following chapters in this book were originally published in *Asia Pacific Business Review*, volume 30, issue 3 (2024). When citing this material, please use the original page numbering for each article, as follows:

Introduction

Reforming Japanese capitalism: introduction
D. Hugh Whittaker and Yoshifumi Nakata
Asia Pacific Business Review, volume 30, issue 3 (2024), pp. 421–432

Chapter 1

Has Japan's corporate governance reform reached a turning point? Some cautionary notes
John Buchanan and Simon Deakin
Asia Pacific Business Review, volume 30, issue 3 (2024), pp. 433–450

Chapter 2

Japan's quest for a sustainable, virtuous circle of growth and innovation
D. Hugh Whittaker
Asia Pacific Business Review, volume 30, issue 3 (2024), pp. 451–466

Chapter 3

Society 5.0 and new capitalism: complementarities and contradictions
Sébastien Lechevalier
Asia Pacific Business Review, volume 30, issue 3 (2024), pp. 467–484

Chapter 4

The transformation of science, technology and innovation (STI) policy in Japan
Tateo Arimoto
Asia Pacific Business Review, volume 30, issue 3 (2024), pp. 485–498

Chapter 5

Japan's triple sustainability challenge
Tokutaro Nakai
Asia Pacific Business Review, volume 30, issue 3 (2024), pp. 499–513

Chapter 6

Evidence-based policy making in Japan's public expenditure: compatibility of fiscal health and investing for the future
Nobuo Akai
Asia Pacific Business Review, volume 30, issue 3 (2024), pp. 514–527

Chapter 7

Much to be done in Japan's family and gender equality policies
Nobuko Nagase
Asia Pacific Business Review, volume 30, issue 3 (2024), pp. 528–542

Chapter 8

Can affirmative action overcome STEM gender inequality in Japan? Expectations and concerns
Hiromi M. Yokoyama, Yuko Ikkatai, Euan McKay, Atsushi Inoue, Azusa Minamizaki and Kei Kano
Asia Pacific Business Review, volume 30, issue 3 (2024), pp. 543–559

Chapter 9

Remedying Japan's deficient investment in people
Yoshifumi Nakata
Asia Pacific Business Review, volume 30, issue 3 (2024), pp. 560–576

Chapter 10

The 'new trinity' reform of labour markets in Japan
Fangmiao Zou
Asia Pacific Business Review, volume 30, issue 3 (2024), pp. 577–595

Chapter 11

Japan's 'consensual' variety of digital capitalism and its global relevance
Harald Kümmerle and Franz Waldenberger
Asia Pacific Business Review, volume 30, issue 3 (2024), pp. 596–612

For any permission-related enquiries please visit:
www.tandfonline.com/page/help/permissions

Notes on Contributors

Nobuo Akai, Professor of Public Policy at Osaka University, publishes in the fields of public economics, public policy and finance, local public finance, and fiscal and tax policy. He sits on several government panels, including the Financial Policy Council and the Tax Deliberation Council.

Tateo Arimoto is Principal Fellow at the Center for Research and Development Strategy at Japan Science and Technology Agency (JST-CRDS) and a visiting professor at the National Graduate Institute for Policy Studies (GRIPS). He is a Fellow of the International Science Council and former Director General of S&T Policy Bureau at the Ministry of Education, Culture, Sports, Science and Technology (MEXT), Japan.

John Buchanan is Research Associate at the Centre for Business Research at the University of Cambridge. He has been a non-executive director of J-Power, a Japanese electrical utility, since 2016. Beginning in 2002 he has undertaken research primarily in two areas: Japanese corporate governance and hedge fund activism. His background prior to academic work was as a commercial banker for 13 years and as an investment banker specializing in mergers and acquisitions for 15 years.

Simon Deakin is Professor of Law and Director of the Centre for Business Research at the University of Cambridge. He specializes in labour, corporate and private law. His books include *The Law of the Labour Market* (2005, with Frank Wilkinson), *Hedge Fund Activism in Japan: The Limits of Shareholder Primacy* (2012, with John Buchanan and Dominic Chai), and *Is Law Computable? Critical Perspectives on Law and Artificial Intelligence* (2021, with Christopher Markou).

Yuko Ikkatai is Associate Professor at the Institute of Human and Social Sciences, Kanazawa University. Her current interests include citizens' participation and gender diversity in science and technology. She has published several papers in journals including the *Journal of Science Communication*, *Public Understanding of Science*, *AI and Ethics*, and *Physical Review Physics Education Research*.

Atsushi Inoue is Associate Senior Fellow at the Nippon Institute for Research Advancement. His research interests include the economics of education and education policy. He has published in journals such as *Education Economics*, *Asian Economic Papers*, *PLOS One*, and the *International Journal of Science Education*.

Kei Kano is Professor in Science Communication Laboratory, Faculty of Education, Shiga University, Director of the Nissan Global Foundation and Director of Japanese Society of Science Education. He focuses on inclusive, culturally relevant science communication/ public engagement with women and the deaf community, and has been involved in the production of science education TV programmes by NHK.

Harald Kümmerle is Senior Research Fellow at the German Institute for Japanese Studies (DIJ) in Tokyo. His research interests include the history of mathematics, digital humanities, new materialism, and critical data studies. Publications related to this work include 'Japanese Data Strategies, Global Surveillance Capitalism, and the "LINE Problem"' (2022, in *Matter: Journal of New Materialist Research*) and 'More Than a Certification Scheme: Information Banks in Japan Under Changing Norms of Data Usage' (2023, in A. Khare and W. W. Baber (eds.) *Adopting and Adapting Innovation in Japan's Digital Transformation*).

Sébastien Lechevalier is Professor at the School of Advanced Studies in Social Sciences (EHESS) in Paris, specialized in the study of Asian Capitalisms, with a focus on the relations between technologies and societies. He is the president of the Fondation France-Japon de l'EHESS (FFJ), editor of *Socio-Economic Review*, and monthly columnist for *Le Monde*. His publications include *The Great Transformation of Japanese Capitalism* (Routledge, 2014) and *Innovation Beyond Technology* (2019).

Euan McKay is Project Associate Professor in the Strategic Planning Office at Kobe University. His research interests include issues related to diversity, minority experiences in higher education, and the history of Anglo-Japanese relations.

Azusa Minamizaki is Project Assistant Professor at the Global Multi-campus, Nagoya University. Her research interests are in science communication and STEM gender issues. She is particularly interested in the environment of middle and high school female students and school teachers.

Nobuko Nagase is Professor of Labour Economics and Social Policy at Ochanomizu University, Tokyo. Her comparative research interests include wage structure and work choice, labour market regulation and social security, tax and other institutional effects on work and gender, marital behaviour, and child-birth timing. She has published in *Japanese Economic Review*, *Asian Economic Policy Review*, *Demographic Research Econometric Review*, and *The Quarterly of Social Security Research*, among others.

Tokutaro Nakai is the Executive Advisor of Nippon Steel Corporation, Japan. He joined Japan's Ministry of Finance in 1985 and was transferred to the Ministry of the Environment (MOE) in 2011. From 2020 to 2022 he was Vice Minister of MOE.

Yoshifumi Nakata is Professor of Strategic Human Resource Management at the Graduate School of Policy and Management as well as the Director of Research Institute of STEM at Doshisha University, Kyoto. His research interests focus on relation between work environment and engineers/software engineers' performance.

Franz Waldenberger is Director of the German Institute for Japanese Studies (DIJ) in Tokyo. He is on leave from Munich University where he holds a professorship in the

Japanese economy. His research focuses on the Japanese economy, corporate governance, and international management. He is editor in chief of the international peer-reviewed journal *Contemporary Japan*. His recent publications include *The Future of Financial Systems in the Digital Age* (2022, co-edited with M. Heckel).

D. Hugh Whittaker is Professor in the Economy and Business of Japan and Director of the Nissan Institute of Japanese Studies at the University of Oxford. His new book is called *Building a New Economy: Japan's Digital and Green Transformation* (2024).

Hiromi M. Yokoyama is Professor at Centre for Data-Driven Discovery (CD3), Kavli Institute for the Physics and Mathematics of the Universe (Kavli IPMU), University of Tokyo. She has led the group for several years and her research interests are in science and technology studies, especially diversity issues, AI ethics, Big science policy, and trust in science.

Fangmiao Zou obtained a DPhil in area studies (Japan) at the University of Oxford, and is currently a research and teaching associate of Japanese economy and business at the Nissan Institute of Japanese Studies, University of Oxford.

Preface

As editors and conference organizers, we were warned by colleagues against giving too much prominence to Japan's 'new form of capitalism,' partly because the concept is vague, and particularly because Kishida Fumio, its champion, was not expected to last long as prime minister. His flagship economic vision would be consigned to history just as quickly, we were assured. While it would be wrong to say that politics and personalities don't matter in Japan, we took the view that the issues taken up in this volume, from Society 5.0, digital transformation (DX), and green transformation (GX), through to the business federation Keidanren's 'sustainable capitalism,' Kishida's 'new capitalism,' and various associated plans like 'digital garden city nation' and 'new trinity' labour market reforms, touch on enduring challenges that need to be addressed by whomever is in power. Japanese prime ministers seek to make a mark with flagship schemes, moreover, but they are almost always from the same political party, and not in the habit of comprehensively tearing up their predecessors' policies out of ideological conviction, posturing, or pique. There is considerable continuity in Japan underneath passing slogans – and prime ministers – so we considered the perspectives we included to be durable rather than fleeting.

In fact Kishida lasted three years, nowhere as long as Abe, to be sure, but a respectable term nonetheless. Kishida's election was greeted by a 7 per cent fall of shares on the Tokyo Stock Exchange, dubbed the 'Kishida shock,' as investors feared that his 'growth and distribution' mantra might mean less structural reform and higher taxes. His successor, Ishiba Shigeru, was likewise greeted by a 5 per cent fall in late September 2024 on similar fears, his reputation as an Abe opponent, and advocate of government policies to promote rural revitalization, among other reasons. Ishiba's inaugural speech to the Diet was carefully watched for hints of his priorities. Amongst the many issues he touched upon, one that stood out was his use of *anzen* (security) and *anshin* (peace of mind). *Anzen* reflected growing geopolitical tensions. Pay and conditions of those serving in the military would be a priority, and his initial cabinet line-up notably featured three former defence ministers (including himself). *Anshin* signalled attention to rural revitalization, opportunities for youth and women, and a wish to bring the ¥1500 average minimum wage target forward to the end of the 2020s instead of the mid-2030s. Although 'new capitalism' only got a passing mention, the *anshin* priorities suggested considerable underlying continuity with Kishida's 'putting people first,' 'investment in people,' and push for higher wages in 'growth and distribution'.

Ishiba's decision to call a snap election less than a month into his term of office led to his Liberal Democratic Party and its junior coalition partner Komeito losing their parliamentary majority. Ironically perhaps, investors this time largely shrugged the prospective uncertainty off. The outcome was unclear at the time of writing; while commentators speculated on Ishiba's chances of survival, and policy drift, there is conversely a chance that having to work with the Democratic Party for the People will reinvigorate the focus on the policies described in this book. Time will tell. New as well as old challenges will need to be addressed. First, as mentioned, security issues, encompassing defence, cyber, economic, energy, and food, will continue to reshape not only Japan's international relations, but also state structures, processes, policies, and state-business-civil society relations.

Second, as digital and green transformation deepen, the optimistic view of the early 2020s that they are twin wheels of a cart moving in tandem towards Society 5.0 is giving way to a more realistic view that they might actually be getting out of kilter, especially with energy-hungry AI threatening emissions reduction targets. Society 5.0 remains a beacon, but can it really accommodate both digital and green, and will it really embody an innovation system oriented towards solving social needs as Society 5.0's proponents insist, or rather competitiveness challenges, which do not necessarily coincide either…

Third, systemic tensions in the 'growth and distribution' mantra also persist, most obviously between the maintenance of neoliberal economic management and the adoption of post-neoliberal sustainable/new capitalism policies. Despite his personal convictions, Kishida effectively placed his bets on both horses following the 'Kishida shock.' Chagrined by Tokyo's plunge in the Global Financial Centre Index, the central and Tokyo metropolitan governments have vowed to restore Tokyo to its former position, to intensify efforts to turn dormant savings into investments, and to make companies ever more responsive to shareholder interests through corporate governance reform. The sale of assets and reciprocally held shares, share buybacks, and efforts to boost share price-to-book value ratios continues apace.

As Whittaker (2024) puts it, there are three 'spirits' of contemporary Japanese capitalism – financialized, (new developmental) state, and communitarian or stakeholder-oriented – which pull in different directions, but are in a dynamic, and *potentially* constructive relationship. Development Bank of Japan (DBJ) surveys suggest that domestic capital spending by large companies is on an upward trend, buoyed in 2023–24 by manufacturing sector investment in electric vehicles and semiconductors, as well as city-centre redevelopments. The '2024 logistics crisis,' in which a shortage of drivers was compounded by the tightening of labour regulations, saw an upturn in digitalization, joint delivery, and other productivity-enhancing measures in industries affected. R&D spending is up too, and greater attention is being paid to recruitment and retention of human resources. Indeed, the buds of productivity and real wage growth are beginning to appear after more than two decades of stagnation. If sustained, they may point to a definitive break from the 'lost decades,' and a new trajectory of 'growth and distribution.' And if so – another, big, 'if' – it may be that Japan manages to achieve a dynamic balance in its capitalisms as it seeks to build Society 5.0.

The contributors to this book would urge caution in this regard. They point especially to ongoing challenges, especially in reversing the stultifying effects of wage suppression, 'portfolio employment' dualism, and lack of investment in people. Population ageing and decline might provide a powerful incentive for change, but a vibrant labour market and employment in which women (and non-Japanese) can 'shine' to borrow Abe's expression also requires changes to social policy and attitudes which are deep-rooted. Multiple issues need to be addressed simultaneously to achieve economic, social, and environmental sustainability. The country is not alone in this quest. As we argue in the Introduction, Japan is worth studying not because it has a new model, as was the post-war manufacturing-centric set of institutions, or because it is exotic and different, but because it is struggling with challenges common to other 'mature' economies, often in sharper relief.

D. Hugh Whittaker and Yoshifumi Nakata
October 2024

Reference

D.H. Whittaker (2024), *Building a New Economy: Japan's Digital and Green Transformation*, Oxford: Oxford University Press.

Introduction: reforming Japanese capitalism

D. Hugh Whittaker and Yoshifumi Nakata

ABSTRACT

Is Japan creating a new economic model through digital and green transformation which will overcome its 'lost decades' lethargy and demographic challenges? Do Society 5.0, DX, GX, 'new/sustainable capitalism', Digital Garden City Nation and other initiatives represent a well-intentioned mish-mash, or something new and potentially coherent which other countries should take notice of? These questions animated a conference held in Oxford in February 2023, and subsequently informed the 11 articles in this special issue by European and Japanese academics and policy makers. The collection identifies tensions and contradictions but also significant changes in in corporate governance, innovation, public policy and human resources, which may point to a new direction for Japanese capitalism.

Introduction

In 2021 Japan's incoming Prime Minister Kishida Fumio[1] called for Japan to adopt a 'new form of capitalism' to recreate a virtuous circle of growth and distribution. He subsequently set out four priority areas: people; science, technology and innovation (STI); startups; and digital and green transformation. In particular, he emphasized the first of these: 'Investment in human capital is at the heart of the growth strategy of the Kishida Administration', he stressed in his May 2022 Guildhall speech in London.

The call was not universally welcomed. In fact, the reaction from investors was swift – the value of shares on the Tokyo Stock Exchange plunged by almost 7% in just over a week, in what some called the 'Kishida shock'. Investors did not like mention of the word 'distribution', especially if they might be expected to provide some of it. The Prime Minister modified his message, putting more emphasis on the 'growth' part of his formula.

There are echoes in the 'new form of capitalism' of Japan's post-war high growth economic model which was centred on manufacturing. This model achieved a high degree of institutional coherence at the macro- and micro-levels of the economy. The economic landscape of the 2020s, however, is quite different. Japan is undergoing digital and green transformations. It is a mature economy, indeed one which is demographically ageing and shrinking, and one in which an increasingly large share of gross national income is earned from overseas investments. If Japan is to achieve a new growth model, it will be with a quite different institutional configuration than the post-war model.

Other countries are also undergoing digital and green transformations, are demographically ageing and/or facing structural labour shortages, with sluggish productivity growth, and derive substantial income from overseas investments, the UK being one such example. Japan is not unique, but the rapidity of change may be. And there are distinctive features in Japan's approach to structural change, including the concept of Society 5.0, which is a kind of future-oriented beacon, and seeks to balance state, market and social relations in the country's transformations, and to achieve a new form of macro- and micro-level institutional coherence.

Outside Japan little is known about these efforts to build a new economy. The 'lost decades' narrative, in which institutional coherence was lost, growth faltered and inequality surged, combined with demographic pessimism over Japan's future, colours most discussions, admittedly not without reason. While former Prime Minister Abe's cry of 'Japan is back' and his three arrows garnered much attention in the 2010s, any lessons for outside observers tended to focus on how to avoid deflationary 'Japanization', a complete turnaround from the learn-from-Japanese-management 'Japanization' of the 1980s.

With less fanfare however, from around 2015, a series of policy initiatives have begun to re-orient the economy in a new direction, with the aim of building a new growth model around a digital and green economy. 'Society 5.0', digital and green transformation (DX, GX), 'green growth strategy', Suga's decarbonization targets and (Japan Business Federation) Keidanren's 'sustainable capitalism' laid the path for Kishida's 'new form of capitalism'. A question is, however, whether all these initiatives are simply a clamour born of desperation to escape from more lost decades, or whether they are beginning to create something new, something coherent, and something worth taking notice of. Are they disparate and lacking ideational and institutional cohesion; or do they have the potential to really set Japan on a new path?

This was the overarching question which a conference in Oxford on 17–18 February 2023 was organized around, with the title 'Reforming capitalism, going digital and green: Does Japan hold answers?' 'Answers' here meant both for Japan, and potentially for others. A group of mainly Japanese and European academics and policy makers gathered to present their views and debate this. In addition to giving presentations and commentary at the conference, sufficient interest was generated to turn their thoughts into articles, which have been assembled in this special issue, with the addition of two further papers. Individually the articles cover different aspects of Japan's current economic transformation; collectively they present a unique view of current developments in the Japanese economy, and the challenges to building Society 5.0 and a new, post-neoliberal, form of capitalism.

One powerful impetus for change mentioned in several of the articles, was the experience of the triple earthquake, tsunami and nuclear disaster of 11 March 2011, and subsequent natural disasters, which highlighted the need for socio-economic resilience at the local level. Another was the Global Financial Crisis, and the advent of Trump and Brexit in neoliberalism's heartlands, adding to unease about growing inequality and social division within Japan. Yet another was unease about the digital transformation, both in terms of the perception that Japan was falling behind, but also that Japan needs to chart a path between domination by oligopolistic 'Big Tech' on the one hand, and an overbearing state on the other, represented by the US and China respectively.

The coherence and adequacy of Japan's responses are questioned in the collection of papers. There are tensions, as well as contradictions – in labour market policy, corporate governance reform, in approaches to decarbonization, and so on. Yet there are also strengths which are apparent, including increasingly strong but supple coordination measures and policy continuity. Both are meaningful for other countries which face similar challenges to take notice of.

The remainder of this Introduction gives a brief overview of the papers, and more importantly, how they fit together, and the logic of the order in which they are presented.

Overview of the articles

Institutions and the way they fit together – or do not – are an important factor in determining whether Japanese capitalism has changed. The French Régulation school refers to 'viable institutional configurations' in which institutions become complementary, but some institutions are more influential than others. This influence and the configuration can change over time. In particular, the wage-labour institutional nexus which was central to post-war Fordism was supplanted in the late 1970s to 1990s by a new monetary and financial configuration in many countries, accompanied by deregulation and the relative demotion of secure employment (Boyer and Saillard 2001). This happened partially in Japan, with the result of declining institutional coherence. The question addressed in this special issue is whether this partial monetary and financial configuration is persisting, or whether a new institutional configuration is starting to take shape, and if so, what are its contours.

The first two papers take up this question through the lens of corporate governance, and indeed show a continued trajectory of financialization and emphasis of shareholder interests rather than their curtailment, as 'new/sustainable capitalism' would have. It is possible to say, as Whittaker (2024a) does, that corporate governance and investor relations have become the key institutional nexus, *and* an axis of tension, as employment relations were in the post-war period. In the latter case these tensions resulted in considerable institutional innovation which was at the heart of 'Japanese-style management' and was an important factor in Japanese economic growth centred on manufacturing. Could the same happen again, with a creative resolution to these tensions?

The first paper, by Deakin and Buchanan (2024), gives a careful account of the evolution of Japan's corporate governance over the past two decades, focusing in particular on the introduction of the Stewardship Code and Corporate Governance Code in 2014 and 2015, respectively, as 'two wheels of the cart' of corporate governance reform. These codes have undergone subsequent revision, and as the authors show, the direction of travel has been a shift from a principles-based, 'comply or explain' approach towards one which is rules-based and prescriptive, driven by the Financial Services Agency and the Tokyo Stock Exchange, and hence increasingly favourable to shareholder interests.

The original authors of the Corporate Governance Code expected that it would 'contribute to the development and success of companies, investors, and the Japanese economy as a whole through individual companies' self-motivated actions so as to achieve sustainable growth and increase corporate value over the mid- to long-term'. While increasingly prescriptive disclosure criteria have come to include diversity and ESG (environment, social, governance), Deakin and Buchanan argue that 'by the time of the 2021 revision elements that seem designed to please investors were increasingly salient'. Drawing on studies from other countries, moreover, they question whether this will increase 'corporate value over the mid- to long-term', or contribute to the vitality of 'the Japanese economy as a whole'. Employee interests, in particular, have become casualties. It is important to note, moreover, that despite alleging that 'people' are at the heart of his 'new form of capitalism', Prime Minister Kishida has maintained this direction of travel, indeed stating to investors at the New York Stock Exchange in 2022 that Japan will 'accelerate and further strengthen corporate governance reforms in Japan'.

Evidence of the shift in corporate governance towards shareholder interests was provided to the New Form of Capitalism Realization Council for its first meeting in November 2021, as reported by Whittaker (2024b) in the second special issue article. Corporate profits of large companies capitalized at ¥1 billion or more doubled between 2000 and 2020, while labour costs and capital expenditure were flat but internal reserves trebled and dividends rose six-fold, the latter almost equalling capital expenditure. These figures do not include foreign direct investment (FDI), which increased more than five-fold over that time, returns from which now contribute significantly to Japan's current account, nor do they include investment in intangible assets. However, investment in intangible assets also appears to have stalled, ironically in areas of past Japanese strength – organization innovation, and investment in human resources. These suggest a reactive, cost-cutting approach to corporate Japan's competitive and balance sheet challenges.

The second half of Whittaker's paper zooms out to a more macro-level perspective, asking whether the initiatives from Society 5.0, DX, GX, 'new form of capitalism' and 'restoring the middle class' are likely to make a difference to this picture, and ultimately to create a virtuous circle of growth and distribution, i.e. a new growth model. Without negating the possibility of this happening, he implies that this will be difficult unless the cross-currents in these initiatives – such as marketization of employment on the one hand and corporate commitments to invest in skills on the other – are acknowledged and addressed. At the same time, he draws attention to new developments in state–market relations, including a revival of the use of industrial policy instruments, albeit in a different form from those of the post-war developmental state, and the possibility of these being pulled in a new direction by geopolitics and security concerns, something that some of the later papers also hint at.

The third paper takes up some of the same issues, while shifting the focus from corporate governance to innovation. The 'lost decades' represent a crisis, Lechevalier (2024) affirms, but a crisis of what? Adopting a Régulation perspective, in which institutional dissonance is the norm rather than the exception, he argues that it is not a crisis caused by a lack of structural reform, as many 'mainstream' economists would have it, as there has been significant reform. However, this has resulted not just in a loss of institutional coherence, but a loss of balance, coordination, and inclusivity in the economy, already pointed out in Lechevalier (2014). Abenomics restored some policy cohesion, but it failed to restore coordination, and maintained a neoliberal trajectory. As well, the innovation system suffered from trying to emulate the Silicon Valley model, when it should have been following the logic set out by Society 5.0, of addressing social needs rather than technology-push in pursuit of competitiveness.

Next, Lechevalier agrees that Society 5.0 on the one hand, and 'sustainable capitalism' and 'new capitalism' on the other, point broadly in the same direction at an ideational level, but institutionally there are tensions within and between them, mainly because Society 5.0 has not freed itself from neo-Schumpeterian innovation, and new capitalism from financialized, shareholder capitalism, which has undermined state capacity to bring about change through the financial system. Digital transformation consequently proceeds fitfully along a neoliberal trajectory. The contradictions can be addressed, he argues, if the government – and Keidanren – actually commit to placing care (elderly care, child care ...) at the centre of Japan's innovation system, turning this into a stakeholder model of innovation, complemented by a stakeholder form of capitalism. This would create a distinctive, human-centric 'anthropogenic mode of development'.

The following papers venture further into Japan's innovation system, and the role of the government in its transformation, after first situating these as a response to global environmental, health and humanitarian crises. Arimoto (2024), whose career has spanned a wide range of roles within Japan's Science and Technology Agency (STA) and related institutions, as well as METI and the Cabinet Office, asserts that STI has become more central in government policy as a result of these crises, but echoing Lechevalier, that it needs to shed its neoliberal economic focus to address them. This simultaneously requires the joining up of policies across ministerial jurisdictions, in the form of 'mission-oriented innovation policy' (MOIP), a process that was accelerated under the Fifth STI Basic Plan (2016–21) which introduced the concept of Society 5.0, and further under the revised STI Basic Law of 2020 which replaced the 1995 S&T Basic Law, and its implementing Sixth STI Basic Plan (2021–26).

Arimoto describes in further detail the Strategic Innovation Programme (SIP), a precursor to these developments introduced in 2014, and more briefly the Moonshot Programme of 2020, both under the direction of the Cabinet Office, which has come to play a key coordinating role for MOIP. Based on his direct involvement, he describes the SIP-adus (autonomous driving for universal services) project which required collaboration across ministries and regional entities, as well as a pro-active approach to legal reform based on a 'public-private intelligent transport system roadmap'. Such projects further need an adaptive approach of continuous learning and adjustment mechanisms, rather than relying on static post-project evaluation, as well as mechanisms to encourage stakeholder participation. The transition to MOIP in Japan, Arimoto concludes, is a work in progress – which will be reflcted in the forthcoming 7th STI Basic Plan (2026–30) – and requires new forms of intelligence and boundary bridging, human resource development, and international collaboration.

The next paper focuses on environmental policy, which Nakai (2024), who moved from the Finance Ministry to the Ministry of Environment following the triple earthquake, tsunami and nuclear disaster in 2011, became Vice Minister and had a large role in shaping the policies he describes. Nakai first sets a context of simultaneous global crises, of the environment, infectious diseases and species extinction, which threaten our own survival, before giving an overview of the evolution of Japan's environmental policy. The latter depicts a shift from seeing environmental protection and economic growth as trade-offs, to insisting on the need for an integrated approach to the environment, economy and society. This was developed in the wake of the triple disaster, leading to the Fifth Environmental Basic Plan of 2018, in which environmental policy would be aligned with 'new growth' and vice versa. One concrete expression was the 'Green Growth Strategy' of late 2020. Another was the Regional Decarbonization Roadmap of 2021, which seeks to achieve carbon neutrality in the civil sector in 100 localities by 2030.

Inheriting new greenhouse gas reduction pledges by the Suga administration in 2021, the succeeding Kishida administration assembled a GX (green transformation) Implementation Council, which formulated a 'Basic Policy for the Realizing of GX' with a 10-year roadmap for sectoral transformation and green technology development. Central to this is ¥20 trillion of public investment to be raised through 'GX Economy Transition Bonds', which in turn should leverage ¥130 trillion or more of private sector investment, incentivized by 'pro-growth carbon pricing' measures. Nakai's vision, and presumably that of the Ministry of Environment, is for a three-layer or stage transformation, to a carbon neutral society; to a circular economy; and to a 'nature-positive, nature-revitalized, decentralized society that co-exists with nature'. Although Japan has much to do to achieve this vision, continuity in policy and its integrated approach make it a promising GX agenda worthy of serious attention.

The hefty sums envisaged in the Basic Policy for the Realizing of GX, as well as other initiatives linked to Kishida's New Form of Capitalism, including child and family policies designed in part to raise the birth rate and slow population shrinkage, heighten the need for effective and efficient public expenditure, which is already under strain. The sixth paper, by Akai (2024), analyses the implementation of evidence-based policy making (EBPM) in central ministries in Japan, the role played by the Council on Economic and Fiscal Policy, and by the Committee for the Promotion of Integrated Economic and Fiscal Reform since 2017. EBPM has 'three arrows' – not to be confused with those of Abenomics – namely setting of key performance indicators (KPIs) for policy objectives; evaluation of policy measures; and administrative review of individual projects, using PDCA (plan, do, check, act) cycles.

To secure ¥150 trillion of GX investment, for example, four pillars have been established – upfront investment support using GX Economy Transition Bonds; investment incentives through pro-growth carbon pricing; new financial instruments; and an international and diffusion strategy – each of which requires various types of KPI, including KPIs to measure just how public spending is actually inducing private sector investment, and whether or not ¥150 trillion actually improves industrial competitiveness as well as decarbonization, and so on. Each pillar has different tiers of increasing specificity. There is a concern underlying Akai's presentation, that although Japan has devoted considerable energy to EBPM (no doubt in parallel with the growth of MOIP, described by Arimoto, which crosses ministerial jurisdictions), it still has far to travel on this journey.

The special issue next turns to 'people', allegedly at the heart of Society 5.0 and new capitalism, but realistically more in rhetoric than reality. Long touted as Japan's biggest asset, people have in fact become its biggest challenge, and not just in terms of a declining and ageing population. Two articles which address the roles of women in particular highlight this. Nagase (2024) critically examines family and gender equality policies, which are undergoing change from a (male) breadwinner employment and social model. Behind this change are stubbornly low birth rates, but also changing attitudes of younger generations: the value attached to marriage and having children has decreased, while a higher proportion of women expect to work throughout their adult lives. Social welfare policies introduced in the 1980s no longer fit social realities.

Abe's 'womenomics' and work-style reforms failed to bring about fundamental changes to employment and work–life balance. 'Regular' long-term employment still imposes long working hours and other restrictions on shared family life, while increasing female labour force participation has been disproportionately in 'non-regular' employment, with lower wages and limited advancement prospects, and as such is socially wasteful. After considering these, Nagase turns to the tax and welfare policies that impede change, particularly those which grant full time housewives and women earning under ¥1.3 million annually public health and pension coverage through the contributions of their spouse, creating a disincentive for women to earn above this ceiling, and likewise for employers, who avoid paying premiums themselves. Attempts to reform the system in 2000–2001 failed, and of the current options being considered, Nagase favours reducing such treatment of housewives when their children reach a certain age, and incentivizing employers to increase hourly wages of non-regular employees but including the latter in employee insurance.

The following paper addresses another conundrum, of the low proportion of women in STEM (science, technology, engineering and mathematics) university courses, and subsequently STEM-related careers. Yokoyama et al. (2024) situate this in a context of Japan's declining research capacity, low proportion of STEM students – male and female – per se, lower proportion of women than men entering university, and declining population, raising the stakes for addressing the issue of women in STEM. They explore reasons behind the low proportion of women in STEM through a series of surveys, which they summarize. Japanese female school students score well in international tests like TIMSS and PISA, and as well as Japanese boys in primary school, but divergence in maths scores begin to appear during middle school. These are linked to characteristic and gender stereotypes attached to subjects and occupations – 'logical thinking' and 'mathematical ability' are associated with masculinity, 'understanding the needs of society' with femininity, and so on. Physics, Yokoyama's own field, is strongly associated with masculinity. The surveys also show that gender stereotypes and views on equality held by girls and their mothers in particular matter.

Changing social attitudes is no easy matter, and in the late 2010s a number of Japanese universities began to introduce womens' quotas for STEM courses based on different entry criteria. There was a surge in 2023, including leading universities like Tokyo Institute of Technology, Tokyo University of Science and Nagoya University. Womens' universities have also started introducing new STEM-related departments. Affirmative action has brought familiar debates, about reverse discrimination and stigmatization of women, including those entering through the normal route, while quotas sometimes remain unfilled. On the faculty and leadership side, targets for increasing the proportion of women are being announced, and the University of Tokyo made headlines in 2021 when women became a majority of its Board members. Further change will require significant stakeholder commitment to create a 'multi-layered information environment with a focus on gender equality'.

The third article to focus on 'people' addresses Japan's surprising lack of investment in human resources. Nakata (2024) first notes Japan's declining population and declining births – from late marriage and non-marriage, or marriage avoidance – which means fewer children and youths in education. He also shows, however, that entry rates into higher degrees (masters and doctorate level) are comparatively low in Japan; that indirect labour costs, and specifically training costs (or investments) of Japanese companies are lower than counterparts in comparative countries, and have declined since 2000; and that public expenditure on education as a proportion of GDP is low in Japan.

Worryingly, while higher education costs for families have increased, income inequality has also increased. Japan experienced the highest growth of income share of the top quintile, and biggest drop in the lowest quintile of comparator countries between 2000 and 2018, and similarly for the fourth and second quintiles, meaning that the ability of lower income families to put their children through higher education has decreased. In the corporate sector, Nakata argues that changes in financial markets have forced employers into a short termist, cost-cutting stance, and that digital transformation and increased job changing have reduced incentives to invest in training, while long working hours leave workers with little appetite to invest in themselves. Kishida's policies, moreover, are time-limited and overly targeted, and sometimes contradictory. Greater consistency and coordination of people-related policies is needed. As is a clear target: 'Attention should be focused on Japanese workers, not their employers, and on young people, not their parents' (or grandparents). Opportunities should be provided regardless of economic background, giving talented youth the opportunity to contribute to society.

Kishida's new capitalism and Keidanren's sustainable capitalism both aspire to restore the vitality of the middle class, *in principle* addressing some of the issues raised by Nakata. This is taken up in the final article on 'people' by Zou (2024), who focuses on the 'new trinity' labour market reforms proposed by Kishida, so-called because they have to be tackled together. The trinity consists of reskilling and upskilling; promotion of job mobility; and job-based (as opposed to 'membership-based') employment. The first is self-evident, although who funds reskilling and upskilling is not. Increasing job mobility addresses the concern that many workers are trapped in ill-suited or low-productivity jobs with little incentive to move. Job-based employment – and reskilling – will supposedly make it easier for them to do so, since it will be skills that are rewarded, not seniority or length of service. The combination, then, will improve the allocative efficiency of labour markets, improve productivity, improve worker satisfaction, as well as reduce the discrimination against women as described by Nagase.

In theory at least. After describing potential contributions of the 'new trinity', and the enabling legislation on unemployment benefits, pensions and tax, Zou proceeds to highlight the 'challenges', including the obvious one of why employers would boost their training – or promote side-jobs for employees – and at the same time countenance higher labour turnover. 'Job-based' wages and employment remains ambiguous but seems to resemble the *shokumu kyū* (pay for the job done) which was rejected in the 1960s. Workers are not necessarily as interested in career development as the model assumes, and an information infrastructure resembling the Danish system would need considerable development and investment. On a more optimistic note, Zou sees a bigger role for labour market intermediaries, pointing out that employment agencies in Japan are already attentive to worker needs. A new model may yet emerge from Japan.

The final article extends this optimism into the realm of digital transformation. Kümmerle and Waldenberger (2024) reject the tendency to frame data regulation regimes as a US market-driven and Chinese state-driven bipolar divide, or even a tripolar divide, adding the EU's rights-driven approach. Japan, they argue convincingly, has created a fourth, consensus-based type, reflecting Japan's approach to regulation in general, and avoiding the dangers to democracy of surveillance capitalism (Zuboff 2019). They advance their argument by first looking at domestic 'information banks' in which individuals *deposit* data with intermediaries which then *lend* it in aggregated form to third parties to derive *value* from it. The transactions involve a high degree of disclosure and consent, and the 'value' can be pecuniary or social, for example for use in medical research or regional projects. Elements of a market-driven and rights-driven approach are combined.

Their second example elevates the consensual approach to the international sphere, as Data Free Flow With Trust, unveiled by Abe at the World Economic Forum in 2019, in which Abe proposed that certain types of data should be put under careful national protection, while other types should be allowed to flow freely across borders. The concept gained traction in 2021 by emphasizing the opt-in of like-minded countries. Kümmerle and Waldenberger cite this as an example of Japan's 'neo-middle-power diplomacy'. Their third example of consensual governance is Japan's approach to the COVID-19 pandemic, in which obligatory lock-downs were avoided through the use of self-restraint and a distinctive approach to data which preserved the 'privacy first' principle, contributing to the country's low mortality rates. They identify key features of Japan's approach to data as 'soft regulations, multi-stakeholder involvement and consensus orientation'.

Conclusion

Kümmerle and Waldenberger's article allows us to see some of the other, more critical contributions, in a different light. The consensual approach they identify can also be seen in proposals for the 'agile governance' of Society 5.0, in which multiple systems interact with each other through interoperability, with input from multiple stakeholders based on a hierarchy of ultimate goals, core values and concrete objectives (METI 2021; Whittaker 2024a). It can also be seen in the Basic Policy (and Plan) for the Realization of GX, and the 'pro-growth carbon pricing' measures outlined by Nakai. Indeed, in his historical study of energy markets in Japan, Samuels (1987) identified 'reciprocal consent' – as opposed to top-down industrial policy – as a key characteristic. Relatedly, Whittaker's article describes the quest for consensus over shared wage and price increases through the Partnership Construction Agreement. That is not to say that consensus can always be reached, and 'consensus' does not always apply to out-groups, but it is the preferred modus operandi of governance.

Some of the more critical contributions in this special issue point to contradictions in Japanese policies, institutions and reforms, including:

- In corporate governance, promotion of shareholder-favouring policies by the Financial Services Agency and Tokyo Stock Exchange while the government and Keidanren claim this has gone too far, and needs to be reined in;
- In innovation, advocating a social-needs orientation while continuing to fund competitiveness-oriented technology-push;
- Advocating 'people-centred' Society 5.0 and rebuilding the middle class while continuing to allow dualization of the labour market and failing to address the causes of growing inequality;

- Expecting employers to fund reskilling and upskilling while at the same time promoting job mobility.

In the main, these represent a conflict between the maintenance of neoliberal approaches to economic management and the adoption of a post-neoliberal Society 5.0 approach which is coordinated through visible hands (based on consensus, balance between cooperation and competition, and pragmatism). But it also seems to represent a preference for not posing contradictions and tensions as such, and creating room for negotiation to reach consensus. Corporate governance is an example; the Stewardship and Corporate Governance Codes were presented in terms of shared investor and management interests in growing 'corporate value' over the medium term, despite underlying tensions. Doing so *may* create space for a creative resolution of tensions and the creation of a new model, in much the same way that employment (capital-labour) tensions were defused in the post-war period to create 'Japanese-style management', which proved highly competitive, and at the same time built a large middle class.

Likewise, conceiving of green and digital as 'two wheels' of economic transformation, and the insistence on not seeing environmental protection, economic growth and social wellbeing as trade-offs, creates space for negotiated consent, and thence commitment and durable policies. This stands in stark contrast to the way Brexit, for example, was handled in the UK, and the UK's flip-flopping over environmental policy, indicative of a trade-off stance between green transformation and economic (especially fiscal) health, as well as the social polarization over reproductive rights and other social issues in the US. From this admittedly optimistic view, the contradictions and tensions identified in the articles of this special issue are not a reason to dismiss Japan's efforts to forge a new direction; on the contrary, as several of the authors suggest, they are reason to take Japan seriously. If, as Lechevalier notes, crisis and conflict are normal states of an economy, and growth regimes 'emerge from the (constructed or much more often along an unexpected fit) alignment between different institutions', perhaps the Japanese approach offers a better chance of achieving this, especially when crises we are facing such as climate change and environmental degradation are so complex. Similarly Japanese pragmatism may lack ideological purity, but it also avoids ideological polarization and accompanying culture wars.

But, and this is an important caveat, simply asserting that people are at the centre of an economic model, or that an innovation system is oriented towards social needs, does not make them so. Japan is facing a crisis of social sustainability. Its post-war economic growth which propelled a rapid demographic transition has now turned into rapid demographic ageing and population decline. This is not unconnected with the roles of women in Japanese society, and the conflicts identified by Nagase and Yokoyama. Nor is it unconnected with the growing role of foreign labour in Japan, and immigration, for which Japan is still ill-prepared. If Japan can turn these tensions into a positive-sum outcome, for women and non-Japanese, and Japanese society and economy, it will be truly noteworthy, and relevant for other countries which are grappling with intense socio-economic tensions which have crystallized into open political and social conflict. Here, as Nakata indicates, pragmatism in the form of temporary or restricted budget and policy measures needs to be significantly stiffened, which will require not just stakeholder engagement, but real political leadership as well.

We hope that this special issue will help to update views on the evolution of the Japanese economy and capitalism, and stimulate reflection on similar challenges faced by other countries.

Note

1. Japanese names in this special issue appear with the surname first and given name last, except for the names of the authors of the articles following the title.

Acknowledgement

The authors would like to thank Chris Rowley for his encouragement in this project, and Fangmiao Zou for help in preparing the articles.

Disclosure statement

No potential conflict of interest was reported by the author(s).

References

Akai, N. 2024. "Evidence-Based Policy Making in Japan's Public Expenditure: Compatibility of Fiscal Health and Investing for the Future." *Asia Pacific Business Review*. https://doi.org/10.1080/13602381.2024.2320543.

Arimoto, T. 2024. "The Transformation of Science, Technology and Innovation (STI) Policy in Japan." *Asia Pacific Business Review*. https://doi.org/10.`080/13602381.2024.2320539.

Boyer, R., and Y. Saillard. 2001. *Regulation Theory: The State of the Art*. London: Routledge.

Deakin, S., and J. Buchanan. 2024. "Has Japan's Corporate Governance Reform Reached a Turning Point? Some Cautionary Notes." *Asia Pacific Business Review*. https://doi.org/10.1080/13602381.2024.2320535.

Kümmerle, H., and F. Waldenberger. 2024. "Japan's 'Consensual' Variety of Digital Capitalism and its Global Relevance." *Asia Pacific Business Review*. https://doi.org/10.1080/13602381.2024.2320553.

Lechevalier, S. 2014. *The Great Transformation of Japanese Capitalism*. London: Routledge.

Lechevalier, S. 2024. "Society 5.0 and New Capitalism: Complementarities and Contradictions." *Asia Pacific Business Review*. https://doi.org/10.1080/13602381.2024.2320538.

Ministry of Economy, Trade and Industry (METI Study Group on New Governance Models in Society 5.0). 2021. *Governance Innovation 2.1: A Guide to Designing and Implementing Agile Governance*. Tokyo: METI.

Nagase, N. 2024. "Much to Be Done in Japan's Family and Gender Equality Policies." *Asia Pacific Business Review*. https://doi.org/10.1080/13602381.2024.2320546.

Nakai, T. 2024. "Japan's Triple Sustainability Challenge." *Asia Pacific Business Review*. https://doi.org/10.1080/13602381.2024.2320541.

Nakata, Y. 2024. "Remedying Japan's Deficient Investment in People." *Asia Pacific Business Review*. https://doi.org/10.1080/13602381.2024.2320549.

Samuels, R. 1987. *The Business of the Japanese State: Energy Markets in Comparative and Historical Perspective*. Ithaca: Cornell University Press.

Whittaker, D. H. 2024a. *Building a New Economy: Japan's Digital and Green Transformation*. Oxford: Oxford University Press.

Whittaker, D. H. 2024b. "Japan's Quest for a Sustainable, Virtuous Circle of Growth and Innovation." *Asia Pacific Business Review*. https://doi.org/10.1080/13602381.2024.2320537.

Yokoyama, H. M., Y. Ikkatai, E. McKay, A. Inoue, A. Minamizaki, and K. Kano. 2024. "Can Affirmative Action Overcome STEM Gender Inequality in Japan? Expectations and Concerns." *Asia Pacific Business Review*. https://doi.org/10.1080/13602381.2024.2320547.

Zou, F. 2024. "The 'New trinity' Reform of Labour Markets in Japan." *Asia Pacific Business Review*. https://doi.org/10.1080/13602381.2024.2320550.

Zuboff, S. 2019. *The Age of Surveillance Capitalism: The Fight for a Human Future at the New Frontier of Power*. New York: Public Affairs.

∂ OPEN ACCESS

Has Japan's corporate governance reform reached a turning point? Some cautionary notes

John Buchanan and Simon Deakin

ABSTRACT

Japan has identified corporate governance as an important element in its attempt to reform its economic system. A combination of political will and sustained implementation by civil servants has produced a corporate governance code and associated mechanisms to sustain and refine the changes that have been introduced in order to raise corporate profitability and stimulate the whole national economy. Meanwhile, the direction of reform has shifted from an initially principles-based approach towards an increasingly proscriptive, rules-based one, favouring the interests of investors over those of other stakeholders. Whether this will achieve the desired results is increasingly being questioned within Japan and runs counter to experience from markets where shareholder primacy already prevails. Japan's own prior experience of trying to transplant laws and institutions from these markets suggests a need for caution.

Introduction

Since 2013 Japan has made a major and sustained effort to revitalize and even reconstruct its corporate governance. Political will has imposed initial reform and created an enduring mechanism to review and adjust the resulting framework thereafter. At the core of this effort is a code of conduct for corporate governance, supported by a complementary code for investors. The tone of reform initially borrowed heavily from the UK experience, incorporating the concept of comply or explain initiated by the Cadbury Report to bring flexibility, and relying on investor pressure to improve corporate responses. Subsequently it has veered further towards the explicitly shareholder-favouring ideas that have characterized the US, the UK, and other markets influenced by agency theory and the interests of institutional investors, diverging from a principles-based approach towards greater reliance on prescription. After proceeding at a remarkable pace for ten years, the outward appearance of radical reform is striking. However, the degree to which these outward changes are influencing the practical behaviour of managers, and whether they are producing the national economic revival that was originally declared to be their ultimate objective, is less clear. The debate underpinning the next review exercise, originally expected for spring 2024 under the timetable observed hitherto but now likely to be delayed (Daiwa Sōken 2023), has revealed uncertainties that need to be addressed.

This is an Open Access article distributed under the terms of the Creative Commons Attribution License (http://creativecommons.org/licenses/by/4.0/), which permits unrestricted use, distribution, and reproduction in any medium, provided the original work is properly cited. The terms on which this article has been published allow the posting of the Accepted Manuscript in a repository by the author(s) or with their consent.

Political support for the reform initiative

A distinguishing feature of recent efforts to reform Japanese corporate governance is the strength of political support. Soon after its return to power in 2012, the Liberal Democratic Party (LDP) established its Japan Economic Revival Headquarters (hereafter 'JERH'), publishing a Japan Revitalization Strategy in 2013 which listed corporate governance reform among its eight areas of concern and proposed amendments to the Companies Act designed, among other concerns, to strengthen the role of external or 'outside' directors. In 2014 the JERH published a Japan Revitalization Vision which contained detailed proposals for a corporate governance code and in the same year a revised Revitalization Strategy confirmed that this would be drafted. Meanwhile the prime minister, Abe Shinzō, had explicitly included corporate governance in his 'Abenomics' programme as part of the structural reforms needed to achieve economic revival (see, for example, Miyajima and Saitō 2020). The combination of Abe's enthusiasm for corporate governance at a strategic level and the diligence of other LDP politicians who progressed the detailed process of reform through the civil service and expert committees led to a series of related developments in 2014 and 2015, beginning with the Stewardship Code and the Itō Review in 2014, followed by the Corporate Governance Code in 2015. In 2017 a further element was introduced when the JERH's Future Investment Strategy announced the Council of Experts Concerning the Follow-up of Japan's Stewardship Code and Japan's Corporate Governance Code (hereafter the 'Follow-up Committee') to oversee periodically the development of the Stewardship and Corporate Governance Codes. Through this rapid progression of reforms the LDP succeeded in establishing a seemingly robust system to influence, monitor and adjust corporate governance practices.

This achievement contrasts with the general lack of progress that preceded it, where promotion of optional new corporate structures, admonitions, and guidelines had mostly failed to produce radical change. Dissatisfaction with Japan's post-war corporate governance regime, with its emphasis on the interests of the company and those stakeholders seen as directly contributing to its success, grew during the 1990s, after the bursting of the equity and real estate 'Bubble', but did not deliver immediately transformative change. Attention focused on US governance practices, on the assumption that they were driving the US's contemporary economic success, but this enthusiasm was initially restricted to theoretical debate. The first practical change came in 1997, when Sony reduced its board of directors and created a new role of executive officer, effectively focusing its newly reduced board on supervisory duties and delegating control of daily operations to its new executive officers, most of whom would formerly have served as junior directors contributing to the board's overpopulation and unwieldiness as a forum for debate. This reform was widely copied, though perhaps more for practical reasons than from any doctrinaire desire to split supervision and execution (Dore 2000). For example, it addressed the problem of excessively large boards that had become commonplace where board membership was seen as a final reward for loyal service. In 1998 the Japan Corporate Governance Forum (since 2012 part of the Japan Corporate Governance Network and not to be confused with the official body of the same name established in 2022, discussed below) issued its Corporate Governance Principles, calling for more accountability to shareholders, transparency, differentiation between supervision and execution, and a majority of non-executives on boards. In 2002 the internal auditor (*kansayaku*) system was strengthened to increase external membership, a reform which has probably raised the quality of supervision but was seen at the time as an attempt by traditionalists to reinforce the existing system at the expense of more radical reform. Soon afterwards, in 2003, the Company with Committees, with three independent committees, each comprising a majority of outside directors, to handle audit, nomination and remuneration, was introduced as an optional alternative to the existing corporate structure overseen by *kansayaku*. This was envisaged by reformers as a platform to introduce the enlightened corporate governance in the US style that many of them favoured but opposition from corporate interests, expressed through the Keidanren (Japan Business Federation), ensured that it became only an optional structure and adoption proved limited (Imai 2001; JCAA 2009). In 2004 the Listed Company Governance Committee assembled by the Tōkyō Stock Exchange (TSE) issued its Principles of Corporate Governance for Listed Companies, which called for more effective governance within the existing framework. Yet, despite all these initiatives, and a general feeling shared by many civil servants, academics, investors, and some corporate managers that change was needed to repair an inadequate system, the state of corporate governance at most Japanese companies around 2010 was not markedly different from that in 1990 (see, for example, Nakamura 2016).

The LDP has managed to change this situation, partly because it focused on a corporate governance code enforced through the TSE and thereby linked to listed status, and partly because it established a robust mechanism under the Financial Services Agency (FSA) to review the continuing state of governance and initiate change. Under Kishida Fumio's government, political support has been maintained. At his speech to the New York Stock Exchange in September 2022, Kishida drew special attention to corporate governance reform as an indication of Japan's increased attraction as an investment target: 'One very important policy is corporate governance reform ... We will accelerate and further strengthen corporate governance reforms in Japan ... ' (Kishida 2022). Thus a supervisory structure has been created and momentum achieved, with every appearance of continuing political will to sustain it. Let us now consider the nature of this structure and where its reform efforts seem to be leading.

The first initiative 2014–15

The mechanism created by LDP politicians to drive corporate governance reform is presided over by the FSA in collaboration with the TSE and operates formally through the Follow-up Committee of experts (described above) whose members debate and define reform proposals. The choice of the FSA to oversee this process, rather that the Ministry of Economy, Trade and Industry (METI), is a departure from the traditional division of responsibilities among the ministries. METI regulates economic affairs and would seem the logical choice to reform the governance of Japanese companies; it has its own advisory committee, the Corporate Governance System Study Group (the 'CGS Study Group'), which continues to issue periodic guidelines on corporate governance practice. Nevertheless, an LDP politician involved in the preparations that led to the first Corporate Governance Code of 2015 commented that the FSA was chosen because it was the financial regulator (which oversees the TSE, among other responsibilities) and also precisely because it was considered to be less enmeshed with corporate interests.

Japan's first Corporate Governance Code, issued in March 2015, was the core of the reform exercise but it was preceded by Japan's first Stewardship Code, in February 2014 and the Itō Review in August 2014. While this sequence of timing may have been intentional, it was suggested by an officer of the FSA in early 2017 that the need to coordinate the Corporate Governance Code with amendments to the Companies Law delayed its finalization, whereas the other initiatives were able to proceed at their own pace. The Stewardship Code, closely modelled on the UK Stewardship Code, was described as a compliment to the Corporate Governance Code with the two codes depicted as 'the two wheels of a cart'; it was an explicit call for institutional investors to exercise responsible stewardship towards the companies in which they invested, in much the same way that the UK's Cadbury Report had seen investors as the natural invigilators of sound corporate governance (Cadbury 1992). The Itō Review is a related but separate exercise, organized by METI rather than by the FSA, and drawing inspiration from the UK's Kay Review of 2011, which examined the role of equity markets in the UK and questioned whether they were promoting good corporate governance to sustain long-term profitability and whether short-termism was undermining this effort. The Itō Review undertook a similarly broad examination of investors' interactions with companies in the face of persistently low returns from Japanese equities but in practice it attracted attention for its premise that Japanese companies' generally low return on equity (ROE) was caused primarily by low profitability and for its recommended target of minimum 8% ROE.

The Corporate Governance Code was published in March 2015 (the '2015 Code') against this background. It differed from previous admonitions for improved governance in several important ways. As explained, it was associated with the Stewardship Code, in the hope that investor pressure would ensure a satisfactory response from companies. It was based on principles rather than rules and gave the option either to comply or explain reasons for non-compliance. Its purpose was declared to be the promotion of medium- to long-term corporate growth, thereby contributing to national economic revival. Finally, and most importantly, it was overseen by the FSA and implemented through the TSE, positioning it as part of listing requirements, and a regime was established to review it periodically. This was clearly a reform that amounted to more than mere guidelines and it could not be ignored by any company that valued listed status. The new code was generally well received by corporate managements because it focused on concepts of best practice that were already widely understood and did not attempt to sweep away existing ideas of how governance should be handled. One practical advantage that it enjoyed over previous initiatives was that corporate administrators charged with compliance matters (usually general affairs departments) now had to deal with a body of explicit requirements linked to their companies' listings for which they had either to comply or explain non-compliance, channelling them into a familiar pattern of analysing the requirements against their existing practice, summarizing implied changes, and making recommendations to senior management, which ensured that boards were fully aware of the new Code and its implications for their governance (Buchanan, Chai, and Deakin 2019).

Subsequent developments 2018–21

In June 2018 the first revision to the Code was published (the '2018 Revision'). In contrast to the 2015 Code, a more didactic tone was apparent, moving beyond general principles to recommend specific actions in key areas of governance: reduction of cross share-holdings, CEO succession planning, independent nomination and remuneration commit-tees, board diversity, disclosure of business strategies, and cost of capital awareness. Compliance levels fell in all of these areas, suggesting that many companies found difficulty in complying (see Buchanan 2022). The next revision was published in 2021 (the '2021 Revision'). Didacticism increased and became explicit prescription in many areas. The 2021 Revision was moreover linked to qualification for the TSE's new Prime Market, which opened in April 2022, effectively making compliance mandatory for com-panies with ambitions to be listed there; in theory companies seeking Prime Market listings could still opt not to comply, offering explanations instead for non-compliance with any of the Code's articles, but few seem to have done so. The next revision was expected in 2024, although there is now uncertainty regarding the exact timing. It is likely to be informed by findings from the new Japan Corporate Governance Forum (JCGF) which Kishida mentioned in his September 2022 speech in New York as part of Japan's continuing corporate governance initiative. This body was duly established by the FSA and had conducted six forum meetings with investment bodies as of June 2023.

The development of the Corporate Governance Code from 2015 to 2021 suggests the direction of travel that the FSA and its advisers appear to favour; the declared objectives and methodology of the 2015 Code seem to have been superseded. The objectives of the codification exercise were stated in the introduction to the 2015 Code as follows: This Corporate Governance Code establishes fundamental principles for effective corporate governance at listed companies in Japan. It is expected that the Code's appropriate implementation will contribute to the development and success of companies, investors and the Japanese economy as a whole through individual companies self-motivated actions so as to achieve sustainable growth and increase corporate value over the mid- to long-term'. It implies that corporate success and national economic revival are major objectives and that corporate initiatives appro-priate to individual companies' circumstances should be the drivers of reform. The same text was repeated unmodified in the introductions to both the 2018 and 2021 Revisions. In explanation of its methodology, the 2015 Code emphasized that 'the Code does not adopt a rule-based approach, in which the actions to be taken by companies are specified in detail. Rather, it adopts a principles-based approach so as to achieve effective corporate governance in accordance with each company's parti-cular situation'. Moreover 'It is necessary to bear fully in mind that companies subject to the Code are not required to comply with all of its principles uniformly'. However, the growing didacticism evident from the 2018 Revision appears to contradict these statements and the 2021 Revision, by linking many new or amended requirements to the Prime Market, effectively moves in many instances to a rules-based formula where complying companies have to adopt specific practices and demonstrate that they have done so. Notable among these are disclosure of policies and measurable goals for personnel diversity, disclosure of sustainability goals linked to the standards of exter-nal organizations such as the TCFD, raising the proportion of independent non-executive directors to at least one third of board membership, establishing independent nomination and remuneration committees, and disclosing the nomination process for directors, together with a 'skills matrix' statement. Most of these requirements are linked to the Prime Market, but the hope was expressed that companies listed on other markets would be encouraged to follow similar practices. None of these requirements seem detrimental to good corporate governance but the very fact that they are requirements threatens to undermine the whole concept of principles-based corporate governance. The tenor of the Corporate Governance Code appears to be shifting to a rules-based approach in which the FSA and its advisers decide how companies should be governed and decree appropriately.

Another important aspect of these developments is the apparent tilt towards shareholder primacy and prioritization of the interests of investors in general. The 2015 Code made clear that shareholders were an important constituency when it expressed the hope that its implementation would 'contribute to the development of companies, investors and the Japanese economy as a whole'. But at this stage the emphasis on benefit to companies and to the national economy still seemed strong. With hindsight, the choice of the FSA, acting through the TSE, rather than METI, to oversee the reform process hints at especial concern for investors' interests but the flexibility and pragmatism of the 2015 Code tended to draw attention away from this aspect. But by the time of the 2021 Revision elements that seem designed to please investors were increasingly salient. Transparency and supervision by outside directors are the keynotes of this Revision, expressed in increasingly intrusive and explicit terms that require companies to observe certain practices and demonstrate their compliance. In theory companies may also explain their non-compliance but the link to Prime Market requirements makes this a difficult choice for any but the most determined of boards. If corporate governance is seen as a mechanism to protect investors' interests and ensure appropriate treatment of shareholders, then this approach is understandable. Dore observed the spread of these ideas globally in 2008: 'Increasing efforts on the part of government to promote an "equity culture" in the belief that it will enhance the ability of its own nationals to compete internationally' (Dore 2008). This idea has certainly become an accepted orthodoxy for many academics and practitioners in markets that favour shareholder primacy, such as the US or the UK, but it runs counter to the intuitive viewpoint of most Japanese managers who see the company as the focus of concern (see, for example, Nikkaku 2021). If corporate governance is seen as the set of mechanisms by which boards administer companies to ensure long-term success for the business while generating prosperity equitably for all stakeholders, as implied by the 2015 Code, then this is a major divergence in favour of a single stakeholder group.

Success of the reforms to date

As explained above, the forms of Japanese corporate governance have been changed and there is now an increasing tendency to demand adherence to the exact formats that regulators and their expert advisers consider appropriate. However, formal change does not necessarily alter the way that governance is actually carried out within companies and opinion appears to be divided as to whether the reforms are contributing to improved corporate performance, with the majority view being that they are not. Research has focused particularly on increases to the numbers of outside directors, as promoted by the Corporate Governance Code.

Ishida and Kōchiyama studied how Japanese companies increased the number of their outside directors to comply with the corporate governance reforms during the period 2015–2017 and noted a pronounced tendency to repurpose external *kansayaku* as outside directors, often shifting from an audit board to a company with audit committee structure at the same time: 'Overall our findings suggest that the Japanese reforms increased the unnatural selection of outside directors and had a limited impact on changing the substance of the corporate governance system' (Ishida and Kōchiyama 2022). From this evidence, one wonders how many other aspects of the reforms have been finessed by Japanese companies to permit them to continue with familiar practices.

Some researchers have concluded that the reforms, particularly with regard to the increased numbers of outside directors, have improved corporate performance: 'Our study shows that increasing the participation of independent members in supervisory boards has had a positive impact on the performance of Japanese companies measured by corporate profitability, asset productivity, dividend payouts, acquisitions' value, and valuation multiples' (Mielcarz, Osiichuk, and Pulawska 2021) but the authors also note that these improvements in performance may be at the expense of job security for the workforce.

Other studies have reached less favourable conclusions. Miyajima observes: 'According to my joint study with Keio University Associate Professor Takuji Saito, although the ROE rose during the period of the Abe administration, the degree to which the corporate governance reform uniquely contributed is negligible ... the only clear change was an increase in returns to shareholders, including dividends and share repurchases' (Miyajima 2021). Yanagida reports a similar result in his study on the effects of increasing the numbers of outside directors at Japanese companies during the period 2014–5: 'I find no evidence that an increase in the number of outside directors significantly affects future performance' (Yanagida 2022). Mitsudome makes a subtle distinction in his analysis: ' ... I find that the percentages of outside directors on the boards are positively associated with annual stock returns, but not with the returns on assets or Tobin's Q. This suggests that shareholders view increases in the presence of outside directors as a positive sign since it would mean better oversight over the management, but the outside directors may not directly contribute to the profitability or the increases in the market values relative to the book values of the net assets' (Mitsudome 2023).

Thus the reforms appear to be influencing corporate behaviour in a direction that satisfies shareholders, through increased distribution of profits and improved transparency, but the majority of observers see little evidence so far of contribution to corporate profitability or national economic revival. From the narrow viewpoint of shareholder primacy, these reforms may be judged a success but their effect on the fundamental efficiency of companies is, at best, unclear. Moreover, as Ishida and Kōchiyama's research indicates, there are doubts as to how effectively some of the reforms are really being implemented within companies.

The tenor of future revisions

Having established the mechanisms of corporate governance reform, the LDP is no longer evident in the operation and development of those mechanisms. These aspects are controlled by the FSA, working with the TSE, and the process of reviewing and debating the issues that comprise and surround corporate governance, feeding into periodic revisions of both the Corporate Governance Code and the Stewardship Code, are nominally entrusted to the Follow-up Committee. A further element was introduced in 2022 through the JCGF, described above, which invites opinions on corporate governance issues and holds meetings with investor groups, presumably advising its findings to the Follow-up Committee. METI's contributions through its CGS Study Group are not directly linked to the FSA's processes, but the Follow-up Committee and the CGS Study Group have some common members so it seems likely that there is at least an unofficial flow of ideas from METI's proposals into the FSA's debates.

Outwardly, the review mechanism based around the Follow-up Committee seems to be dominated by investor interests. Roughly 24% of the committee were from corporate backgrounds as of 19 April 2023, whereas investors, academics, and advisers (including a lawyer) each made up approximately the same percentage, effectively outnumbering commercial interests by three to one (Follow-up Committee 2023b). Moreover the aim of the JCGF, as described by Kishida and reiterated by the FSA, is to 'hear from investors from around the world' implying a bias in favour of the interests of institutional investors. Nevertheless, the reality may be more nuanced. The Follow-up Committee's Action Program for Accelerating Corporate Governance Reform: From Form to Substance, published on 26 April 2023 shows the likely tenor of future developments. The document lists three groups of current issues for consideration:

(1) Management issues, such as encouraging the management with an awareness of profit-making and growth based on the cost of capital and promoting initiatives relating to sustainability, including investment in human capital;
(2) Issues related to the effectiveness of independent directors, such as improving the effectiveness of the board, the nomination committee and the remuneration committee, and improving the quality of independent directors; and
(3) Issues related to dialogues between companies and investors, such as enhancement of information disclosure as well as dealing with legal issues, and market environment issues (Follow-up Committee 2023a).

Of these current issues, (1) and (2) above suggest continued attention to internal aspects of corporate governance and imply increasingly invasive measures to ensure compliance with the model of governance that the experts favour. It is possible to see (3) in the same way but the references to legal and market environment issues may equally refer to concerns raised by the Keidanren on behalf of its member companies, as described below. Two recent opinions submitted to the Follow-up Committee, from investor and corporate interests, respectively, illustrate the dynamics of this situation. An opinion dated 19 April 2023 from the International Corporate Governance Network (ICGN), whose CEO is a Follow-up Committee member, expresses general satisfaction with the direction of travel, summarily dismisses concerns expressed to the Committee that corporate governance reforms hitherto have not demonstrated any effect on corporate performance, and calls for stronger action in areas such as disclosure and the reduction of strategic shareholdings (ICGN 2023). This is essentially what might be expected from an investors' advocacy organization such as ICGN and can be interpreted as an encouragement to greater prescription and regulation. However, an opinion submitted on the same date by Committee member Matsuoka Naomi (who is Chair of the Sub-Committee on Capital Markets at the Keidanren's Committee on Financial and Capital Markets and is thus assumed to be transmitting the views of the Keidanren) draws attention to a number of points that appear to be causing concern among Japanese corporate managements, stating, 'the corporate governance reform that is needed today is not to set detailed rules in the Corporate Governance Code (Governance Code), but rather to increase the effectiveness and substance of the reforms already in place, and to support steps taken by companies based on their own initiatives to improve mid- to long-term profitability and productivity'. The opinion moreover emphasizes that 'we want to reemphasize the importance of adhering to the principles based approach and the comply-or-explain approach of the Governance Code'. Further comments deal with points such as the need for companies to avoid short-sighted policies to improve balance sheet ratios and the need to permit flexibility in sustainability compliance. The latter part of the document calls for improvements in investor behaviour through allocation of better resources to stewardship activities, more careful investigation by proxy advisers before they issue potentially influential guidance to investors, and the need for companies legally to be able to identify their ultimate shareholders (Keidanren 2023). None of these three latter points seems likely to enthuse investors who see corporate governance primarily as a tool to sustain shareholder primacy but perhaps most of interest is the Keidanren's clear focus in its initial comments on the need to reduce prescriptive rules, to return the initiative to companies to determine their best choices, and to adhere to the principle-based approach of comply or explain; this appears to be a call for reversion to the spirit of the 2015 Code while reducing the didacticism and prescription increasingly evident since the 2018 Review.

The Keidanren's concerns appear to have entered the debate concerning future policies and this suggests that the Follow-up Committee is not wholly focused on shareholder primacy and investors' interests. The Action Program appears to be reflecting at least some of these concerns when it states: 'It is vital to move the focus of reform from form to substance in resolving the above issues. Sufficient results cannot be expected only by satisfying form. Substance matters. Furthermore, it has been pointed out that further detailed requirements, if introduced, may undermine the original purpose of the "comply or explain" approach and may cause corporate governance reform in practice to lose its substance. Thus, it is desirable that effective solutions to individual companies' corporate governance problems be considered in the context of reality, by identifying individual issues through constructive dialogues between companies and investors. It is also important for self-motivated changes to take place in the mindsets of companies and investors. To this end, it is necessary to create an environment that promotes such changes, as well as to make the dialogues between companies and investors more productive and more effective'. Interestingly, the Action Program also hints that revisions to the codes may not continue to follow the triannual cycle observed hitherto, implying a more pragmatic response to specific issues. A similar trend is evident also in a recent Nikkei editorial which notes the decision by the UK's FRC to withdraw certain intrusive amendments that were planned for the UK corporate governance code and makes the following observation regarding developments in Japan: 'Japan's governance code, through a series of amendments, has progressively raised the hurdles regarding board composition. This has resulted in greater management transparency but, at the same time, one cannot overlook the ill-effects of formalism with regard to aspects such as the increase in outside directors whose specialist knowledge is questionable' (Nihon Keizai Shimbun 'Nikkei' 13 December 2023).

Japanese corporate governance reform in comparative perspective

Japan's corporate governance reforms have not been taking place in isolation from developments in other countries. To a large extent they are intended to replicate or mimic a model of shareholder-orientated corporate governance which is associated with American and, to a lesser extent, British practice. Strengthening shareholders' rights to hold managers to account should, in theory, reduce agency costs and so drive down the cost of capital, thereby fuelling innovation and growth. 'Radical' innovation of the kind associated with Silicon Valley is sometimes attributed to the willingness of shareholders to assert their influence over corporate decision making (Summers 2001), and the designers of Abenomics appear to have expected some kind of similar outcome in Japan. So far, however, there is little or no sign of this happening (Miyajima and Saitō 2020). To see why it is helpful to put the Japanese reform programme in the context of wider trends in corporate law and regulation, and to consider the state of the art in the empirical literature on the economic and social effects of shareholder protection laws.

A first point to note, which may seem surprising in the light of the current Japanese debate but is well established empirically, is that Japan's corporate laws are by no means among the weakest when it comes to shareholder rights. In fact, just the opposite, as we can see from Figure 1. At the beginning of the 1990s Japan had some of the most pro-shareholder laws in the world, comparable to those in the US and UK and significantly stronger than those in force, for example, in China and Germany at this point. Japan's proximity to the US should not occasion any surprise when it is borne in mind that while Japan has a civil law system which was modelled on the German civil code as part of Meiji era modernization at the end of the nineteenth century, Japan's corporate laws derive from a US model which was put in place during the period of the American occupation, post-World War Two, with only minor subsequent amendments (West 2001). On paper, at least, Japanese shareholders enjoy similar legal rights to those of their American and British counterparts when it comes to such matters as electing directors and preventing the dilution of voting and dividend rights.

There are certain differences between Japan, on the one hand, and the US and UK, on the other, when it comes to the governance of takeover bids. During the 1980s and 1990s, hostile takeovers in the US and UK proved to be a highly effective means, on the one hand, of empowering shareholders in their relations and dealing with boards, and, on the other, of releasing reserves which would otherwise be tied up as retained earnings on corporate balance sheets (Armour and Skeel 2005). Since the 2000s, takeover bids or the threat of them have been frequently used by activist hedge funds in America and Britain in an attempt to induce target companies to declare increased dividends or initiate share buybacks. When this tactic was tried in Japan in the same period, however, it largely failed to bring about the expected corporate restructurings (Buchanan, Chai, and Deakin 2012). This was in part because the Japanese courts gave target boards greater leeway to adopt and trigger defensive measures including 'poison pills' which would have the effect of

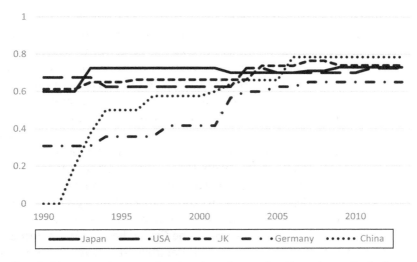

Figure 1. Shareholder protection over time in selected countries. Note: the vertical axis measures the extent of shareholder protection set out in corporate law and corporate governance standards as measured by the CBR Extended Shareholder Protection Index (SPI), with a higher score indicating more protection. The SPI is a composite of ten indicators measuring different aspects of legal and regulatory shareholder protection. See Deakin et al. (2018) for further details.

deterring bids by making them infeasibly expensive. In litigation around the *Livedoor* (2005) and *Bull-Dog Sauce* (2007) cases, Japanese judges took a sceptical view of takeovers, in some instances characterizing bidders as 'abusive' where they had no strategic plan for the company, other than breaking it up through asset disposals (Hayakawa and Whittaker 2009). This was not the sort of language that a judge in the Delaware Court of Chancery would ever have used, and while poison pills may in theory be triggered in the context of a US takeover, it seems that this has never actually happened there, contrary to the situation in Japan, where poison pills were widely adopted in the aftermath of the Bull-Dog Sauce ruling and were used to deter unwelcome approaches (Milhaupt 2009).

Until recently, the concrete reality of the Japanese poison pill as a real defence to a takeover bid was clear a point of difference to its largely symbolic status in US law and practice. UK practice was even more clearly against the poison pill, with its Takeover Code more or less explicitly ruling out this kind of ex ante defence (Armour and Skeel 2005). There are, however, some signs that the Japanese courts are shifting their position on poison pills. Although in 2021 the Japanese Supreme Court affirmed, in the *Tōkyō Kikai* case, a poison pill which had operated as an anti-takeover device, a subsequent decision, *Mitsuboshi*, saw the Court strike down an anti-activist poison pill on the grounds that it unduly infringed shareholders' rights. There have been a handful of successful hostile bids since 2019 and hedge fund activism is on the rise again. Assessing these developments, Milhaupt and Shishido (2023, 355) foresee a 'measure of convergence' between Japanese and US courts' interpretations of the poison pill, while noting that the two systems remain on different paths.

The distinct approaches of courts and regulators to takeover bids in Japan and other countries is only part of the reason for their relative rarity in Japan. In the Bull-Dog Sauce case, what ultimately enabled the company to deflect the assault of the hedge fund targeting it, Steel Partners, was the reluctance of its shareholders to go along with Steel's plans to increase dividends through the sale of corporate assets. These shareholders were predominantly financial services companies, strategic allies or commercial partners of Bull-Dog Sauce, who had no interest in seeing it broken up. This pattern was repeated in other failed hedge fund interventions in Japanese companies at around the same time (Buchanan, Chai, and Deakin 2012). The structure of ownership and the resulting coalition of interests in listed Japanese companies was then at odds with the logic of takeover bids and hedge fund activism of the kind that transformed corporate governance, and the wider economy, in the US and UK, in the 1980s. Unless there is a more fundamental shift in these wider economic variables, changes to 'soft law' corporate governance codes of the kind recently initiated in Japan, or even to the 'hard law' of legislation and judicial interpretation, cannot realistically be expected to have a similar impact.

Change may be coming. In November 2023, the Cosmo Energy Group decided not to activate a poison pill defence in the face of a determined activist investor campaign, seemingly because the board was not convinced that the company's other shareholders would support doing so. An article in *Nikkei Asia* promptly announced a 'requiem' for the poison pill as an anti-takeover defence (Givens 2023). It remains to be seen how far Japan has approached what the same article described as a 'turning point'. The corporate governance debate has undoubtedly moved on from where it was two decades or so ago when Japan's first hostile takeover movement was effectively halted in its tracks by a combination of judicial and regulatory intervention. However, takeover bids and activist campaigns remain relatively rare in Japan by comparison to the situation in other developed market economies, and turning points have been predicted before. Toray CEO Nikkaku Akihiro's less charitable view of the rules 'made in foreign countries' (Nikkaku 2021) suggests that not everyone is convinced that hostile takeovers and hedge fund activism are the answer to Japan's corporate governance dilemmas.

The idea that Japan should modernize its current model by copying other systems seems to owe more to dogma than to experience. The evidence from other countries is that empowering shareholders through the mechanism of corporate governance reform has decidedly mixed effects. Even in the US and UK cases where hostile takeovers have been most commonly deployed as mechanisms of corporate restructuring, they do not consistently produce superior profits or returns to target companies (Cosh and Hughes 2008). The main beneficiaries, in a financial sense at least, are the targets' shareholders, who get an immediate gain which is somewhat in the nature of a windfall for accepting the bidder's offer to buy them out for a premium over the price at which their shares were previously trading. The performance of targets post-takeover demonstrates considerable variance, ranging from spectacular gains in some cases to catastrophic losses in others, so that on average gains and losses largely cancel each other out. Even in those cases where target companies demonstrate improved performance and profitability, leading to higher returns for shareholders, wages and employment tend to fall, suggesting that the gains from higher productivity are not evenly shared (Conyon et al. 2002). The evidence from hedge fund activist interventions in the US and UK is similar: on average they generate increased returns for shareholders, which may be evidence of improved or at least more profit-focused management (Brav et al. 2008, 2015), but reduced ones for bondholders and creditors, and for employees (Klein and Zur 2009, 2011). In Japan, aggressive hedge fund interventions have not, on average, generated gains even for shareholders (Buchanan, Chai, and Deakin 2020).

What of that other talisman of pro-shareholder corporate governance, the independent board? In the US case, it has been difficult to find evidence linking the presence of independent directors to superior corporate performance (Bhagat and Black 2002). If anything, companies with a higher proportion of independent directors appear to underperform their industry peers during recessions and crises (Anginer et al. 2018). In the UK, there is similar uncertainty over the impact of the 'comply or explain' approach of the Cadbury code and its successors. Companies which neither comply nor explain actually outperform those observing the code, at least where there is a dominant shareholder. Where ownership is dispersed, the result is reversed (Arcot and Bruno 2018). In the case of companies which choose to explain their non-compliance, the quality of disclosures is generally low in the sense of being standardized and uninformative with respect to features of the reporting company (Arcot, Bruno, and Faure-Grimaud 2010).

While going against the grain of conventional wisdom on the inherent desirability of external or independent boards, on reflection these results are, again, not so surprising. Independent or outside directors are, by definition and even in a sense by design, less knowledgeable about the companies whose boards they sit on than executives and other employees. Non-executive directors may have sector expertise and they may also benefit from the experience of sitting as independents on multiple boards at the same time, but they will not have, and cannot be expected to have, an insider's understanding of the company's strategy and the risks it may be facing. They will be critically dependent on the CEO and other senior executives (not all of whom will be board members) for such knowledge as they do have. This dependence places non-executive directors in a precarious position when it comes to making strategic judgements on the company's behalf, and even more so in a crisis which puts the company's future on the line. The finding, repeated across several econometric studies (Anginer et al. 2018; Beltratti and Stulz 2012; Fahlenbrach and Stulz 2011), that US banks with a proportionately higher number of outside directors were more likely to enter into bankruptcy during and immediately after the financial crisis of 2008, confirms what was already known from studies of high profile corporate failures from the earlier 'dotcom' bubble and crisis of a decade before, the Enron case being simply the most high profile of several such events (Bratton 2002).

Just as the activist hedge fund turned out to be a 'plant flowering out of season' in the Japan of the 1990s and early 2000s (Buchanan, Chai, and Deakin 2012, ch. 8, discussing the so-called Murakami Fund), so the external or outside director model may be a transplant that the Japanese corporate governance system is prone to reject or at best co-opt to its own way of working. The large, executive-dominated board which the recent Japanese reforms have been seeking to marginalize and ultimately suppress arose in a context in which large industrial companies, so-called 'community firms' (Inagami and Whittaker 2005), operated as productive coalitions, seeking to find common ground between the interests of labour and finance, and focused in the final analysis on product quality rather than shareholder returns. Whatever their other shortcomings, insider-dominated boards were not easily swayed by charismatic CEOs, and regarded finance as one input or interest among many, neither prior to nor subordinated by the interests of employees. This model served the cause of incremental innovation well enough in the period when large Japanese industrial firms dominated world markets in a range of sectors from vehicle production to consumer electronics. While that era is no more, the move made by many Japanese companies over the past two decades in the direction of smaller boards with specialized sub-committees and a higher quota of outside directors has not been entirely seamless. At the point when the US-style company with committees system was being introduced in the early 2000s, along with a separation between board-level directors on the one hand and senior corporate managers outside the board on the other, concerns were already being expressed over the risks inherent in this transition, which would leave CEOs relatively less constrained by the type of collegiate decision making which had previously been the norm, and had the potential to detach boards from their companies' wider organizational and managerial processes (Buchanan and Deakin 2008, 2009). While Japanese companies have not experienced high-profile corporate failures on the scale of those which became a regular occurrence in the US after the turn of the millennium, this would seem to have been in spite of rather than because of the adoption of board structures modelled on US practice.

In any assessment of Japan's move towards a more shareholder-friendly form of corporate governance, account should be taken of the wider societal implications of this direction of travel. Shareholder protection norms were widely adopted around the world in the 1990s and 2000s, being enshrined in international guidelines such as those produced by the OECD, and in transnational standards including several EU directives (Deakin, Sarkar, and Siems 2018). The areas of law and regulation showing the fastest rate of change were those relating to independent boards and takeover bids, with both moving in a markedly pro-shareholder direction in the decade prior to the 2008 financial crisis. As these laws have now been in force in a large range of countries for over a decade, it has become possible to get some understanding of their long-term effects.

Shareholder dominance over corporate decision making in the US has been linked to anti-competitive outcomes and lower quality of goods and services, suggesting that corporate governance reform is not necessarily a positive sum game as far as customers are concerned (Azar, Schmalz, and Tecu 2018). A similar point applies to the interest of workers. Shareholder protection laws are positively correlated with rising inequalities of income, as measured by the Gini coefficient, and by a rise in the capital share, that is, the proportion of national income going to rents and dividends, at the expense of the labour share of national income, that is, the part going to wages and salaries (Sjöberg 2009). Second-order effects of these growing disparities include negative health impacts; through the mediating effect of income inequality, a higher level of shareholder protection in a country is associated with indicators of chronic illness, such as obesity and mental illness, and with rising child mortality (Ferguson et al. 2017).

Conclusion

The LDP has fulfilled its promise to reform Japan's corporate governance and the mechanism it has created seems sufficiently robust to ensure that the process of supervision and adjustment will continue. However the system that has been created faces a problem neatly illustrated by the essentially contradictory opinions above submitted to the Follow-up Committee by the ICGN and the Keidanren: no one has ever succeeded in defining corporate governance in any but the most general terms without encountering the problem that different actors see corporate governance systems in very different ways. After the initial flexibility of the 2015 Code, the FSA and the Follow-up Committee have increasingly promoted a style of governance that implies a belief in adversarial relationships between investors and management predicated on agency theory and relying on rules and disclosures at the expense of principles. As the Keidanren has pointed out, substance is more important than outward form; increasingly invasive rules, often at variance with Japanese managers' tacit understandings of good governance, threaten to undermine the legitimacy of the Corporate Governance Code and encourage purely formal compliance. Rather than intensify the weight of rules and disclosures, this seems the moment to consider how the reforms to Japanese corporate governance promoted hitherto can be given the maximum substance in actual managerial practice. It is also an opportune moment for the FSA and Follow-up Committee to consider whether corporate governance should really be seen primarily as an aid to investors and whether the direction they have taken over the past few years can really help corporate profitability and national economic revival without greater concessions to the viewpoint of corporate management.

Although the numbers of outside directors on Japanese boards is increasing, partly in response to the pressures engendered by successive amendments to the corporate governance codes noted above, it would appear that they have a largely advisory role, and do not occupy the strategic position they are often accorded on US and British boards. This may be no bad thing: a system in which outside directors can decide the fate of a company in response to a takeover bid or activist hedge fund intervention, tipping the scales in favour of asset disposals or share buybacks to placate shareholder demands, is one in which short-term financial pressures are likely to prevail over more enduring investment needs. Co-opting the outside director model to the organizational ethic of the Japanese firm may end up providing the best of both worlds, but the imposition of outside directors and related features of Anglo-American corporate governance through external regulatory pressure could equally be a distraction from efficient management and an obstacle to the long-term planning which larger Japanese firms have up to now been able to practise, with some notable successes as well as the occasional failure.

If Japan has so far mostly avoided some of the social and economic downsides of corporate governance reform, which include growing inequality, this may be because these reforms have so far had comparatively little impact in the Japanese case. If the direction of change is maintained and enforcement becomes stricter over time, with more prescription and fewer opportunities to respond flexibly to guidance, the reforms can be expected to begin to alter the behaviour of corporate actors. Takeover bids and shareholder activist campaigns may yet prove to the catalysts for wider changes in assumptions and practices. In that event, business practices which have transformed economies and societies elsewhere, beginning with share buybacks and dividend increases and extending to downsizing and rising wage inequality, will most likely become familiar features of the Japanese scene. The implications for Japan's economy are difficult to predict but it cannot be assumed that they would be beneficial, a point which applies also to their wider social consequences.

Acknowledgments

We are grateful for comments received at the 'Reforming Japanese Capitalism' conference held at the Said Business School, Oxford, on 17–18 February 2023, and to Mari Sako and Hugh Whittaker for feedback on an earlier draft.

Disclosure statement

No potential conflict of interest was reported by the author(s).

References

Anginer, D., A. Dermiguc-Kunt, H. Huizinger, and K. Ma. 2018. "Corporate Governance of Banks and Financial Stability." *Journal of Financial Economics* 130 (2): 327–346. https://doi.org/10.1016/j.jfineco.2018.06.011.

Arcot, S., and V. Bruno. 2018. "Corporate Governance and Ownership: Evidence from a Non-Mandatory Regulation." *Journal of Law, Finance, and Accounting* 3 (1): 59–84. https://doi.org/10.1561/108.00000023.

Arcot, S., V. Bruno, and A. Faure-Grimaud. 2010. "Corporate Governance in the UK: Is the Comply-Or-Explain Approach Working?" *International Review of Law and Economics* 30 (2): 193–201. https://doi.org/10.1016/j.irle.2010.03.002.

Armour, J., and D. Skeel. 2005. "Who Writes the Rules for Hostile Takeovers and Why? The Peculiar Divergence of US and UK Takeover Regulation." *University of Pennsylvania Law Review* 95: 1727–1794.

Azar, J., M. Schmalz, and I. Tecu. 2018. "Anticompetitive Effects of Common Ownership." *The Journal of Finance* 73 (4): 1513–1565. https://doi.org/10.1111/jofi.12698.

Beltratti, A., and R. Stulz. 2012. "The Credit Crisis Around the Globe: Why Did Some Banks Perform Better?" *Journal of Financial Economics* 105 (1): 1–17. https://doi.org/10.1016/j.jfineco.2011.12.005.

Bhagat, S., and B. Black. 2002. "The Non-Correlation Between Board Independence and Long-Term Firm Performance." *Journal of Corporation Law* 27 (2): 231–273. https://doi.org/10.4236/ajibm.2012.24020.

Bratton, W. 2002. "Enron and the Dark Side of Shareholder Value." *Tulane Law Review* 76:1275–1361. https://doi.org/10.2139/ssrn.301475.

Brav, A., W. Jiang, and H. Kim. 2015. "The Real Effects of Hedge Fund Activism: Productivity, Asset Allocation, and Labor Outcomes." *The Review of Financial Studies* 28 (10): 2723–2769. https://doi.org/10.1093/rfs/hhv.037.

Brav, A., W. Jiang, R. Thomas, and F. Partnoy. 2008. "Hedge Fund Activism, Corporate Governance, and Firm Performance." *Journal of Finance* 63 (4): 1729–1775. https://doi.org/10.1111/j.1540-6261.2008.01373.x.

Buchanan, J. 2022. "Japan's Corporate Governance Code 2015–2021: Legitimacy and the Transition from Principles to Prescription." *Zeitschrift Für Japanisches Recht/Journal of Japanese Law* 27 (53): 19–44.

Buchanan, J., D.-H. Chai, and S. Deakin. 2012. *Hedge Fund Activism in Japan: The Limits of Shareholder Primacy*. Cambridge: CUP.

Buchanan, J., D.-H. Chai, and S. Deakin. 2019. "Taking a Horse to Water? Prospects for the Japanese Corporate Governance Code." *Zeitschrift Für Japanisches Recht/Journal of Japanese Law* 24 (47): 69–108. https://doi.org/10.17863/CAM.35815.

Buchanan, J., D.-H. Chai, and S. Deakin. 2020. "Unexpected Corporate Outcomes from Hedge Fund Activism in Japan." *Socio-Economic Review* 18 (1): 31–52. https://doi.org/10.1093/ser/mwy007.

Buchanan, J., and S. Deakin. 2008. "Japan's Paradoxical Response to the New 'Global standard' in Corporate Governance." *Zeitschrift Für Japanisches Recht/Journal of Japanese Law* 13 (26): 59–84.

Buchanan, J., and S. Deakin. 2009. "In the Shadow of Corporate Governance Reform; Change and Continuity in Managerial Practice at Listed Japanese Companies." In *Corporate Governance and Managerial Reform in Japan*, edited by D. H. Whittaker and S. Deakin, 28–69. Oxford: OUP.

Cadbury. 1992. *Report of the Committee on the Financial Aspects of Corporate Governance*. London: Gee.

Conyon, M. J., S. Girma, S. Thompson, and P. Wright. 2002. "The Impact of Mergers and Acquisitions on Company Employment in the United Kingdom." *European Economic Review* 46:31–49. https://doi.org/10.1016/S0014-2921(00)00086-6.

Cosh, A., and A. Hughes. 2008. "Takeovers after 'Takeovers'." In *Issues in Finance and Industry: Essays in Honour of Ajit Singh*, edited by P. Arestis and J. Eatwell, 215–236. London: Palgrave Macmillan.

Daiwa Sōken (Daiwa Institute of Research) Report. 2023. Suzuki: *Futatsu no kōdo no magarikado – teikiteki saisokuteki kaitei no toriyame e (Two Codes at a Turning Point – Towards Abandonment of Previsions of Detailed Rules)*, July 3.

Deakin, S., P. Sarkar, and M. Siems. 2018. "Is There a Relationship Between Shareholder Protection and Stock Market Development?" *Journal of Law, Finance, and Accounting* 3 (1): 115–146. https://doi.org/10.1561/108.00000025.

Dore, R. 2000. *Stockmarket Capitalism: Welfare Capitalism - Japan and Germany versus the Anglo-Saxons*. Oxford: Oxford University Press.

Dore, R. 2008. "Financialization of the Global Economy." *Industrial and Corporate Change* 17 (6): 1097–1112. https://doi.org/10.1093/icc/dtn041.

Fahlenbrach, R., and R. Stulz. 2011. "Bank CEO Incentives and the Credit Crisis." *Journal of Financial Economics* 99 (1): 11–26. https://doi.org/10.1016/j.jfineco.2010.08.010.

Ferguson, J., D. Power, L. Stevenson, and D. Collinson. 2017. "Shareholder Protection, Income Inequality and Social Health: A Proposed Research Agenda." *Accounting Forum* 41 (3): 253–265. https://doi.org/10.1016/j.accfor.2016.12.005.

Follow-up Committee. 2023a. *Kōporēto Gabanansu Kaikaku No Jisshitsuka Ni Muketa Akushon purōguramu. Suchuwādoshippu kōdo Oyobi kōporēto Gabanansu kōdo No forōappu Kaigi, Ikensho (6)* [Action program for accelerating corporate governance reform: from form to substance. the council of experts concerning the follow-up of japan's stewardship code and japan's corporate governance code. opinion statement no.6]. Dated April 26, 2023.

Follow-up Committee. 2023b. "List of Members of Council of Experts Concerning the Follow-Up of Japan's Stewardship Code and Japan's Corporate Governance Code: As of April 19, 2023."

Givens, S. 2023. "Time for a Requiem to Japan's Poison Pill Takeover Defence." *Nikkei Asia*, November 23. Accessed January 6, 2024. https://asia.nikkei.com/Opinion/Time-for-a-requiem-to-Japan-s-poison-pill-takeover-defense.

Hayakawa, M., and D. H. Whittaker. 2009. "Takeovers and corporate governance: three years of tensions." In *Corporate Governance and Managerial Reform in Japan*, edited by D. H. Whittaker and S. Deakin, 70–92. Oxford: OUP.

ICGN. 2023. (Letter to 28th Council of Experts) "ICGN Response to the FSA's Proposed Action Program for Substantiating Corporate Governance Reforms." Dated April 19, 2023.

Imai, T. 2001. *Arata na keizai shakai no kōzō* [Building a new economic society]. Keidanren: Chairman's speech at Imperial Hotel, Tokyo, June 20.

Inagami, T., and D. H. Whittaker. 2005. *The New Community Firm: Employment, Governance and Management Reform in Japan*. Cambridge: CUP.

Ishida, S., and T. Kōchiyama. 2022. "Unnatural Selection of Outside Directors: Consequences of Japanese Corporate Governance Reforms." *European Financial Management* 28 (2): 1–30. https://doi.org/10.1111/eufm.12361.

JCAA. 2009. *Iinkai setchi kaisha risuto* [List of companies with committees]. Nihon Kansayaku Kyōkai (Japan Corporate Auditors Association 'JCAA') [Japan Audit and Supervisory Board Members Association after 2013].

Keidanren. 2023. "Opinion Statement on the 'Action Program for Substantiating Corporate Governance Reforms (Draft)' of the Council of Experts Concerning the Follow-Up of Japan's Stewardship Code and Japan's Corporate Governance Code." Dated April 19, 2023.

Kishida, F. 2022. "Speech to New York Stock Exchange." Posted September 22, 2022, Accessed January 4, 2024. https://www.mofa.go.jp/na/na2/us/shin4e_000044.html.

Klein, A., and E. Zur. 2009. "Entrepreneurial Shareholder Activism: Hedge Funds and Other Private Investors." *The Journal of Finance* 64 (1): 187–229. https://doi.org/10.1111/j.1540-6261.2008.01432.x.

Klein, A., and E. Zur. 2011. "The Impact of Hedge Fund Activism on the Target Firm's Existing Bondholders." *Review of Financial Studies* 24 (5): 1735–1771. https://doi.org/10.1093/rfs/hhr016.

Mielcarz, P., D. Osiichuk, and K. Pulawska. 2021. "Increasing Shareholder Focus: The Repercussions of the 2015 Corporate Governance Reform in Japan." *Journal of Management & Governance*. https://doi.org/10.1007/s10997-021-09619-0.

Milhaupt, C. 2009. "Bull-Dog Sauce for the Japanese Soul? Courts, Corporations and Communities – a Comment on Haley's View of Japanese Law." *University of Washington Global Studies Law Review* 8 (2): 345–361. https://openscholarship.wustl.edu/law_globalstudies/vol8/iss2/12

Milhaupt, C., and Z. Shishido. 2023. "The Enduring Relevance of the Poison Pill: US-Japan Comparative Analysis." *Stanford Journal of Law, Business & Finance* 28:336–358. https://doi.org/10.2139/ssrn.4339701.

Mitsudome, T. "Corporate Governance, Outside Directors and Firm Performance: Evidence from Japan." Available at SSRN. Last revised 13 February 2023, Accessed December 12, 2023. https://papers.ssrn.com/sol3/papers.cfm?abstract_id=4334208.

Miyajima, H. 2021. "Crucial Viewpoint on Corporate Governance: Developing a 'New Japanese model'." *RIETI*, Accessed December 12, 2023. https://www.rieti.go.jp/en/papers/contribution/miyajima/10.html.

Miyajima, H., and T. Saitō. 2020. "Corporate Governance Reforms Under the Abenomics: The Economic Consequences of Two Codes." Available at SSRN. Posted October 20, 2020, Accessed December 12, 2023. https://ssrn.com/abstract=3684372.

Nakamura, M. 2016. "The Security Market and the Changing Government Role in Japan – Corporate Governance Issues." *Asian Education and Development Studies* 5 (4): 388–407. https://doi.org/10.1108/AEDS-09-2015-0044.

Nikkaku, A. 2021. ""Tōray shachō ga ken'o suru ōbeiryū kigyō keiei e no geigō, 'rūru zukuri wa kaigai ga yaru to iu kankaku wa ikenai'" [Tōray CEO abhors accommodation of business management to Euro/American fashion: 'The idea that rules are made in foreign countries is wrong']. (Interview in Tōyō Keizai 10 July)."

Sjöberg, O. 2009. "Corporate Governance and Earnings Inequality in the OECD Countries 1979–2000." *European Sociological Review* 25 (5): 519–533. https://doi.org/10.1093/esr/jcn069.

Summers, L. 2001. "London Stock Exchange Bicentennial Lecture, London." (copy on file with authors).

West, M. 2001. "The Puzzling Divergence of Corporate Law: Evidence and Explanations from Japan and the United States." *University of Pennsylvania Law Review* 150 (2): 527–601. https://doi.org/10.2307/3312972.

Yanagida, T. 2022. "Effect of the 2015 Code Revision to the Corporate Governance Code on Japanese Listed Firms." *Asian Academy of Management Journal of Accounting and Finance* 18 (2): 41–61. https://doi.org/10.21315/aamjaf2022.18.2.3.

ᗙ OPEN ACCESS

Japan's quest for a sustainable, virtuous circle of growth and distribution

D. Hugh Whittaker

ABSTRACT
Large Japanese corporations which have accumulated substantial reserves are now under pressure to spend them, but on what, or on whom? Should they increase their (domestic) capital and R&D expenditure, which languished between 2000 and 2020; or invest more in their employees, whose wages have stagnated; or increase their shareholder returns, which have already surged; or raise executive remuneration closer to overseas counterparts? This article examines tensions in recent developments in Japan's political economy, from Society 5.0 to Kishida's 'new form of capitalism' and Keidanren's 'rebuilding the middle class', from the perspective of these dilemmas.

Introduction

Acknowledging the virtues of capitalism and the market economy, in 2023 Japan's main business federation Keidanren nonetheless lamented that an 'excessive focus on shareholder capitalism and market fundamentalism has brought about various social issues, such as the destruction of the global environment and ecosystems, and the expansion and reproduction of inequality' (Keidanren 2023). Earlier, in 2020, it had opined that 'the updating of Japanese capitalism and the realization of growth that is sustainable and resilient against various types of risk would make Japan a pioneer in establishing a new vision for capitalism around the world' (Tokura 2020). Here the business federation was proposing measures to rebuild Japan's once-expansive middle class.

These views dovetailed with the 'new form of capitalism' agenda of Prime Minister Kishida, whose New Form of Capitalism Realization Council was confronted with the following statistics in their November 2021 meeting. Between 2000 and 2020, in large firms capitalized at ¥1 billion or more:

- Labour costs declined from ¥51.8 to ¥51.6 trillion
- Capital investment declined from ¥21.8 to ¥20.7 trillion
- Operating profits almost doubled, from ¥19.4 to ¥37.1 trillion
- Cash and deposits almost doubled, from ¥48.8 to ¥90.4 trillion
- Internal reserves almost trebled, from ¥88.0 to ¥242.1 trillion

---

This is an Open Access article distributed under the terms of the Creative Commons Attribution-NonCommercial-NoDerivatives License (http://creativecommons.org/licenses/by-nc-nd/4.0/), which permits non-commercial re-use, distribution, and reproduction in any medium, provided the original work is properly cited, and is not altered, transformed, or built upon in any way. The terms on which this article has been published allow the posting of the Accepted Manuscript in a repository by the author(s) or with their consent.

- Dividends rose *sixfold*, from ¥3.5 to ¥20.2 trillion.[1]

Together, the government and Keidanren have proposed the reform of Japanese capitalism, and more recently, rebuilding of its depleted middle class. Kishida's growth strategy had four broad emphases: innovation through science and technology; infrastructure development plan for a Digital Garden City Nation; realization of 'carbon neutral'; and economic security. It also had three distribution policies: strengthening of distribution for workers; enlargement of the middle class and countermeasures to the falling birthrate; and improved income for workers in nursing and daycare (Kishida 2021; Yamakoshi 2023). When it was first mooted, the 'distribution' side provoked a sharp sell-off of stocks – dubbed the 'Kishida shock' – and was promptly amended. 'Income doubling' became '*investment* income doubling', and the new capitalism priorities were simplified to people; science, technology and innovation (STI); startups; and digital and green transformation (DX and GX) (Kishida 2022).

Are the government and big business serious about changing Japanese capitalism, and about creating a new growth model which is 'people-centred', or is this wishful thinking, or posturing? Restated for the purpose of this article, what are the prospects of Japan creating a new 'virtuous circle of growth and distribution', with a different configuration to that of the post-war model? That model was progressively undermined from the 1980s, and the intervening decades were characterized by partial financialization and, with exceptions, a conservative approach to addressing new competitive challenges, with domestic investment hesitancy and cost-containing people management.

Since 2014–15, however, an increasingly coordinated approach has sought to steer Japan in a new direction – towards Society 5.0 through DX, GX, and more recently sustainable and new capitalism. Seen from the perspective of corporate internal reserves, however, there are tensions, and indeed potential contradictions, in part arising from Japan's interconnectedness with the global economy. These tensions, partly submerged under the appeal for growth – increasing the size of the pie before deciding how to divide it – are nonetheless real, and threaten to compromise the reform agenda.

The article is organized as follows. The first half looks at the background of the statistics above, starting with corporate finance and investment, then corporate governance and returns to shareholders, and finally employment relations. The second half turns to the macro level, and attempts to create a new 'virtuous circle of growth and distribution', starting with Society 5.0, DX and GX, followed by the reform of capitalism, including recent pronouncements on rebuilding the middle class and 'new trinity' labour market reforms. As well, it will consider the implications of the growing emphasis on various forms of security – defence, cyber and economic – which could pull Japan in yet a different direction. The Conclusion asks: Which way forward for Japan?

Finance and innovation

Let us start with the statistics given in the introduction, and add some more. First, as noted, capital expenditure of large firms was flat between 2000 and 2020, even as their profitability was restored. Instead of investment, the profits appear to have been squir-relled away, or distributed to shareholders, whose dividends increased sixfold. In terms of corporate activity, however, and especially in terms of innovation, this picture is partial, in at least two senses, namely overseas investments, and investment in intangible assets.

Japan's outbound foreign direct investment (FDI) increased massively between 2000 and 2022 – from $32 billion to $172 billion on a net, flow basis.[2] On the one hand, this generated an income and contributed to Japan's current account surplus. In the decade to 2022 income derived from outbound FDI and portfolio investment almost trebled to ¥50 trillion ($378 billion), an amount equivalent to almost 10% of Japan's GDP, creating a significant gap between gross national income (GNI) and gross domestic product (GDP). Much of the economic activity resulting from FDI, including capital expenditure, innovation and employment generation, accrues to the GDP figures of the recipient countries rather than to Japan. If this were balanced by inbound FDI it would not matter, but that is not the case. In terms of the inbound to outbound FDI ratio, and inbound FDI as a proportion of GDP, Japan falls near the bottom of UNCTAD's country rankings (cf. Katz 2021). Consequently, Japan has become an investment powerhouse abroad, but depends on its own corporations for domestic investment, which has languished.

A second caveat is that capital expenditure is not necessarily an accurate indicator of innovation, since the latter includes intangible assets which may contribute substantially to productivity growth. Intangible assets are difficult to measure, and standardized statistics in Japan are lacking. Researchers have used the methodology of Corrado, Hulten, and Sichel (2005, 2006), who propose three major categories of intangible assets: computerized information (e.g. software, databases), scientific and creative property (R&D, mineral exploration, copyright and licence costs, other product development, design and research expenses), and economic competencies (brand equity, organization structure, firm-specific human resources). Using this methodology, Fukao et al. (2009), estimated that the share of intangible asset investment rose in Japan during the 1990s and first half of the 2000s to over 10% of GDP, but this was lower than in the US. Miyagawa and Kim (2010) produced similar figures, and found that Japan scored relatively low on the third category, which is ironic because Japanese companies were once renowned for organizational innovation and their firm-specific human resources (cf. Iwao 2023; Itami 2024; Lechevalier 2024 in this collection). More recently Kim (2023) found that the intangible asset to GDP ratio had hardly changed by 2018, and that in contrast to the US, where intangible asset investment overtook investment in tangible assets in the late 1990s, this had not happened in Japan.

Taking just two of the above intangible asset components, first, science and technology R&D investment as a proportion of GDP in Japan is by no means low in international comparisons, but since the Global Financial Crisis it has remained largely flat, vacillating between 3.3 and 3.6% of GDP, a similar share to company R&D investment relative to turnover (Sōmushō tōkeikyoku 2021). While R&D investment in real terms grew by 70% in the US and Germany between 2000 and 2019, however, and in the UK by 50%, in Japan (and France) it only grew by 30%, and hardly at all since 2008. Similarly, whereas university R&D expenditure more than doubled in the US, Germany and the UK between 2000 and 2018, and increased in France by 80%, in Japan it only increased by 10%.[3]

Second, despite Japan's reputation for on-job training (OJT) in the 1980s, its recent firm-specific investment in human resources is even bleaker. A survey cited in the 2018 White Paper on Labour reported that the US, France, Germany, Italy and UK spend at least one percent of GDP on off-job-training, while in Japan it declined from 0.4% in 1995–99 to just 0.1% in 2010–14 (Kōsei rōdōshō 2018, 89). On-job training (OJT) is very difficult to measure, but a 2017 survey cited in the same White Paper showed that the number of

Japanese companies which carried out OJT in 2017 was significantly less than the OECD average (87). Inoki (2016) disputes such claims by arguing that roughly 10% of working hours in Japan can be considered OJT, but Miyagawa (2018) in turn argues that OJT is mostly about learning existing work, and not learning new skills or knowledge which might link it to innovation – DX, for example – hence there is a disconnect between skills and innovation, which impedes growth of intangible assets.

Miyagawa further points to the delay in cleaning up the financial aftermath of the bubble burst, which dragged on through the 1990s, and impeded structural changes in the economy, including the shift to investment in intangible assets. Companies opted instead to curb labour costs, most strikingly by increasing their reliance on non-regular employees, whose share of the labour force grew from less than 20% in the late 1980s, to almost 40 in the late 2010s, *in spite of* an increasingly tight labour market and growing labour shortages (cf. Nakata 2024 in this collection).

Finance and corporate governance

The financial turbulence of the late 1990s and early 2000s brought about substantial changes in corporate finance. Companies reduced their borrowing and curtailed their investments as they set about rebuilding their balance sheets.[4] Banks faced paper-thin margins on loans and deposits, as interest rates hovered around zero. Households kept more than half their financial assets in bank deposits, despite earning no interest.[5] The ¥1 quadrillion of household savings (in 2020) was used by banks to purchase government bonds, or held as reserves at the Bank of Japan, both in amounts roughly equivalent to Japan's GDP. Part of the government's goal of doubling income investment hinges on encouraging households to make use of NISA (Nippon Individual Savings Account), while banks have increasingly turned their attention to startups, a particular emphasis of new capitalism (cf. Katz 2024).

Meanwhile, after their balance sheets were rebuilt and profitability was restored, large companies began to amass internal reserves. These grew by 80% in the decade to 2021, to over ¥500 trillion, also just shy of Japan's GDP. Not only did large companies shun bank loans, they also reduced their bond and share issues. Yet they were not free from market pressures, especially from shareholders. Internal reserves make a tempting target for activist shareholders, of course, but there are other reasons why investor relations emerged to become the key institutional nexus for managers, replacing employment and industrial relations of the post-war period.

These are set out by Deakin and Buchanan (2024) in this collection. In brief, the changes began in the 1990s, when companies, and especially banks, began to sell off reciprocally held 'stable shares' to improve their balance sheets, and foreign investors stepped in to purchase them. Legal reforms in the late 1990s and early 2000s enabled corporate restructuring and choice in corporate governance structures, and activist share-holders began to challenge insider (management) control. A new wave of reforms came under the second Abe administration, with the Stewardship Code and Corporate Governance Code. Ostensibly these were meant to enhance 'corporate value and sustain-able growth through constructive engagement', in the words of the Stewardship Code, but the background was a campaign to enhance returns on investment (ROE), from a Topix average of 6% to 10%, thereby making Japanese stocks more attractive to international investors. Over time the Corporate Governance Code's 'comply or explain' requirements were tightened, making 'soft' law increasingly hard. Shareholders have become increasingly emboldened to challenge managers on the provisions, and corporate strategy.

This is the background to the sixfold rise in shareholder dividends that we saw in the introduction, as well as a rise in share buybacks. De-regulated in the US in the early 1980s, the latter have been widely used there to drive up stock prices, and to boost executive compensation. According to Lazonick (2014, 4), the 449 S&P500 Index companies which were publicly listed from 2003 to 2012 spent 54% of their profits on share buybacks. In Japan they were legalized in 1994, and in FY2022–23 listed companies spent ¥9 trillion on them, which was almost half as much as dividends. Together they accounted for 84% of net profits.[6] While this suggests a swing towards shareholder primacy, Miyajima and Ogawa (2022) argue that buybacks in Japan are different from the US, in that they are often used by restructuring companies, especially banks, wishing to sell relational shares, and that they are mostly retained as treasury stocks to raise new funds later, for M&A, or allocation to third parties, including managers and employee shareholding associations. Hara (2009, 2017), on the other hand, who has influenced Kishida's 'new capitalism', sees them as an importation of US corporate governance practices to Japan, and advocates restrictions on both share buybacks and on decision-making rights of short-term shareholders. Meanwhile, the surge of dividends and buybacks continued in 2023 and is expected to continue in 2024. The justification has moved from ROE to price-to-book (P/B) ratio, as the Tokyo Stock Exchange (TSE) is now requiring disclosure by prime listed companies with a ratio of less than 1, and measures to raise it (*Nikkei Asia* 2023b).

Such pressures are said to be a contributing factor in the rising number of delistings from the TSE, as well as the rise of domestic mergers and acquisitions (M&A), which rose by 80% in the first half of 2023. Although the buyout of Toshiba by the domestic consortium Japan Industrial Partners, and photoresist company JSR by the largely government Japan Investment Corporation, stole headlines, some 2000 M&A cases were recorded in that period. This rise will continue if the Ministry of Economy, Trade and Industry (METI) Fair Acquisitions Study Group has anything to do with it. The group is 'eager to compile guidelines from the logic of financialization that would make sense to people in capital markets', according to the responsible METI official (*Nikkei Asia* 29 December 2023; 2023d; cf. *Japan Times* 2023).

M&A, and buy-outs, can have a positive effect on corporate value through creating synergies, accelerating restructuring and building scale, not to mention providing an exit for owners with no successors. And facilitators like private equity (PE) firms have shed the 'vulture' image of the 2000s, with some gaining legitimacy, and indeed respect (Schaede 2020). But the METI official cited seems oblivious to the controversies surrounding 'financialization' and its connection to growing inequality, in contrast to the stated aims of the government.[7]

Demise of the employee-favouring firm

During the 1990s Japan entered an 'employment ice age'. With almost two job seekers for every job advertised, fresh graduates found it difficult to secure regular jobs. Without fresh graduates, however, workforce ageing accelerated, and so did seniority-linked labour costs. To curb labour costs older workers were 'loaned' or transferred to subsidiaries, or offered early retirement. The portfolio of employment types proposed by the employer federation Nikkeiren's (1995) *Shinjidai no Nihonteki keiei* (Japanese Style Management for a New Era) was gradually realized through labour market de-regulation, and the number of non-regular workers surged. Companies once depicted as 'employee-favouring' (Dore 2000) and practising 'human capitalism' (Itami 1987), now responded to their competitive, corporate governance and payroll challenges by curbing investment, including investment in employee education and training, and hiring non-regular workers. Wage growth stalled. Between 2000 and 2018 the labour share of value added in large firms (capitalized at ¥1 billion or more) fell from 60.9 to 51.3%, before recovering somewhat to 54.9% in 2019.[8]

The government and companies were not oblivious to the negative effects of all this, including deflation. As early as 2006, after Koizumi's neo-liberal reforms, policy began to change, and it accelerated under the second Abe administration from 2012. In the words of Vogel (2018, 262–63) policy became 'more interested in improving working conditions than in helping firms to cut costs, because this would help increase the workforce and raise productivity. It was more interested in raising the status of women and nonregular workers than in giving employers more flexibility in hiring nonregular workers, because this would make it easier for women to combine work and childrearing. And it was more interested in raising wages than in suppressing them, because this could lift consumer demand'.

In particular, the government became concerned about how to increase the workforce as the population began to decrease. This would require bringing more women, elderly and non-Japanese into the workforce, each of which posed challenges to 'Japanese-style' employment. Employers by and large opted to ignore the challenges and placed the three groups into 'non-regular' employment. Most of the growth of women's employment in the 1990s was in part time work, and from 2005 to 2020 the proportion of women who were in non-regular employment rose from 45% to 54%.[9] By this time the female labour force participation rate had risen to over 77%, so women were no longer a vast, untapped reserve, at least quantitatively. Older workers, too, on reaching their company's mandatory retirement age, were generally placed on annual contracts at a much lower rate of pay. And most of the roughly two million non-Japanese workers in Japan were also in non-regular categories, including so-called 'trainees'.

The negative effects of such dualism were also recognized, not least in terms of productivity loss. Abe promised to create a 'dynamic society of 100 million people', a 'society in which all women shine'. His Council for the Realization of Work Style Reform introduced a package of policy measures targeting work-life balance, childcare, parental leave and the gap in wages and conditions between regular and non-regular workers, which was passed in the 2018 'Work Style Reform' Diet. The legislation was the result of compromise, however, and the provisions on overtime, equal pay for equal work and exemption were contentious. Critics pointed to contradictions, loopholes, and scope for evasion and exploitation (cf. Weathers 2018), and the package prodded employers to change rather than forcing them to do so.

As in other countries, moreover, the employed – self employed binary in Japan has been eroded by the rise of quasi-employment or contracting, an ever-growing category which includes gig and spot work. Such work is often undertaken in addition to other work – by necessity or by choice – but it can also be the main source of income. The number of people registered for spot work with four leading agencies reached 10.7 million in May 2023, although this figure includes multiple registrations (*Nikkei Asia* 2023c). Overall, the growth of this type of work has extended the 'low road' trajectory from the 1990s, of growing polarization and inequality accompanying flexibilization (cf. Lucács 2020; Shibata 2023).

Let us conclude the first part of this paper, which focuses on the statistics considered by the New Form of Capitalism Realization Council, cited in the Introduction. The reasons for corporate restraint on capital expenditure, curtailment of labour costs, increase of reserves and savings, and leap in shareholder returns are multiple, but are a far cry from the dynamic growth model of the post-war period. They point to a reactive approach to Japan's competitive challenges, which include the emergence of China, and the new US model centred on venture-capital-backed Silicon Valley IT firms, and growth of global value chains linking the two (Sturgeon 2002). The loss of confidence in Japan's post-war model and the assertion of US interests abroad saw corporate governance and investor relations gain increasing prominence, ultimately leading to the latter becoming the key institutional nexus, replacing the wage-labour nexus (Boyer and Saillard 2001). The 'employee-favouring firm' was replaced by the 'shareholder-favouring firm', albeit not yet shareholder interest *maximization*.

At the policy level, as Japan struggled to exit deflation, the second Abe administration from 2012 provided much-needed continuity. The 'three arrows' of Abenomics' halted deflation but did not get Japan to its 2% inflation target, and the third arrow – 'growth strategy to promote private investment' – achieved some results, but did not ultimately provide a new growth model. The question for us to consider now is whether the flurry of new reforms which have gained momentum in recent years is likely to prove any different, and create a new 'virtuous circle of growth and distribution'.

From society 5.0 to 'new form of capitalism' and beyond

Away from the trumpets and fanfare of the three arrows, and now a largely-forgotten second set of arrows launched in 2015, the Council for Science, Technology and Innovation (CSTI) produced the 5th STI Basic Plan (2016–20), which introduced the concept of 'Society 5.0'.[10] This was peremptorily dismissed by some as one-upmanship vis-à-vis Germany's Industrie 4.0, but it gained considerable traction. One reason is that it provided a future-oriented direction to Japan's reform efforts, at least in terms of innovation, and it opened the way for an approach which balances market incentives, government direction, and industry-based collaboration, which had been missing hitherto. It also called for a change of approach in Japan's STI policy, from a focus on technology-push, to focus on social issues, like societal ageing and depopulation, and flexibility to respond to unpredicted events like Japan's earthquake, tsunami and earthquake triple disaster of 2011.

The concept spread to other government policy documents, and to Keidanren (Japan Business Federation) and its members, which is not surprising since a prominent member of the CSTI, Nakanishi Hiroaki, was also the chairman of Keidanren, and of the Hitachi group. Keidanren's (2017) 'Revitalizing Japan by Realizing Society 5.0' proposed an action plan to 2030. An economic analysis it subsequently commissioned claimed that the individual and combined impacts of investing in 57 emerging technologies critical for Society 5.0 – in next generation healthcare, smart mobility, energy, AI, etc. – would grow the economy from ¥531 trillion in 2015 to ¥900 trillion by 2030, as against ¥650 trillion for 'business as usual' (Nomura 2020).

Society 5.0 started as a vision of Japan's digital future, and the subsequent 'digital transformation' campaign (DX) became a vehicle for its realization. It began to incorporate other elements as well, however, especially 'green transformation' (GX) and realization of the UN's Strategic Development Goals (SDGs). DX and GX became the 'two wheels' driving Japan's economic transformation, according to the Green Growth Strategy, first released in December 2020 (Cabinet Office and 9 Ministries and Agencies 2021). Keidanren (2020), the Government Pension Investment Fund and the Institute of Future Initiatives at Tokyo University issued a joint report in 2020 which argued that if Society 5.0 and ESG (environment, social, governance) are combined, 'the problem-solving innovation ecosystem will evolve autonomously, Society 5.0 will be realized, and SDGs will be truly achieved' (14).

Reforming capitalism

Growth strategies alone, however, are insufficient to address deep-seated social issues, including growing inequality, demographic decline, and the need for rural revitalization. Concerns within Japan echoed growing calls for the reform of capitalism outside Japan, from the likes of BlackRock CEO Larry Fink, the US Business Roundtable, the World Economic Forum, the *Financial Times*, and more, who called on companies to serve a social purpose through stakeholder governance, and not just serve the pecuniary interests of their shareholders.

Abe had begun to address some of Japan's social issues, as well as wage stagnation, but Kishida more explicitly took up the 'distribution' side of 'growth and distribution'. As noted in the introduction, his new growth strategy was balanced by distribution policies, although he backtracked on income doubling when investors took fright.[11] If *investment* income doubling is really implemented, this would *increase* rather than decrease income and wealth disparities. Kishida was not pursuing the reform of capitalism in isolation. Before he came to power, Keidanren had announced its 'new growth strategy' and stakeholder-oriented 'sustainable capitalism', eliding the two and declaring that 'the extension of our current path of gradual reform offers no future for capitalism, and we intend to take bold steps to embark on this new strategy' (Tokura 2021). Indeed, government and Keidanren pronouncements were increasingly synchronized. Nor did Kishida give up. By the spring wage bargaining round of 2023 the more traditional understanding of 'growth and distribution' – that productivity growth should come first, and distribution should come from the resulting profits – was reinterpreted to assert that without wage growth there would not be productivity growth. In the *shuntō* wage round the government, supported by Keidanren and the trade union confederation Rengo, urged employers to give *above-inflation* wage increases wherever they could. Some did so, with headline-grabbing double-digit increases, but the problem was that overall, wage increases were subsequently nullified by rising inflation, so the recipients often found themselves no better off, and sometimes worse off.

A further concern was that large firms would be able to raise their prices, and wages, but small firms, lacking market power, could not. In fact, large firms might abuse their power to raise their prices and wages at the *expense of* their suppliers. The government and Keidanren organized a campaign called the *partnership kōchiku sengen* (partnership construction declaration), in which signatories promised to negotiate with their suppliers over price increases in good faith. By early 2023, over 22,000 companies had signed the declaration, and by late 2023, over 38,000 companies. A *Nikkei* company survey in late 2023 found not just a greater prospective willingness to concede above-inflation wage increases in 2024, but also acceptance of higher prices from suppliers so they could do the same (*Nikkei Asia* 2023e). In other words, the government and big business were playing a (cautious) role in wage and price coordination – echoing 1970s *shuntō* and corporatism, or alternatively a distinctively Japanese approach to coordinated capitalism (Witt 2006), with Rengo (Japan Trade Union Confederation) incorporated as a junior partner.

The wage increase push was part of an effort to restore the health of Japan's middle class. Acknowledging the role of capitalism and the market economy in bringing about unprecedented development, Keidanren (2023) nonetheless criticized the 'excessive focus on shareholder capitalism and market fundamentalism' that had depleted the middle class and 'created various social problems, such as environmental and ecosystem destruction, and the expansion and reproduction of inequality'. Shareholders and corporate governance were not the main focus of its proposals to rebuild a 'thick' middle class however. Shareholders were only mentioned three times in the report, and dividends not at all. By contrast, wages were mentioned fifteen times, and labour mobility eight times, echoing New Form of Capitalism Realization Council's 'new trinity labour market reform' proposals, announced just two weeks earlier (cf. Zou 2024 in this collection).

Dismantling "Japanese-style' employment

From around 2018 Keidanren had begun to call for its members to shift from 'membership-based' to 'job-based' employment. Following Hamaguchi (2009), post-war 'Japanese-style', 'lifetime employment' was now presented as 'membership-based', which no longer made sense because it trapped employees in companies and jobs they could no longer contribute to, and lacked incentives to draw them into emerging growth areas – especially IT and AI – after reskilling. Labour productivity would be improved, and wages would rise if the institutional obstacles to mobility were removed, so the argument went, but these deep-rooted and intertwined obstacles required a multi-pronged ('trinity') approach to reform. This consisted of 1) opportunities for re-skilling, which would enable workers to change jobs; 2) reform of the employment and wage system, especially moving from 'seniority-based' wages and promotion – the perennial bogeyman – to a 'job-based' system which would reward those acquired skills; and 3) support for labour mobility, especially to growth sectors.[12] Fundamentally, as the New Form of Capitalism Realization Council put it, it was a shift from 'careers as given by the company' to 'each individual chooses his or her own career'. This would require measures to make pensions portable to reduce tax on lump sum retirement or severance payments, reduce the time for receiving unemployment benefit, better career consulting and job changing advice, increase the hiring of mid-career workers and wage reform by companies, and most importantly, increase the provision of reskilling, both by companies, and the government.

Ironically, while both the government and Keidanren have been critical of financialized 'shareholder capitalism' for depleting the middle class, together their proposals advocate its companion – 'marketization' (Dore 2008), of labour markets. They are doing so for several reasons, including the need to attract skilled overseas workers, managers and entrepreneurs, for whom 'membership-based' employment does not make sense; the need to open corporate doors to the skills of women more widely; as well as a chronic shortage of skills in digital technologies. Kishida acknowledges the skills problem: 'The reality is that investment in education and training in the corporate sector in Japan is much lower than in other countries. My government has already introduced a three-year, 400 billion yen package' to support vocational education and training and recurrent education (Kishida 2022).

In fact, one survey found shareholders to be more interested in employee education and training as a means of raising corporate value than managers. Both groups were asked to list three top mid-to-long-term investment and financial priorities from a list of nine. Shareholders chose IT investment, R&D investment and just behind, investment in people. This was only the fifth choice of managers, well behind capital investment, IT investment, R&D investment, and investor returns! (*Nikkei shinbun* 2022). Perhaps the nature of the survey influenced the responses, but when put together with the meagre off-JT and OJT figures cited earlier, it seems that managers need to regain some of the virtues of the post-war system, rather than trying to jettison it.

As does the government, which has also under-invested in VET, and universities, for many years. Japan has one of the highest rates of private funding of universities among OECD countries, but the lowest rate of public sector expenditure, at a mere 40% of the OECD average (MEXT 2016). And university investment in research has been flat – it was ¥3.70 trillion in 2013 to ¥3.68 trillion in 2020, with the public sector contributing less than half of that amount (Sōmushō tōkeikyoku 2021). There will no doubt be a divergence of opinions about who is primarily responsible for 'reskilling' part of the trinity (why would companies invest in training only to lose employees through mobility, Rengo's chairperson pointed out?), and in practice if not in aspiration Japan remains far from being a social investment state which 'focuses on human capital and the labour market as anchors for individual well-being' (Leoni 2016, 196; cf. Kamimura 2021).

Evolving state-business relations

The government will have to play a more active role in labour market matters, such as investing more in its career advisory and job placement services, as well as public training facilities. In fact the agenda from Society 5.0 to new capitalism and beyond points to a bigger role for the state in other areas also. On the one hand, Lechevalier (2024) in this volume argues that financialization has weakened the government's ability to carry out these new roles, and that it may also be weakened by the widely reported exodus of younger bureaucrats, reportedly to startups. Yet it is also evident that Asia's first developmental state has been resurrected, albeit in a modified form which is less likely to ruffle the features of the country's trade and investment partners. The Green Growth Strategy (GGS), for example, not only asserts that GX and growth are compatible, but is explicitly presented as industrial policy, based on five policy tools (grants, tax incentives, finance guidance, regulatory reform and international collaboration) and targeting fourteen 'growth sectors' in energy, transport, manufacturing, home and office. An initial government ¥2 trillion pump priming allocation, designed to elicit ¥15 trillion worth of private sector investment, was subsequently raised to ¥20 trillion in the more comprehensive GX Realization Basic Plan in 2023. International development initiatives complementing the GGS include the Asia Energy Transition Initiative (2021) and Asia Zero Emissions Community (2022) (See Arimoto 2024; Nakai 2024, in this collection for more details).

Further, however, Japan's security environment has changed dramatically, both in terms of geopolitics, and cybersecurity, which in turn have implications for economic security. Defence-related security, cybersecurity and economic security have all been given substantial boosts, and are increasingly integrated, conceptually, and administratively under the Kantei, or Prime Minister's Office, which has grown to become the 'control tower' of Japan's new developmental state. The shifts gained momentum under the second Abe administration, and have been given added urgency under Kishida.

Long sheltered under the US security umbrella, Abe began to shift Japan's security stance with the establishment of the National Security Council in 2013. Article 9 of the Constitution was subsequently re-interpreted to include 'collective self-defence', and Kishida has proposed developing counterstrike capabilities and increasing defence spending to 2% of GDP by 2027. A Japanese version of the (US) Defence Advanced Research Projects Agency (DARPA) is mooted. The Cybersecurity Strategic Headquarters was also strengthened, while METI and its IT Promotion Agency began to issue Cybersecurity Management Guidelines to companies in 2015. Japan is still seen as a cybersecurity laggard – IISS (2021) for example, placed Japan in its bottom capability tier – and a serious breach of defence networks in 2020 and 2021, allegedly by China, shows much remains to be done in this area. More recently Japan passed the Economic Security Protection Act (2022), and appointed a cabinet-level Economic Security Minister. The law focuses on the stable supply of critical materials, critical infrastructure, critical technologies, and has a secret patent provision. The National Security Secretariat added an economic division to its existing six divisions in 2020, and by 2022 it had become the largest division.

Japan is increasingly closely coordinating its various security measures with its allies, especially the US, but also the Quad, which includes Australia and India, Chips 4 (US, Japan, Korea, Taiwan), US-Japan-South Korea, the EU. ... How far this goes will depend on geopolitics and geoeconomics, including the securitization of trade and investment, but given that even seemingly innocuous technologies and products can be used for military purposes, the potential for further tightening of economic security is real. In sum, state-market relations are moving back towards a larger role for state-coordination, in innovation, distribution, and security, although this movement is not without contradictions. Bold rhetoric, cautious initiatives and a nascent new developmental state have not (yet) halted or reversed the march of financialized, shareholder capitalism.

Which way forward?

Companies have accumulated significant internal reserves, roughly equivalent to Japan's GDP. There are growing pressures on them to deploy these reserves, but in which direction will they flow? There are some signs that large companies are regaining their appetite for (domestic) capital expenditure. The Development Bank of Japan's annual survey found that companies were planning to increase their capital spending in 2022–23 by 27%. The next year's survey found they had actually increased it by a more modest 11%, and the following year's planned 21% increase will probably be tempered as well, but DX and GX have set a direction, and much of the investment is concentrated in electric vehicles, semiconductors, production equipment and decarbonization (DBJ 2023). They are also spending more on wages increases, although to date this has largely been negated by inflation. And when asked whether their provision of human resource development spending had changed over the past 3 years, 61% of human resource management (HRM) managers to a 2023 Recruit survey responded no, while only 21% reported any increase (Recruit 2023). Many reported the need for substantial revision to their human resource development systems. This remains a weak link in the growth and distribution circle concept.

Shareholders and executives, on the other hand, have benefited most from profit distribution and companies dipping into their internal reserves. In the year to March 2023 shareholders received the highest ever dividends for a second year in a row, which is expected to be repeated in 2024. Share buybacks are closing in on ¥10 trillion. Executive compensation jumped by a massive 33%, ostensibly through linking compensation to performance (in a rising stock market), and the quest to secure top non-Japanese talent. According to one calculation, average executive pay in firms with a turnover of ¥1 trillion or more was ¥270 million ($1.8 million), roughly one third of the level of UK, German and French executives, and one seventh of the US level (*Nikkei Asia* 2023a, 2023b). Pointedly, it is rare to find a comparison of executive compensation with average or new employee compensation in Japan nowadays – this was once a typical measure of the 'employee-favouring firm'.

At the national, policy level there is evidence that policy making has become less siloed, and more joined up under the the Kantei. And yet, while the Kishida administration and Keidanren call for curbing shareholder capitalism and the restoration of a broad middle class, with a greater distribution to labour, the Financial Services Agency, together with the Tokyo Stock Exchange, continue their drive to make Japanese companies more attractive to investors, particularly overseas investors, now with their demand for P/B ratios above 1. This contradiction, which is partly structural due to Japan's integration into the US-led global economy, is seldom commented on. This might reflect the assertion by the architects of the Stewardship and Corporate Governance Codes that shareholders and managers share a common interest in increasing 'corporate value' for the medium-to-long term, or at least an 'increase-the-pie-first' strategy. The assertion of unitary values is drawn into question by cases like Toshiba, but on the other hand, it may be an attempt to create the very norms they are asserting. Private equity (PE), decried in the 2000s as vulture capital, has acquired a certain respectability in the intervening years by adhering to the norms of corporate value creation, thereby diverging from PE behaviour in other countries (Schaede 2020). If anyone can reconcile these seemingly divergent forces, it may be Japan, but it is a big 'if', and a more fundamental rethink of corporate governance may be needed.

Although Society 5.0 and 'new capitalism' claim to be people-centred, there is a long way to go before reality meets the aspiration. Japan is still far from being a social investment state. It can claim to have a revivified developmental state, promoting digital and green technologies, with evolved tools such as guidelines and codes, and mission-oriented industrial and innovation policy, and the promotion of startups, but it could also be pulled in a different direction if the security situation in East Asia deteriorates further.

Japan may not have created its new growth model which is equitable and green yet, but in terms of avoiding the extremes of Big Tech market oligopoly and financialized capitalism on the one hand, and an overbearing state on the other, it is worth taking its attempts to build Society 5.0 and reform its capitalism seriously.

Notes

1. Naikaku kanbō atarashii shihonshugi jitsugen honbu jimukyoku (November, 2021) 'Chingin, jinteki shihon ni kansuru dētashū' (Data on Wages and Human Capital), p. 2. 'New capitalism' will be used here rather than the government's preferred 'new form of capitalism'.
2. https://www.jetro.go.jp/en/reports/statistics.html accessed 27 December, 2023. The figures are listed in US$.
3. OECD figures for 2019 put Japanese R&D expenditure at 18 trillion; Japanese estimates are ¥19.6 trillion. Over the same period South Korean R&D expenditure more than quadrupled, and Chinese R&D expenditure grew more than twelve-fold. NISTEP 2021 and 2020: https://www.nistep.go.jp/sti_indicator/2021/RM311_11.html and https://www.nistep.go.jp/sti_indicator/2020/RM295_15.html accessed 14 August 2023.
4. In the first half of the 2000s alone they reduced their borrowing from banks by ¥40 trillion: T. Kawanami in *Nikkei shinbun* 17 December 2022 ('Semaru Reiwa no ginkō no saihen' [Looming Reiwa Bank Re-organization]).
5. In 2020 Japanese households held 54% of their financial assets in cash and bank deposits, compared with 14% in the US and 37% in the Euro 19: Kurosawa, (2020, 6).
6. Sumitomo Mitsui DS Asset Management Market Daily figures (5 July 2022, in Japanese). https://www.smd-am.co.jp/market/daily/marketreport/2022/07/news220705jp/ accessed 15 August 2023.
7. Financialization is 'the increasing role of financial motives, financial markets, financial actors and financial institutions in the operation of domestic and international economies' (Epstein 2005, 3), or 'a pattern of accumulation in which profits accrue primarily through financial channels rather than through trade and commodity production' (Krippner 2005, 12).
8. In smaller firms labour's share is higher, and the fall was less, but still substantial. Naikaku kanbō atarashii shihonshugi jitsugen honbu jimukyoku, 2021.
9. Dalton (2017); https://www.gender.go.jp/about_danjo/whitepaper/r03/zentai/html/zuhyo/zuhyo01-02-07.html accessed 16 August 2023. The proportion of men in non-regular employment increased from 9 to 22% over the same time period. Cf. Nagase (2024) in this volume.
10. Simply put, Society 5.0 is 'a human-centered society that achieves both economic development and solutions to social issues through a system that highly integrates cyberspace and physical space'. https://www.openaccessgovernment.org/japans-6th-science-technology-and-innovation-basic-plan/120486/ accessed 14 June 2022. Society 5.0 follows hunting and gathering (1.0), agricultural (2.0), industrial (3.0) and information (4.0) societies.
11. Income doubling was an echo of the 1960s policy of Ikeda Hayato, Prime Minister and head of Kishida's LDP faction. This policy linked growth and distribution through the *shuntō* wage bargaining mechanism.
12. In fact, as Nakata (2023) points out, the membership- versus job-based employment dichotomy is a false one; the careers of the majority of workers are already occupationally-based. And 'seniority-based' wages and promotion is misleading, as there has long been an ability or performance component in wages.

Acknowledgments

I would like to thank Kurosawa Yoshitaka for helpful discussions related to finance and investment in Japan. This paper draws on parts of my book *Building a New Economy: Japan's Digital and Green Transformation* (Oxford University Press, 2024).

Disclosure statement

No potential conflict of interest was reported by the author(s).

References

Arimoto, T. 2024. "The Transformation of Science, Technology and Innovation (STI) Policy in Japan." *Asia Pacific Business Review*. https://doi.org/10.1080/13602381.2024.2320539.

Boyer, R., and Y. Saillard. 2001. *Regulation Theory: The State of the Art*. London: Routledge.

Cabinet Office and 9 ministries and agencies. 2021. "2050 nen karbon nyūtoraru ni tomonau guriin seichō senryaku [Green Growth Strategy for 2050 Carbon Neutral]." Tokyo.

Corrado, C., C. Hulten, and D. Sichel. 2005. "Measuring Capital and Technology: An Extended Framework." In *Measuring Capital in the New Economy*, edited by C. Corrado, J. Haltiwanger, and D. Sichel, 11–46. Chicago: University of Chicago Press.

Corrado, C., C. Hulten, and D. Sichel. 2006. "Intangible Capital and Economic Growth." NBER Working Paper No. 11948. Cambridge, MA: NBER.

Dalton, E. 2017. "Womenomics, 'Equality' and Abe's Neo-Liberal Strategy to Make Japanese Women Shine." *Social Science Japan Journal* 20 (1): 95–105. https://doi.org/10.1093/ssjj/jyw043.

Deakin, S., and J. Buchanan. 2024. "Has Japan's Corporate Governance Reform Reached a Turning Point? Some Cautionary Notes." *Asia Pacific Business Review*. https://doi.org/10.1080/13602381.2024.2320535.

Development Bank of Japan. 2023. "2023 nendo setsubi tōshi keikaku chōsa [Survey on Capital Investment Plans for FY2023]." Accessed August 14, 2023. https://www.dbj.jp/pdf/investigate/equip/national/2023_summary.pdf.

Dore, R. 2000. *Stock Market Capitalism, Welfare Capitalism: Japan and Germany versus the Anglo-Saxons*. Oxford: Oxford University Press.

Dore, R. 2008. "Financialization of the Global Economy." *Industrial and Corporate Change* 17 (6): 1097–1112. https://doi.org/10.1093/icc/dtn041.

Epstein, G. 2005. "Introduction." In *Financialization and the World Economy*, edited by G. Epstein, 3–16. Cheltenham: Edward Elgar.

Fukao, K., T. Miyagawa, K. Mukai, Y. Shinoda, and K. Tonogi. 2009. "Intangible Investment in Japan: Measurement and Contribution to Economic Growth." *Review of Income and Wealth* 55 (3): 717–36. https://doi.org/10.1111/j.1475-4991.2009.00345.x.

Hamaguchi, K. 2009. *Atarashii kōyō shakai: Rōdō shisutemu no saikōchiku e* [A New Employment Society: Rebuilding the Labour Sysytem]. Tokyo: Iwanami shoten.

Hara, J. 2009. *Atarashii shihonshugi: Kibō no taikoku, Nihon no kanōsei* [New Capitalism: Country of Hope, Possibilities for Japan]. Tokyo: PHP.

Hara, J. 2017. *Kōeki shihonshugi: Eibeigata shihonshugi no shūen* [Public Interest Capitalism: The End of UK-US-style Capitalism]. Tokyo: Bungei shunjū.

IISS (International Institute for Strategic Studies). 2021. "Cyber Capabilities and National Power: A Net Assessment." London: IISS.

Inoki, T. 2016. *Zōho gakkō to kōjō: Nijuisseiki no jinteki shigen* [Supplement, Schools and Factories: Human Resources in the Twentieth Century]. Tokyo: Chikuma gakugei shobō.

Itami, H. 1987. *Jinponshugi kigyō: Kawaru keiei kawaranu genri* [Human Capital-Ism: Changing Management, Unchanging Principles]. Tokyo: Chikuma shobō.

Itami, H. 2024. *Nihon kigyō: Doko de, nani o, machigae, meisō shita no ka* [Drifting Japanese Companies: Where and What Have Been the Mistakes and Straying?] Tokyo: Toyo Keizai.

Iwao, S. 2023. *Nihon kigyō wa naze 'tsuyomi' o suteteiru no ka*a [Why are Japanese Companies Discarding Their 'Strengths'?]. Tokyo: Kobunsha.

Japan Times, The. 2023. "Japan's Powerful METI 'Eager' for Guidelines That Spur M&A, Official Says." April 18.

Kamimura, Y. 2021. "Hataraku koto no imi to hogo: Jizokukanō na deisento uaku no kōsō [The meanings and Protection of Work: Making Decent Work Sustainable]." Nihon rōdō kenkyū zasshi, No. 736, 77–86.

Katz, R. 2021. "Why Nobody Invests in Japan: Tokyo's Failure to Welcome Foreign Capital is Hobbling Its Economy." *Foreign Affairs*, October 13.

Katz, R. 2024. *The Contest for Japan's Economic Future: Entrepreneurs versus Corporate Giants*. New York: Oxford University Press.

Keidanren. 2017. "Revitalizing Japan by Realizing Society 5.0: Action Plan for Creating the Society of the Future." Tokyo: Keidanren.

Keidanren. 2023. "Sasutenaburu na shihonshugi ni muketa kōjunkan no jitsugen: Buatsui chūkansō no keisei ni muketa kentō kaigi hōkoku [Achieving a Virtuous Circle Toward Sustainable Capitalism: Report of the Deliberation Council on Forming a Thick Middle Class]." Tokyo.

Keidanren, Tokyo University and GPIF. 2020. "The Evolution of ESG Investment, Realization of Society 5.0, and Achievement of SDGs: Promotion of Investment in Problem-Solving Innovation."

Kim, Y.-G. 2023. "A Series of Seven Articles in the *Nikkei Shinbun*." July 21-29.

Kishida, F. 2021. *Kishida bijyon: Bundan kara kyōchō e* [Kishida Vision: From Division to Cooperation]. Tokyo: Kodansha.

Kishida, F. 2022. *Guildhall Speech*, May 5. London.

Kōsei rōdōshō. 2018. *Heisei 30 nen ban rōdō hakusho* [2018 White Paper on Labour]. Tokyo.

Krippner, G. 2005. "The Financialization of the American Economy." *Socio-Economic Review* 3 (2): 173–208. https://doi.org/10.1093/SER/mwi008.

Kurosawa, Y. 2020. "Nihon keizai: Teitai no 30 nen no gen'in – chōwa ga torenai baburu [The Japanese Economy: Causes of 30 Years of Stagnation]." *Toshika kenkyū kōshitsu, Rondan* 12:1–8.

Lazonick, W. 2014. "Profits Without Prosperity: Stock Buybacks Manipulate the Market and Leave Most Americans Worse Off." *Harvard Business Review*.

Lechevalier, S. 2024. "Society 5.0 and New Capitalism: Complementarities and Contradictions." *Asia Pacific Business Review*. doi:10.1080/13602381.2024.2320538

Leoni, T. 2016. "Social Investment as a Perspective on Welfare State Transformation in Europe." *Intereconomics* 51 (4): 194–200. https://doi.org/10.1007/s10272-016-0601-3.

Lucács, G. 2020. *Invisibility by Design: Women and Labour in Japan's Digital Economy*. Durham, NC: Duke University Press.

MEXT (Ministry of Education, Culture, Sports, Science and Technology). 2016. "K [Investment Supporting Higher Education: Related Material]." Accessed August 18, 2023. https://www.mext.go.jp/content/1413715_018.pdf.

Miyagawa, T. 2018. *Seisansei to wa nanika: Nihon keizai no katsuryoku o toinaosu* [What is Productivity: Reconsidering Japanese Economic Vitality]. Tokyo: Chikuma shinsho.

Miyagawa, T., and Y.-G. Kim. 2010. "Mukei shisan no keisoku to keizai k [Measurement of Intangible Assets and Their Economic Effects: Analysis at the Macro, Industry and Company Levels]." RIETI Policy Discussion Paper Series 10-P-014.

Miyajima, H., and R. Ogawa. 2022. "Atarashiii shihonshugi to jishakabukai kisei [New Capitalism and Regulation of Share Buybacks]." RIETI Special Report. Accessed July 17, 2022. https://www.rieti.go.jp/jp/special/special_report/169.html.

Nagase, N. 2024. "Much to Be Done in Japan's Family and Gender Equality Policies." *Asia Pacific Business Review*. https://doi.org/10.1080/13602381.2024.2320546.

Nakai, T. 2024. "Japan's triple sustainability challenge." *Asia Pacific Business Review*. https://doi.org/10.1080/13602381.2024.2320541.

Nakata, Y. 2023. "'Jobu-gata koyō o chushin to suru koyō shisutemu no minaoshi no dōkō' [Trends in Revision of the Employment System, Centred on 'Job-Based Employment']." In *Aratana jidai ni okeru keizai no kōjunkan jitsugen ni mukete* [Towards the Realization of a Virtuous Economic Cycle in a New Age], edited by R. Sōken 192–95. Tokyo: Rengo-RIALS.

Nakata, Y. 2024. "Remedying Japan's Deficient Investment in People." *Asia Pacific Business Review*. https://doi.org/10.1080/13602381.2024.2320549.

Nikkei Asia. 2023a. "Compensation for Japan's Top Executives Up Record 33% in 2022." August 16.

Nikkei Asia. 2023b. "Japan Inc. Annual Dividends at Record Levels Again." June 8.

Nikkei Asia. 2023c. "Japan Sees Explosion in 'Spot Workers' in Hotels, Bars, Stores." June 22.

Nikkei Asia. 2023d. "M&A Among Japanese Companies Jump 80% in Domestic Restructuring Push." August 15.

Nikkei Asia. 2023e. "More Japan Business Leaders Expect 5% Wage Hikes in 2024: Poll." December 28.

Nikkei shinbun. 2022. "Hito e no tōshi: Kigyō kachi o sayū, sukoa jōi no kabuka 7 waridaka [Investing in People: Affecting Corporate Value, Share Price of High Scorers 70 Percent Higher]." August 7.

Nikkeiren. 1995. *Shinjidai no Nihonteki keie* [Japanese Style Management for a New Era]. Tokyo: Nikkeiren.

Nomura, K. 2020. "Society 5.0 for SDGs: Sōzō suru mirai no Keizai hyōka [Society 5.0 for SDGs: An Economic Analysis of Future Created]." Tokyo: 21st Century Research Institute.

Recruit. 2023. Accessed August 18, 2023. https://www.recruit.co.jp/newsroom/pressrelease/assets/20230726_hr_01.pdf.

Schaede, U. 2020. *The Business Reinvention of Japan: How to Make Sense of the New Japan and Why It Matters*. Stanford: Stanford University Press.

Shibata, S. 2023. "Gender, Precarious Labour and Neoliberalism in Japan." In *Temporary and Gig Economy Workers in China and Japan: The Culture of Unequal Work*, edited by H. Fu, 48–73. Oxford: Oxford University Press.

Sōmushō tōkeikyoku. 2021. *Tōkei de miru Nihon no kagaku gijutsu kenkyū* [Japanese S&T Research in Statistics]. Tokyo: Sōmushō.

Sturgeon, T. 2002. "Modular Production Networks: A New American Model of Industrial Organization." *Industrial and Corporate Change* 11 (3): 451–96. https://doi.org/10.1093/icc/11.3.451.

Tokura, M. 2020. "The NEW Growth Strategy." Accessed January 11, 2024. https://www.keidanren.or.jp/en/policy/2020/108_proposal.html.

Tokura, M. 2021. "The NEW Growth Strategy." Accessed January 11, 2024. https://en.kkc.or.jp/international-platform/20210618.html.

Vogel, S. 2018. "Japan's Labour Regime in Transition: Rethinking Work for a Shrinking Nation." *Journal of Japanese Studies* 44 (2): 257–292. https://doi.org/10.1353/jjs.2018.0039.

Weathers, C. 2018. "The Contradictions of the Womenomics Campaign: Abe Shinzō's Employment Reforms and Japan's Public Service Workers." *US-Japan Women's Journal* 53 (1): 47–71. https://doi.org/10.1353/jwj.2018.0002.

Witt, M. 2006. *Changing Japanese Capitalism: Societal Coordination and Institutional Adjustment*. Cambridge: Cambridge University Press.

Yamakoshi, A. 2023. "'Scene Setting' Address to 'Reforming Capitalism, Going Digital and Green: Does Japan Hold Answers'." Oxford: Saïd Business School, 17–18 February.

Zou, F. 2024. "The 'New Trinity' Reform of Labour Markets in Japan." *Asia Pacific Business Review*. https://doi.org/10.1080/13602381.2024.2320550.

Society 5.0 and new capitalism: complementarities and contradictions

Sébastien Lechevalier ⓘ

ABSTRACT
In a context of proliferation of concepts proposed by the Japanese government and major other stakeholders this paper aims at determining whether it is the sign of an intellectual and political dynamism that would prepare the emergence of a new model or the symptom of a loss of bearings after years of neoliberalism. More precisely, it focuses on the relations between the Society 5.0 vision and the 'new/sustainable' capitalism one. In mobilizing the Régulation theory framework and a non-Schumpeterian approach to innovation, it put into their institutional context several reports that are advocating these visions. Our major conclusion is that, despite some conceptual similarities, several contradictions and dissonance between these visions are major impediments to the development of a new model. What is required is more coherent policies as well as the inclusion of a broader set of stakeholders to define the goals and the path of the reform.

Introduction

Society 5.0, sustainable capitalism, new capitalism, DX, GX ... The least one can say is that there is no scarcity of concepts proposed by the Japanese government to think what should look like the Japanese socio-economic system by the 2030s. Is this proliferation of terms the sign of an intellectual and political dynamism that would prepare the emergence of a new Japanese model or the symptom of a loss of bearings after decades of neoliberal reforms (e.g. liberalization of financial and labour markets, privatization, reform of the State. See Lechevalier (2014) for more details) that have destabilized the previous system but failed to produce a coherent alternative system?

Although it is difficult to give a definitive answer to this question at this stage, a preliminary step can be an effort to make sense of these different terms and associated policy proposals.

In this contribution, we build on Whittaker (2024) to further investigate what this conceptual spreading means in terms of institutional change and of potential emergence of a new Japanese model. To this end, we mobilize a Régulationist framework, mainly the concepts of crises, of institutional complementarities and hierarchy, and of ideational regime (Boyer 2015). More precisely, as Whittaker (2024), *coherence* is the main criterion in our evaluation of the potential emergence of a new model. It is analysed at the institutional level but also at the ideational level, in following the insights from Amable (2003) and from Amable and Palombarini (2009). This is necessary because many of the above concepts are not yet implemented in terms of reforms, and it is meaningful because of the importance of knowledge regimes (Maslow 2018) to complement the institutional dynamics.

More precisely, this article aims at comparing the two visions of, on the one hand, 'new capitalism' (pushed by PM Kishida since 2021) and 'sustainable capitalism' (proposed by Keidanren in 2020) and, on the other hand, of Society 5.0 (introduced in 2015 in the context of the 5th Science and Technology Basic Plan) in order to identify their complementarities and dissonance, in the Japanese institutional context of the early 2020s. Our goal is to discuss the conditions of emergence of an original model of capitalism and of innovation in a post-industrial Japan.

Our argument can be summarized as follows. For about 25 years, in order to solve the innovation crisis that Japan has been facing, a reform of the Japanese innovation system has been introduced to promote convergence towards the so-called Silicon Valley model (theoretically characterized by the major role of startups, deep interactions between industry and academia, as well as the existence of venture capital) but it has failed, and this is not a major problem. From this perspective Society 5.0 corresponds to a major progress in helping to think post-industrial economies and societies (beyond industry 4.0) and the potential of digitalization. This vision on the relation between innovation, technology and society is complementary to a certain form of capitalism (and not only a growth strategy, which is defined at the level of economic policies), which will define the conditions of production, distribution and other important parameters, according to the Régulation theory. This is why it is particularly important to understand whether Society 5.0 and new capitalism do have or not some complementarities or are characterized by some contradictions. Although these two visions are not at the same level,[1] we argue that they proceed from a same thinking on the future of the Japanese economy and society. In doing so, we expect that this paper contributes to the overall work in focusing on two areas, namely the innovation system and the socio-economic system.

Our research strategy mainly relies on an institutional and public policy analysis of innovation policies and structural economic reform in Japan, in critically mobilizing official reports. They are then put in context through an institutional analysis inspired by the Régulation theory. Our approach also mobilizes socio-economics of innovation and Science and Technology Studies (STS), in proposing a non-Schumpeterian view on innovation.

The rest of the paper is built as follows. After having proposed an analysis of the crises of Japanese capitalism and innovation model, we introduce the Society 5.0 and new/ sustainable capitalism visions and interpret them as answers to these crises. Then, we analyse the complementarities and dissonance between the two. A last section concludes.

Which crisis of capitalism and of innovation in Japan? A Régulationist view

The analysis of crises is at the heart of the research programme of the Régulation theory (Amable 2003). Growth regimes in this theoretical perspective emerge from the (constructed or much more often along an unexpected fit) alignment between different institutions, which is nothing but automatic. From this perspective, crisis is the normal state of the economy, as it corresponds to a period where actors are in conflict about the institutional hierarchy of the economy (Amable 2003; Amable and Palombarini 2009).[2]

Although we call for a joint analysis of different aspects of the crisis in the introduction of this article, we look separately in this section at the innovation crisis and at the capitalism crisis, for analytical purpose, but also because their analysis does correspond to two different branches of the literature.

Which crisis of Japanese capitalism?

The nature of the crisis of the Japanese economy since the early 1990s has been the matter of a lively debate. For some economists, the major reason is related to a series of short-term policy mistakes, in particular in the area of monetary policy (see, for example, Bernanke 2000; Koo 2013). On the contrary, other economists focus on structural factors such as the end of catch-up area, an ageing population and the lingering effects of the financial crisis provoked by the bubble (see, for example, Hoshi and Kashyap 2011; Motonishi and Yoshikawa 1999). This second category of explanations has achieved dominance over the past fifteen years. Within this category of explanations, the mainstream view is that this crisis is caused by a lack of structural reforms. In following Lechevalier and Monfort (2018), we argue that this convenient explanation is not validated by facts, given the important number of reforms introduced from the 1980s.

This is why, while emphasizing the importance of structural factors, our view is fundamentally opposed to this mainstream vision: we consider that the crisis of Japanese capitalism is first of all a coordination crisis, which is mainly related to the decay of synergies at the macro and micro levels, as well explained by Whittaker (2024), within a slightly different theoretical framework.

If one looks at the macro level (Figure 1), the differences between Japan, on the one hand, and Europe and the US, on the other hand, is striking when the evolution of nominal GDP is considered. However, once we take into account the demographic evolution and the price dynamics (deflation), Japan is much more similar to Europe. This is when one decomposes the GDP into its components (Table 1) that some characteristics of the Japanese trajectory between 2000 and

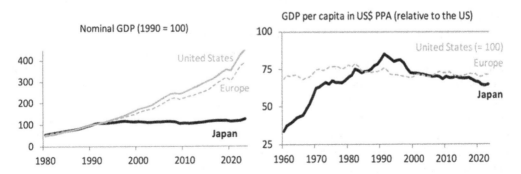

Figure 1. Evolution of the nominal GDP and of the real GDP per capita in Japan, the US and Europe until the early 2020s. Sources: OECD; IMF.

Table 1. Japan's main economic indicators 2001–2023.

	2001–2007	2008–2012	2013–2019	2020–2023
Average annual growth (per cent)				
Gross domestic product	1.3	−0.3	0.9	0.1
Private consumption	1.2	0.4	0.2	−0.1
Private investment	0.8	−2.2	2.0	−0.2
Exports	7.3	0.7	3.4	2.5
Inflation	−0.3	−0.2	0.8	1.2
Memorandum				
Population growth	0.1	0.0	−0.1	−0.3
Unemployment rate	4.7	4.6	3.1	2.6
Public debt (in per cent GDP)	164	206	232	258
Word GDP growth	4.4	3.3	3.4	2.4

Sources: CAO; IMF; author.

2020 appear. Private investment as well as exports are fluctuating around a declining growth trend but the most striking is the continuous decay of the growth rate of private consumption, from 1.2 points at the beginning of the period to −0.1 at the end. This evolution can be partly explained by demographics but it is also informative about the role of consumption in the transformation of the growth regime over this period.

This unbalanced nature of the Japanese growth regime at the macro level is confirmed at the micro level in two ways. First, if one concentrates on key indicators for the performance of large firms (capitalized at ¥1 billion or more) between 2000 and 2020, as Whittaker (2024) does, one gets the following stylized facts: labour costs of large firms have been cut, (domestic) capital investment has continuously declined, whereas operating profits almost doubled. As for the internal reserves, they have been multiplied by a factor of three, and dividends by a factor of six.

The second indicator of this unbalanced growth regime is visible at the supply side: as shown by Ito and Lechevalier (2009), one observes an increasing dispersion of labour productivity of firms in both manufacturing and non-manufacturing sectors for firms of similar size and belonging to the same sector, from the mid-1990s.[3]

To summarize, the crisis that Japanese capitalism is facing is not a matter of collapse but rather of unbalanced development, which is the symbol of end of an inclusive growth regime (Lechevalier and Shibata 2024). The above stylized facts can be certainly analysed in terms of balance sheet recession (Koo 2013) or profit and accumulation without investment (Durand 2017). However, what is striking in the Japanese case is that the lack of coordination between firms with different characteristics leads to poor macro performance. As explained by Lechevalier (2014), without trying to systematically explain the macro performance of economies by some underlying institutional characteristics, it is worth recognizing that the extremely decentralized structure of the Japanese post-war capitalism did require some coordination devices in order to deliver inclusive growth. All these institutions of different nature – such as industrial policy, 'bureaupluralism', keiretsu structure, or *shuntō* (i.e. a coordinated wage bargaining institution) – did experience decay from the 1980s (with a different timing for each of them) in a period of liberalization. Most of them have experienced a revival, under a different form from the 2010s, with the important exception of *shuntō*. We argue that it is a major reason for wage stagnation and thus for deflation and growth slowdown.

Abenomics constitutes a major attempt of better coordination of economic policies as symbolized by the image of 'three arrows'. However, it has not contributed to the 're-coordination' of the economy. In our view, this is because of its ideological and practical continuity with the agenda of 'neoliberal reforms', which has been introduced gradually from the 1980s and has been a source of institutional destabilization (Lechevalier 2014). This is the major reason why it has failed to push towards a new 'growth regime'[4] (Lechevalier and Monfort 2018) – which would be the successor of the post-war inclusive growth regime – which would be supported by a sustainable form of capitalism (Keidanren 2020). This is the major challenge for Post-Abenomics.

Which innovation crisis in Japan?

According to a mainstream view (Branstetter and Nakamura 2003; Nezu 2004), Japan has been facing an innovation crisis from the 1990s because of its backward institutions. The post-war Japanese innovation system has been successful in promoting the catch-up process. However, it did not adjust quickly enough to the end of the catch-up era, when the issue was less to imitate than to innovate; even more importantly, it has become unsuitable for a new technological context, characterized by the emergence of new technologies more crucially linked to science, as part of the emerging knowledge-economy, with shorter innovation cycles (Lechevalier 2014). In this context, there was no other possibility than to reform the Japanese innovation system to promote the convergence towards the best model in this new environment, that of Silicon Valley. It is supposedly characterized by the important role of entrepreneurship, venture capital, and of the collaboration between firms and universities. It seems to have indeed sup-ported the emergence of key technologies such as a new generation of internet and big data–based Information and communication technologies (ICT) or biotech.

A major conclusion of this view is that startups are the drivers of innovation and should be the focus of public policies. This is because of the importance of the mechanisms of creative destruction – according to which innovation is based on the emergence of new actors with new ideas and ways of producing, which will ultimately replace the incumbent players. This is why the relatively small number of startups and the lack of their growth in Japan by comparison to the US has been interpreted as a symbol of the weakness of the Japanese innovation system (Anchordoguy 2000). As a result, it is often concluded that innovation capabilities in Japan have overall declined (Branstetter and Nakamura 2003). Various anecdotal (e.g. the trajectory of Sony) and statistical evidences (e.g. the number of breakthrough innovations born in Japan) are then provided to support this view.

This analysis is inspired by the dominant Neo-Schumpeterian view regarding innova-tion and its role in the prosperity of advanced nations (Lechevalier 2019). By contrast to this mainstream view, our own view, inspired by the Régulation theory (Boyer 2003) and the social system of innovation approach (Amable, Barré, and Boyer 1997) emphasizes the necessary diversity of innovation systems. It can be summarized as follows. The right 'model' for innovation does not exist: it depends on the sector, the technology, etc. If it is difficult to deny that it is in the North of California that major new technologies have emerged during the 1980s-1990s, this is not the end of history. More precisely, we argue that different technologies require different models of innovation; moreover, different models of innovation are required in different industries, even when the same technology is considered (e.g. robotics in industries and in services). Even more importantly, when innovation is considered beyond technology, a very different type of innovation system, which is able to deliver social innovation, is required. As a whole, it defines a non-Schumpeterian approach to innovation (Lechevalier 2019).

To put it differently, we easily recognize that for about 25 years, the reform of the Japanese innovation system has failed to lead to a convergence to the so-called Silicon Valley model (Lechevalier 2014). However, in our view, this is not a major problem, especially in the present context, when ICT and biotech are still major general-purpose technologies: the main issue is rather to apply these technologies to various domains, where there is a real demand.

It does not mean that there is no problem of innovation in Japan. There is indeed an innovation crisis, as in many other countries, but it is not of the same nature than the one emphasized by the above view. Discussing about an innovation crisis might seem at little bit surprising, as there is no week during which a major breakthrough technological innovation is announced. Examples are diverse but range from the quick advance of AI (e.g. the introduction of ChatGPT) to the very rapid and simultaneous launch of several vaccines against Covid-19. Nonetheless, the crisis is of different nature and more about the relationship between the innovation system and society. We argue that there are rising doubts about the dominant Neo-Schumpeterian innovation model and a general decay in the trust in science, which has been particularly visible during the COVID-19 crisis, when several groups have promoted the idea of the existence of a conspiracy. Some components of this crisis are indeed quite general and not specific to Japan, such as the gap between the increasing resources dedicated to innovation and decreasing well-being observed in many cases (e.g. evolution of well-being of patients and nurses in European hospitals, where the investment in up-to-date technologies goes hand in hand budget cut and downsizing of the staff) or various technology-related scandals (e.g. in chemical or pharmaceutical industries).

In short, we argue that the crisis of innovation is the crisis of the relationship between technological innovation and society. While several technologies are potentially extremely beneficial to the society, their negative externalities are not always properly taken into account, which shed doubts on their positive impact. *Ex post* effort in making them more acceptable is clearly not enough, and if (scientific) education is certainly useful to rebuild the link between society and technology, there is no doubt that *ex ante* participation of citizens in the definition of priorities and limits to innovation would have much better outcomes, less in terms of acceptability than in the direction and the nature of innovation (Lechevalier 2019).

Although this crisis is quite global, there are also some characteristics that are specific to Japan. This country, which is among the most technophile and techno-centred, has been shaken by several events that have shed light on the inability of engineers to guarantee safety. The nuclear accident that has followed the Tohoku earthquake is certainly a turning point from this perspective. This has been understood by several key players of the Japanese innovation system, as we observe for about one decade the creation of social sciences and humanities departments in institutions such as the Japan and Science Technology agency (JST), RIKEN or Tokyo Institute of Technology.

Moreover, in relation with what has been identified above as a signal of the crisis of Japanese capitalism as a lack of coordination, Japan's major problem is its failure to diffuse (technological and organizational) innovation, a fact demonstrated by the growing productivity gap separating the nation's most productive firms from the rest of the economy (Lechevalier 2014). From this perspective, technological spillovers are the key for growth in the knowledge economy. Although it is difficult to measure their evolution at the level of the whole economy, it has been shown at the sectoral level, namely in the case of robotics that they can be promoted by government-sponsored research consortia (Lechevalier, Ikeda, and Nishimura 2010).

Ideological answers to crises: reforming the Japanese capitalism and innovation system

Society 5.0 as an answer to the innovation crisis: reconnection between technology and society

Society 5.0 is a concept that has been proposed in the 5th Science and Technology Basic Plan (December 2015) as a future society that Japan should aspire to. According to this vision, thanks to advanced digitalization, it will be possible to promote 'a human-centred society that balances economic advancement with the resolution of social problem by a system that highly integrates cyberspace and physical space'.[5] In short, in order for Japan to regain its Science, Technology and Innovation (STI) edge, it is proposed to apply digital technologies not only to (manufacturing) industries but also to a wide range of services and dimensions of the social life.

In general terms, in trying to better connect social needs and (mainly) technological innovation, the Society 5.0 vision can be considered as an attempt to propose solutions to the innovation crisis that has been described above. It corresponds to a major progress in helping to think postindustrial economies and societies (beyond industry 4.0) and the potential of digitalization. The example of what is expected from digitalization in the fields of healthcare and caregiving is very telling from this viewpoint. The emphasis is put on the role of the analysis of big data (including personal real-time physiological data, or healthcare-site information) through artificial intelligence. Concrete examples of innovation include: using robots to provide living support and conversation partners and to promote an autonomous way of living; using robots to ease the on-site burden of healthcare and caregiving; providing optimal treatment anywhere through the sharing of physiological and medical data. Moreover, it is worth emphasizing that these solutions are also presented as ways to help reducing the social costs associated with healthcare and caregiving and solving labour-shortage problems at healthcare sites.

In our view, the concept of Society 5.0 is now well established and serves as an essential reference to innovation policy and beyond. It is more generally a signal for a wide set of actors, from firms to government through research institution. The Society 5.0 vision has inspired the STI policies, which have been redirected towards a mission-based type (Mazzucato 2018), as it is visible in the Moonshot Research and development programme, which corresponds to the implementation of policies inspired by the Society 5.0 vision.

New capitalism as an answer to the crisis of capitalism: re-coordination

As well explained in the introduction of this volume, the concept of 'new capitalism' has emerged from the fall 2021 campaign for the Liberal Democratic Party (LDP) leadership, which is the crucial step to become Prime Minister. At that time, it was summarized by Kishida Fumio as the necessity of creating a virtuous circle of growth and redistribution through economic and social reform initiatives, in order to correct various flaws that have been generated by capitalism. This accidental context means that the concept is fragile and highly dependent on the fate of PM Kishida.

To put it differently, in our view the new capitalism programme does not correspond to a well-established vision. It has been elaborated by a small circle of advisors (e.g. among them Kihara Seiji), with the goal to differentiate Kishida's programme from Abenomics, the economic programme of former Prime Minister Abe (2012–2020). It has been challenged and criticized by a part of the Japanese elite, as being ambiguous if not in contradiction with some conservative principles, which are the DNA of the LPD. This has been visible in the media after the election of PM Kishida, but also, and even more surprisingly, during the discussion within the 'Council of New Form of Capitalism Realization'. In reading the minutes of this council that have been published,[6] it is possible to identify a narrower vision with an exclusive focus on the promotion of startups, which is the signal of a form of ideological backlash, dominated by the Neo-Schumpeterian vision of innovation and economic growth. After some successful lobbying from the most conservative members of the political and economic elite, this programme has become more standard from a conservative viewpoint, and partly disconnected from the Society 5.0 vision, as introduced previously.

Does it mean that its importance should be neglected and we may predict that its legacy will be very limited? We do not think so, for at least two reasons. First, as well shown by Whittaker (2024), it is in fact very much connected to the Keidanren vision of 'sustainable capitalism', as published in the 'The new growth strategy' report (2020).[7] There is no direct evidence that PM Kishida and his advisors got directly inspired by the concept of 'sustainable capitalism' in the elaboration of the concept of 'new capitalism'. However, there is an obvious convergence as well pointed out by Whittaker (2024, 10).

Second, as the 'sustainable capitalism' vision, it corresponds to some deeply rooted ideas in the Japanese context. We may cite here the 'Godfather' of Japanese capitalism, Shibusawa Eiichi (1840–1931), according to whom capitalism should be fundamentally ethical (*gapponshugi*) and should bring capital, labour, and management together to serve the public interest.

Therefore, if one takes seriously the idea of 'new/sustainable' capitalism, as promoted by PM Kishida and Keidanren, how to define their major characteristics? First, new capitalism is clearly presented as an answer to the crisis of the capitalism, as it has developed from the 1980s. The problem is no more the reform of the post-war capitalism but the 'reform of the reformed Japanese capitalism', which has a strong Neoliberal flavour. It explicitly appears in PM Kishida's speech in May 2022 in London: 'Why does capitalism need upgrading? Because we need to solve two crucial present-day challenges. One is the problem of economic externalities, such as widening inequality, climate change, and issues deriving from urbanization'.[8] It is worth noting that he refers to the Japanese capitalism but implicitly also to the dominant capitalism at the global level. It means that there a defiance on some aspects of shareholder capitalism that goes hand in hand with the promotion of stakeholder cap talism (Whittaker 2024). Does it mean that Japan should head towards the stakeholder model of the post-war period? Despite some references to the 1960s policies of then Prime Minister Ikeda, the new capitalism vision is rather forward-looking, in trying to benefit from digitalization and to overcome the environmental crisis by promoting a more sustainable model. Even more importantly, it put values on the importance of reintroducing coordinating mechanisms and consistent institutional linkages (such as *shuntō*) in order to limit the disconnection between the micro- and the macro-levels and to promote a new form of inclusive growth, which would benefit more or less to all, and not only to capital.

As a whole, these two answers – Society 5.0 and 'new/sustainable' capitalism – go in the same direction of a human-centred mode of development. However, it does not go without tensions and conflict, especially within Keidanren and LDP – the Society 5.0 vision being more consensual – and without contradictions or dissonances, which are analysed in the next section.

Complementarities and disconnection between Society 5.0 and new capitalism: an overall lack of coherence

Complementarities between Society 5.0 and new capitalism

The complementarity between Society 5.0 and 'new capitalism' (especially in its Keidanren version of 'sustainable capitalism') first appears in terms of individuals who have participated in the making of both concepts (Whittaker 2024, 10). Here, the figure of Nakanishi Hiroaki, who has been the president of Hitachi between 2010 and 2014, is absolutely central. As well pointed out by Whittaker (2024), he has been a member of the commission of the Council for Science and Technology Policy (CSTP), from which emerged the concept of Society 5.0. Few years later, in 2018 he became the chairman of Keidanren (Japan Business Federation), until his death in 2021. Under his leadership, Keidanren published a report, 'Revitalizing Japan by Realizing Society 5.0: Action Plan for Creating the Society of the Future', in which a roadmap was defined to reach the goals of Society 5.0, while making it at the same time a key value and a source of revitalization of the economy.

This is again under the leadership of Mr. Nakanishi that Keidanren published its 'New growth strategy', in which it advocates to make capitalism more sustainable.[9] In this report, growth, form of capitalism and Society 5.0 are clearly linked. The legacy of this effort seems to be confirmed, as Tokura Masakazu (Chairman of the Board, Sumitomo Chemical Company), has been designated to be the successor of Mr. Nakanishi, as the Keidanren chairman, and as, at the time of writing, in Fall 2023, there is no sign of discontinuity in the priorities set by Keidanren. Although it is difficult to trace the direct influence of 'sustainable capitalism' on 'new capitalism', the role of one key adviser of PM Kishida, Kihara Seiji, has been underlined.

Beyond the human and intellectual origin of both concepts, are we able to identify ideological commonalities? The answer is positive. If considered seriously, society 5.0 may correspond to a new vision not only of STI policies and of economic development driven by digital technologies but also of capitalism. In context of Society 5.0, the focus is indeed

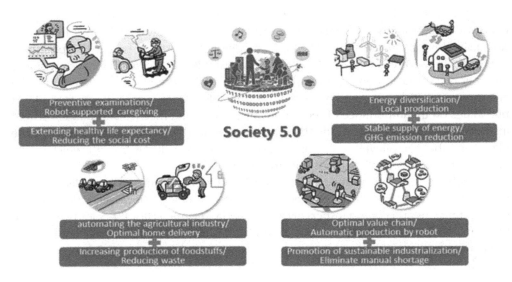

Figure 2. Society 5.0: a vision for post-industrial growth. Source: Cabinet Office (https://www8.cao.go.jp/cstp/english/society5_0/index.html. Accessed on 11 August 2023.

clearly on the improvement of well-being, rather than on GDP growth, as it is visible in Figure 2: this is an issue-oriented vision of Science, Technology and Innovation policies, whose aim is to propose technology-based solutions to various social and economic challenges, such as ageing and health issues, environmental issues, production issues, etc. It means that, at a more ideological level, a real convergence between Society 5.0 and new/sustainable capitalism, is also visible, with an emphasis on human being. In promoting the emergence of a Society 5.0 since the mid-2010s, the Japanese government has not only encouraged the use of digital technologies outside manufacturing plants, for different aspects of social life, but also elaborated a vision, which should logically lead to a discussion about the desirable socio-economic system that should be associated to it.

If these two visions – Society 5.0 and new/sustainable capitalism – are logically connected, how can we summarize their relation? We cannot disagree with the following image: 'As a simplification, if DX and GX are wheels of a cart, and Society 5.0 is the destination, capitalism is the cart itself' (Whittaker 2024, 105). However, our analysis is at both ideational and institutional levels. From this perspective, what is crucial is to analyse the degree of institutional complementarities between the social system of innovation that lead to Society 5.0 and the institutions that are at the basis of new capitalism. From this perspective, a series of dissonance appear that may make it difficult for the car 'new capitalism' to reach its destination 'society 5.0', to use Whittaker's image.

Sources of dissonance between new capitalism and society 5.0

In what follows, we identify four major sources of dissonance: the priority put on startups to promote a human-centred capitalism and society; the gap between the critics on shareholder capitalism and the absence of fundamental reconsideration of the role of corporate governance and investor relations; the unbalanced impact of digitalization; the contradictions between the revival of an ambitious development state and the decay of capabilities of the Japanese state.

First, Society 5.0 requires to be achieved a clear departure from the Schumpeterian view on innovation and of capitalism, as it is the major cause of the innovation crisis, as explained above. This is not yet the case, as it is visible in the emphasis on startups within the Committee for the promotion of new capitalism. Startups as a whole are one of the major contributors to innovation but what is required to reach Society 5.0 is of different nature: the key is less decentralized breakthrough innovation that could become *ex post* acceptable to the public, thanks to various efforts, including marketing, than a coordinated effort to promote innovation that increases wellbeing and that is well diffused in order to increase its impact, if possible in an inclusive way. This inadaptation between the destination and the vehicle is also visible in the way the STI policies inspired by Society 5.0 is organized. Namely, the Moonshot programme is the core of this STI policy and, as a mission-based STI policy framework, it is connected to the goals of Society 5.0. However, although it is organized in 9 goals that cover different social challenges, it is obvious that the drivers are rather technological than social, as it can be seen in the management by different agencies that cover different technological fields (Lechevalier and Kodate 2024).

Second, so far, despite their critics against shareholder capitalism, Kishida and Keidanren are not challenging the dominant institutional form of 'reformed' Japanese capitalism under neoliberal policies at the company level, namely corporate governance and investor relations, as well explained by Whittaker (2024). In Régulationist terms, as employment and industrial relations have been downgraded, the wage labour nexus has lost its centrality and is no more at the top of the institutional hierarchy, where it has been replaced by Corporate governance and investor relations, as well explained by Whittaker (2024). This is not a problem *per se* but it largely explains the unbalanced nature of growth in Japan since the early 2000s (as explained above) and the fact that it does not benefit at all the categories, which is in rupture with the model of inclusive growth that Society 5.0 is trying to revive.

Third, digitalization, as it is promoted in Japan, is aggravating this unbalanced nature of the growth model and may contribute to the reinforcement of a Neoliberal model, despite official efforts from the government and Keidanren to move beyond its limitations. In its present form, digitalization is not a wheel of the car towards Society 5.0. This is visible at the level of government policies. According to Shibata (2022), digitalization is far from pushing towards new capitalism but rather used to achieve a neoliberal agenda, which accelerates the flexibilization of the labour market and ensure profit-oriented restructuring. When one looks at the effects of digitalization at the shop floor level, some benefits appear, but they systematically favour the companies and not the workers. This is, for example, visible in the hospitality sector with the introduction of devices for booking, ordering of food serving, leading to a deterioration of working conditions (Shibata 2022). If some positive effects can be detected from the viewpoints of productivity and monitoring, this is not the case in terms of wellbeing, which contradicts the very concept of Society 5.0, even without assuming that there is a clear intention of the government and of the firms to pursue the neoliberal agenda of flexibilization, because of the lack of unity of these two groups (Whittaker 2024).

It does not mean that digitalization in the Japanese context is just a continuation of the Neoliberal trend. In some cases, it may have contributed to further flexibilization but the degree of deskilling etc. is never the same than in the US, for example. It means that the techno-feudal hypothesis (Durand 2020) is not verified in the Japanese context. There is a diversity of digitalization, because not everything is determined by technology and because institutions matter in this process (Lechevalier and Shibata 2024). Technology itself is not able to fundamentally change the political economy; this is the political economy (e.g. the weakness of unions) that will condition the effect of technological change. As a result, it has some consequences on the model of growth. The inclusive growth regime has experienced a decay much before the first substantial effects of digitalization but, in a later stage, it has been one of the major sources of inequalities in post-industrial Japan, through the emergence and the consolidation of a digital divide, which is far from 'human-centric' society or stakeholder capitalism.

Last but not least, although the Japanese government is showing a new activism in promoting the emergence of society 5.0 and in trying to rebuild some coherence between the form of capitalism and the social system of innovation, we may have some doubts in its ability to succeed. A first indicator is the systematic gap between the numerical targets set by the government (e.g. in terms of startups creation) and the actual number of startups (see for example Hemmert et al. 2022). Rather than a form of strategic hyperbole, an instrument for institutional change (Whittaker 2024, 170), we interpret it as a sign of the decay of both government expertise and efficient implementation of policies. Moreover, in our view, it is deeply rooted in what can be analysed as a decay of state capabilities. One indicator is the attractiveness of the bureaucracy for young graduates from the best universities.[10] More profoundly, as shown by Lechevalier et al. (2019), financialization, which has been promoted by the Japanese government from the 1970s-1980s, has weakened the institutional capabilities of the Japanese state. At a theoretical level, it is possible to identify a weakening complementarity and a changing hierarchy between finance and state (especially in its allocative capability, which is the core of industrial policies), to the detriment of this last one. It means that any revival of the developmental state, as it seems to be the case with the combination of Society 5.0 and new capitalism, will suffer from the dismantlement of its financial arm. Concretely, the privatization of the Post under PM Koizumi has durably weakened the Fiscal Investment and Loan Program (FILP), which has not been replaced by any equivalent. As a result, we may have some doubt on the capability of the state to be the driver of the car leading to Society 5.0: the Japanese government has no more the capacity of influencing the allocation of resources, as it is shown by the systematic failure of promoting startups for more than two decades.

All these sources of contradictions and difficulties do not mean that there is no chance to reach a form of coherence. It rather means that several additional steps are required to reach Society 5.0. The following section is dedicated to the description of one possible path towards more coherence.

Which model of innovation to realize society 5.0? Which model of capitalism for post-industrial Japan?

The goal of this section is not to set a normative view on the Japanese capitalism and innovation system but rather to look at the institutional conditions of realization of Society 5.0 and new capitalism, in taking seriously these two visions.

Towards a care-led innovation model?

Society 5.0 is orienting the innovation system towards the solution to social problems. Among the various social problems, which Japan is facing, ageing society is by far the most crucial. This is why, without surprise, it is central in both the Society 5.0 vision and in its implementation in Moonshot programme, especially the Moonshot Goal 7 ('Realization of sustainable care systems to overcome major diseases by 2040, for enjoying one's life with relief and release from health concerns until 100 years old'), in relation with health issues.

Ageing society is partly related to the increasing longevity of human being. In this context, the issue of long-term care has become a privileged area for the application of technologies, in the spirit of promoting a 'silver economy'. This is particularly the case in the Japanese context, characterized by an important and increasing 'Care gap': with the ageing of population, the needs for eldercare are increasing while the number of potential care staff is stable or decreasing, especially in the context of restrictive immigration policies. This is why the potential contribution of several technologies (notably robotics, artificial intelligence [AI], information and communication technologies [ICT]) has been recognized, as they can partly solve problems of autonomy and vulnerability, whether it concerns communication, mobility or cognitive abilities. However, at the same time, several important limitations have been emphasized (Wright 2023), as well as a gap between the promotion of robots in eldercare by public policies and the real social needs, as industrial policy goals are still dominating social policy goals.

We argue that the difficult introduction of technologies in eldercare is not a one-off problem, but a fundamental impasse related to the way in which social needs and technological responses are articulated, in line with the dominant Schumpeterian paradigm of innovation, as explained above. There is an urgent need to reconnect social and technological dynamics, by proposing concepts and practices of innovation that make well-being the ultimate criterion for innovation, and we believe it is not unachievable in the Japanese context.

Our argument is that achieving the goal of overcoming the eldercare gap, as other social goals, requires a different approach to innovation than the one that has been at work to promote (mainly manufacturing) competitiveness. In order to fully accomplish the Society 5.0 vision, our proposal is to put the concept of *care* at the heart of the innovation process. This concept indeed allows us to clarify and specify social needs, focusing on inter-individual and social relationships and to consider both material and affective dimensions of care situations mobilizing innovative technologies (Lechevalier and Kodate 2024).

It requires defining more precisely the notion of care, in following the work by Paperman and Laugier (2020). It is a material, technical, emotional and affective work, which is done within social, sex, class and race relationships between different types of actors: the care givers, the beneficiaries and those who supervise and prescribe the work. The care is not only a caring attitude but it corresponds to a set of material and relational activities, sometimes intricated with highly specialized curative techniques, whose aim is to give a concrete answer to others' needs. It can be defined as a service, support and assistance relationship, which implies a sense of responsibility vis-à-vis others' well-being.

Bringing users closer to technological innovations is far from being an isolated concern, and the analysis of technological innovations in the field of care for older adults has made significant progress in this respect. However, this approach is still very much influenced by the 'acceptability' perspective. By contrast, the focus here is not on individual users but on inter-individual and social relations.

Although, care-led innovation is at this stage mainly a methodology, whose aim is to improve technologies used in eldercare, it is possible to identify several cases of innovation that do correspond to the principles of care-led innovation (Lechevalier and Kodate 2024). One example is the use of passive monitoring devices (hereafter PMD) to monitor safety and support independent living of older persons (Obayashi, Kodate, and Masuyama 2020).

In short, a model of social innovation is needed to realize Society 5.0; care-led innovation can be this model, if it is extended beyond eldercare and long-term care. It does not exclude the use of new technologies but emphasizes the innovation at a given level of technology. In this model, major actors will not be necessarily startups, which are nonetheless an important actor, but a larger set of stakeholders that includes: users, non-users, communities, and any institution that may help to socialize the costs and the risks while acting for the common good (e.g. governments).

The Japanese way to the emergence of an anthropogenic mode of development

The human centred vision at the core of new/sustainable capitalism is not without any relation with the concept of 'anthropogenic mode of development', as developed by Boyer (2019). This is a concept introduced in the context of discussions regarding successors to the Fordist regime that aims at describing a mode of development, in which three service sub-sectors – healthcare, education, and culture – are central, as seen by the fact that expenditures in these sectors tend to supplant the acquisition of standard goods and services. It focuses on the production of man by human labour and does put at its centre the notion of wellbeing as the key criteria to evaluate the outcome of this new mode of development.

It is itself diverse, as it is visible through the contrast between the costly and unequal US Anthropogenic model and the muted emergence of an Anthropogenic model in Japan. The contrast between these two different forms is striking: putting aside the issue of inequalities that has been well studied (Tachibanaki 2009), an important difference concerns the average life expectancy, which is much higher in Japan in the US, while healthcare expenditures are more than 40% lower than in the United States, which is all the more remarkable since the Japanese population is much more aged than the US one. In terms of education, access to higher education is better in Japan than in the United

States, although some studies reveal some unequal trend (Kariya 2016). However, there are also problems in the emergence of an anthropogenic model in Japan, as revealed by the very low declining Japanese fertility rate, which is a major cause of ageing and shrinking population.

The demographic issue is not a minor one. In our view, this is a symbol of the contradiction between the productive and reproductive sphere (Fraser 2016). It would an illusion to consider that technology alone would be enough to overcome this challenge, as it might be understood from the reading of some reports on Society 5.0. Demography is a domain for which care-led innovation may play a major role, besides the initial focus on eldercare. This is why we may imagine the development of complementarities between this model of innovation and the anthropogenic mode of development, at the condition of rebalancing the hierarchy between the wage-labour nexus and the corporate governance.

Conclusion: society 5.0, a change in innovation policies and a new perspective for Japanese capitalism?

This article has investigated the complementarities and dissonances between the visions of Society 5.0 and of new/sustainable capitalism, which have been introduced within the last decade in Japan. Our purpose is to determine whether they prefigure the emergence of a new model of capitalism and of innovation. Based on a Régulationist framework, our strategy has been to analyse them as answers to crises. What is indeed needed is an analysis of the crisis of Japanese capitalism that does not deny the importance of innovation but that incorporates social changes, which are not only the outcomes of innovation but its precondition.

We argue that the discussion in Japan on Society 5.0 may lead to a major change in opening the door to the emergence of alternative models of capitalism – such as an 'Anthropogenic' mode of development – and of innovation. A model of non-Schumpeterian innovation is needed to realize Society 5.0; care-led innovation can be this model. It does not exclude the use of new technologies in order to solve social problems but rather emphasizes social innovation based on existing technologies.

What can be learnt from the history of the emergence of new regime is that top/down visions are not enough. A participation from various stakeholders is required in order to allow for unexpected fits that are the major conditions for this emergence. In order to achieve the building of Society 5.0, major actors will not be necessarily startups but a larger set of stakeholders.

The major requirement to achieve Society 5.0 is to move from the concept of innovation as a tool for competitiveness to the concept of innovation as a source of well-being. The new model of innovation that should be associated to Society 5.0 is highly complementary to an anthropogenic mode of development. This is in reimagining a form of coherence that Japan can propose a model for the 21st century. Our answer to the initial question is therefore mixed. Although there are complementarities between the visions of capitalism and of techno-society, there are also contradictions and dissonance that are the signals of an overall lack of coherence.

This article has focused on the level of principles in identifying two complementary models of capitalism and of innovation – namely the anthropogenic mode of

Notes

1. Society 5.0 has been gradually elaborated by the Japanese administration in charge of technologies, with the contribution with the academia and other stakeholders, whereas 'new capitalism' is partly an accidental concept, elaborated in the context of a political campaign in order to distinguish a politician from its predecessors, when 'sustainable capitalism' has been proposed, outside the government by the major business federation, but with an emphasized continuity with the concept of Society 5.0.
2. A institutional complementarity can be seen as the synergy between two beneficial constraints. This concept should be distinguished from the one of institutional hierarchy that implies a certain asymmetry between institutions (Boyer 2015; Lechevalier, Debanes, and Shin 2019).
3. This performance dispersion is explained by an 'unobservable' heterogeneity, which has led to further investigation. Among the possible causes, one may cite the interaction between innovation and international strategies (Ito and Lechevalier 2010).
4. The existence of a growth regime is not detected here by the level of GDP growth but rather by its institutional coherence (Whittaker 2024).
5. https://www8.cao.go.jp/cstp/english/society5_0/index.html. Retrieved on 11 August 2023.
6. See for example https://www.kantei.go.jp/jp/101_kishida/actions/202304/25shihon.html. Retrieved on 3 August 2023.
7. https://www.keidanren.or.jp/en/policy/2020/108_proposal.html. Retrieved on 11 August 2023.
8. See https://japan.kantei.go.jp/101_kishida/statement/202205/_00002.html. Retrieved on 5 August 2023.
9. https://www.keidanren.or.jp/en/policy/2020/108_proposal.html. Retrieved on 11 August 2023.
10. We are grateful to Takehiko Kariya for having drawn our attention on a series of articles publishes in *Asahi Shimbun* on this topic: https://www.asahi.com/edua/article/14757614?p=1. Retrieved on 16 September 2023.

Acknowledgments

The author is extremely grateful to Hugh Whittaker and Franz Waldenberger for their constructive comments and to Brieuc Monfort for this help regarding data. Usual caveats apply.

Disclosure statement

No potential conflict of interest was reported by the author(s).

Funding

This work was supported by a French government grant managed by the Agence Nationale de la Recherche under the France 2030 program, reference ANR-23-PAVH-0005.

ORCID

Sébastien Lechevalier (iD) http://orcid.org/0000-0002-1416-0342

References

Amable, B. 2003. *The Diversity of Modern Capitalism*. Oxford: Oxford University Press.

Amable, B., R. Barré, and R. Boyer. 1997. *Systèmes nationaux d'innovations*. Paris: Economica.

Amable, B., and S. Palombarini. 2009. "A Neorealist Approach to Institutional Change and the Diversity of Capitalism." *Socio-Economic Review* 7 (1): 123–143. https://doi.org/10.1093/ser/mwn018.

Anchordoguy, M. 2000. "Japan's Software Industry: A Failure of Institutions." *Research Policy* 29 (3): 391–408. https://doi.org/10.1016/S0048-7333(99)00039-6.

Bernanke, B. 2000. "Japanese Monetary Policy: A Case of Self-Induced Paralysis." In *Japan's Financial Crisis and Its Parallels to US Experience*, edited by R. Mikitani and A. Posen, 149–166. Washington (DC): Institute for International Economics.

Boyer, R. 2003. "The Embedded Innovation Systems of Germany and Japan: Distinctive Features and Futures." In *The End of Diversity? Prospects for German and Japanese Capitalism*, edited by K. Yamamura and W. Streeck, 147–182. Ithaca: Cornell University Press.

Boyer, R. 2015. *Économie politique des capitalismes. Théorie de la régulation des crises*. Paris: La Découverte.

Boyer, R. 2019. "How Scientific Breakthroughs and Social Innovations Shape the Evolution of the Healthcare Sector." In *Innovation Beyond Technology*, edited by S. Lechevalier, 89–119. Singapore: Springer.

Branstetter, L. G., and Y. Nakamura. 2003. "Is Japan's Innovative Capacity in Decline?" In *Structural Impediments to Growth in Japan*, edited by M. Blomstrom, J. Corbett, F. Hayashi, and A. Kashyap, 191–224. Chicago: University of Chicago Press.

Durand, C. 2017. *Fictitious Capital: How Finance is Appropriating Our Future*. London: Verso Books.

Durand, C. 2020. *Techno-féodalisme. Critique de l'économie numérique*. Paris: La Découverte.

Fraser, N. 2016. "Contradictions of Capital and Care." *New Left Review* 100:99–117.

Hemmert, M., A. R. Cross, Y. Cheng, J. J. Kim, M. Kotosaka, F. Waldenberger, and L. J. Zheng. 2022. "New Venture Entrepreneurship and Context in East Asia: A Systematic Literature Review." *Asian Business & Management* 21 (5): 831–865. https://doi.org/10.1057/s41291-021-00163-1.

Hoshi, T., and A. Kashyap. 2011. "Why Did Japan Stop Growing?" *National Institute for Research Advancement (NIRA)*.

Ito, K., and S. Lechevalier. 2009. "The Evolution of Productivity Dispersion of Firms. A Reevaluation of Its Determinants in the Case of Japan." *Review of World Economics* 145 (3): 404–429. https://doi.org/10.1007/s10290-009-0027-0.

Ito, K., and S. Lechevalier. 2010. "Why Some Firms Persistently Out-Perform Others? Investigating the Interactions Between Innovation and Exporting Strategies." *Industrial and Corporate Change* 19 (6): 1997–2039. https://doi.org/10.1093/icc/dtq056.

Kariya, T. 2016. "Understanding Structural Changes in Inequality in Japanese Education: From Selection to Choice." In *Social Inequality in Post-Growth Japan: Transformation During Economic and Demographic Stagnation*, edited by D. Chiavacci and C. Hommerich, 149–165. London: Routledge.

Keidanren. 2020. *Shin seichō senryaku*. Tokyo: New Growth Strategy.

Koo, R. C. 2013. "The World in Balance Sheet Recession: Causes, Cures and Politics." In *Post-Keynesian Views of the Crisis and Its Remedies*, edited by O. Dejuán, E. F. Paños, and J. U. Gonzalez, 46–65. London: Routledge.

Lechevalier, S. 2014. *The Great Transformation of Japanese Capitalism*. London: Routledge.

Lechevalier, S., Ed. 2019. *Innovation Beyond Technology: Science for Society and Interdisciplinary Approaches*. Singapore: Springer.

Lechevalier, S., P. Debanes, and W. Shin. 2019. "Financialization and Industrial Policies in Japan and Korea: Evolving Institutional Complementarities and Loss of State Capabilities." *Structural Change and Economic Dynamics* 48:69–85. https://doi.org/10.1016/j.strueco.2017.08.003.

Lechevalier, S., Y. Ikeda, and J. Nishimura. 2010. "The Effect of Participation in Government Consortia on the R&D Productivity of Firms: A Case Study of Robot Technology in Japan." *Economics of Innovation & New Technology* 19 (8): 669–692. https://doi.org/10.1080/10438590902872903.

Lechevalier, S., and N. Kodate. 2024. "Implementing Society 5.0: Towards a Care-Led Innovation Model in Japan?" In *Crises, Innovations, and Health: Post-Covid Capitalism in Asia and Europe*, edited by S. Lechevalier and J.-P. Gaudillière. forthcoming.

Lechevalier, S., and B. Monfort. 2018. "Abenomics: Has It Worked? Will It Ultimately Fail?" *Japan Forum* 30 (2): 277–302. https://doi.org/10.1080/09555803.2017.1394352.

Lechevalier, S., and S. Shibata. 2024. "The Contribution of Digitalization to Non-Inclusive Growth in Japan. A Régulationist Perspective on Post-Industrial Dynamics." *Competition & Change*. forthcoming.

Maslow, S. 2018. "Knowledge Regimes in Post-Developmental States: Assessing the Role of Think Tanks in Japan's Policymaking Process." *Pacific Affairs* 91 (1): 95–117. https://doi.org/10.5509/201891195.

Mazzucato, M. 2018. "Mission-Oriented Innovation Policies: Challenges and Opportunities." *Industrial and Corporate Change* 27 (5): 803–815. https://doi.org/10.1093/icc/dty034.

Motonishi, T., and H. Yoshikawa. 1999. "Causes of the Long Stagnation of Japan During the 1990s: Financial or Real?" *Journal of the Japanese and International Economies* 3 (4): 181–200. https://doi.org/10.1006/jjie.1999.0429.

Nezu, R. 2004. "Why Did Japanese Industry Lose Out in the Global Competition During the 1990s?: Current Problems and Prospect for Recovery." *Japanese Economy* 32 (1): 45–75. https://doi.org/10.1080/2329194X.2004.11045181.

Obayashi, K., N. Kodate, and S. Masuyama. 2020. "Can Connected Technologies Improve Sleep Quality and Safety of Older Adults and Care-Givers? An Evaluation Study of Sleep Monitors and Communicative Robots at a Residential Care Home in Japan." *Technology in Society* 62:101318. https://doi.org/10.1016/j.techsoc.2020.101318.

Paperman, P., and S. Laugier, eds. 2020. *Le souci des autres: éthique et politique du care*. Paris: Éditions de l'École des hautes études en sciences sociales.

Shibata, S. 2022. "Digitalization or Flexibilization? The Changing Role of Technology in the Political Economy of Japan." *Review of International Political Economy* 29 (5): 1549–1576. https://doi.org/10.1080/09692290.2021.1935294.

Tachibanaki, T. 2009. *Confronting Income Inequality in Japan: A Comparative Analysis of Causes, Consequences, and Reform*. Cambridge: MIT Press Books.

Whittaker, H. 2024. *Building a New Economy: Japan's Digital and Green Transformation*. Oxford: Oxford University Press.

Wright, J. 2023. *Robots Won't Save Japan: An Ethnography of Eldercare Automation*. Ithaca: Cornell University Press.

The transformation of science, technology and innovation (STI) policy in Japan

Tateo Arimoto

ABSTRACT

This note sketches the evolution and growing centrality of Japan's science, technology and innovation (STI) policy over the past quarter century, from the Basic Law on Science and Technology in 1995 to the new Science, Technology and Innovation Basic Law in 2020. It highlights: the shift from a primary emphasis on economic value and competitiveness to encompass social needs, resilience and sustainability; the growing importance of mission-oriented innovation policy (MOIP); the consequent need for new coordination mechanisms across government and at different levels, from local to international; the need for continuous evaluation and adjustment mechanisms as opposed to post-project/programme evaluation; and the need for human resources for these. The Strategic Innovation Programme (SIP) Automated Driving Project is described as a pioneering model of cross-ministerial MOIP, and key challenges for the forthcoming 7th STI Basic Plan (2026–30) are identified.

Introduction

Quietly but profoundly, Japan's science, technology and innovation (STI) policy has changed in recent years. Against a backdrop of deepening crises, disasters and pandemics, STI policy is shedding its prioritization of economic value and competitiveness and becoming more responsive to social needs, even as it becomes central to national power. Mission-oriented innovation policy (MOIP) which addresses cross-cutting issues and requires complex coordination mechanisms with a whole-of-government approach has come to the fore. Japan is responding to the Budapest Declaration from the 1999 World Conference on Science for the Twenty-first Century calling for 'science for society' and 'science in society'.

In this note I will outline the evolution of Japan's STI policy, especially over the quarter century from the passage of the first Basic Law on Science and Technology in 1995 to the Science, Technology and Innovation Basic Law of 2020. The first section provides a global context of current challenges and policy needs. The second section sketches the evolution of Japan's policies from 1995 to 2020, as just noted. The third section probes some cases of Japan's MOIP, particularly from the Strategic Innovation Programme (SIP), which I have been involved in, followed by the expansion of MOIP into other socio-economic transformation initiatives. I conclude by looking ahead to the 7th STI Basic Plan (2026–30), which is about to enter the planning phase, and the challenges which are likely to shape it. STI policy will play a crucial role, overlapping with industrial, environmental, security and foreign policies, in navigating increasingly complex global dynamics and tensions (OECD 2023).

Escalating crises and a call for rethinking modern science and technology

Humanity and our planet face a pivotal moment in history, as we grapple with an existential crisis. The reality of global warming has reached a critical threshold, unleashing uncontrollable natural disasters like hurricanes, floods, and major fires. The devastating impact of the COVID-19 pandemic exceeds the loss of five million lives worldwide, and brought about a profound reassessment of societal governance, challenging both democratic and authoritarian systems. Simultaneously, the Russian invasion of Ukraine and the escalating U.S.-China struggle for hegemony threaten to fracture the world along political, security, and economic lines, rendering the post-World War II international political and economic system dysfunctional.

With this turbulent backdrop, science and technology, which has evolved together with human society, faces unprecedented pressures to transform its values and systems. The current paradigm, constructed since World War II, stands at a crossroads, calling for a re-examination of its purpose, policy-making processes, management, evaluation, and human resources; indeed prompting a critical exploration of the essence of science and the identity of scientists. I would like to propose four perspectives.

(1) *Changing values and the transformation of STI policy*: The dominance of economic values in the purpose of STI policy has persisted for over 30 years under neoliberalism. However, we now witness a notable expansion of its boundaries to encompass sustainability, resilience, well-being, and security (OECD 2023).

(2) *S&T as the foundation of national power*: The Russian invasion of Ukraine and the intensifying U.S.-China technological struggle have propelled S&T policy to the centre of overall national power. No longer confined to the realm of 'soft power', S&T policies must now intricately integrate with other public policies spanning industry, military, energy, environment, health, food and disaster prevention (OECD 2023).

(3) *S&T as a driver for global problem solving*: S&T has become a potent tool for addressing global, regional, national, and local challenges, exemplified by the pursuit of United Nations Sustainable Development Goals. The spotlight on mission-oriented innovation policies (MOIP) intensifies, with heightened expectations following the rapid development and distribution of vaccines during the COVID-19 pandemic. Yet the transformative potential of emerging technologies, such as AI and bioengineering, is accompanied by profound risks, including military applications and exacerbation of societal inequalities. The global political agenda, evidenced at the G-7 and G-20 Summits, revolves around the international competition, cooperation, and governance of these emerging technologies.

(4) *Revisiting the Budapest Declaration*: In the Budapest Declaration of 1999 the International Council of Science (ICSU) set out a 'Commitment of Science in the

21st Century', encompassing 'science for knowledge', 'science for peace', 'science for sustainable development', and 'science for and in society'. A quarter-century later, the global scientific community now faces a call to revisit and re-evaluate the tenets of this foundational declaration.

The elevation of S&T policies to the forefront of national strategies is a global trend (Biden and Sunak 2023), accompanied by increased investment in research and development (R&D), with a concerted effort to expedite the development and societal implementation of cutting-edge technologies such as AI, semiconductors, quantum technology, biotechnology, sensors, and autonomous systems. There is a growing emphasis on strategic intelligence functions, encompassing the analysis of priority areas for technological development, assessment of social impact, and redesigning of international collaborations.

The biannual flagship OECD report 'Science, Technology and Innovation Outlook' encapsulates these trends and provides a thought-provoking overview of contemporary issues in STI policy (OECD 2023). A central theme of the 2023 report is transformation of the objectives of STI policy, expanding beyond a singular economic focus to encompass a diverse array of values, including the promotion of sustainable and resilient societies, enhancement of quality of life, and assurance of security. Notably, the report introduces the concept of 'securitization of STI', highlighting the pivotal role of S&T not only in military applications but also in addressing crises such as climate change, energy, food security, and pandemics. It emphasizes key areas such as technology governance, funding systems, mission-oriented innovation, strategic intelligence and foresight, and the cultivation of dynamic capabilities and diverse career development.

The OECD is scheduled to convene a significant ministerial meeting on STI policy in April 2024. The first gathering of its kind in a decade, it will bring together member countries and representatives from the Global South in Paris to engage in collaborative discussions and elaborate on a declaration outlining a transformative STI policy framework for fostering a sustainable and inclusive future. This strategic initiative underscores the collective commitment to shaping the trajectory of S&T policies at the global, regional, national and local levels in alignment with evolving social needs, geopolitical challenges and technological revolutions in the next decade.

Evolution of Japan's S&T legal framework from 1995 to the STI basic law of 2020

In response to 1980s disputes between Japan and the US and Europe, subsequently exacerbated by globalization and heightened international economic and technological competition following the Cold War, Japan enacted a Basic Law on Science and Technology (S&T) in 1995. This aimed at promoting S&T, and advocated increased investment in R&D, system reforms fostering industry-academia collaboration, and human resource development. Figure 1 shows the evolution of Japan's STI policy and action plans in the past almost 30 years (Cabinet Office 2021c). In 2020, a quarter-century later, the 'Basic Law on Science, Technology, and Innovation' was enacted, signifying a considerable overhaul of the previous 1995 framework. The new law not only continues the promotion of S&T but also introduces 'innovation' as a major purpose. It emphasizes

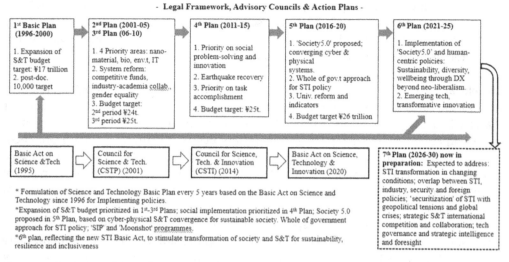

Figure 1. Evolution of Japan's science, technology and innovation policy. Source: Author, based on (Government of Japan 2021).

that S&T should not only address economic concerns but also tackle broader social problems (Arimoto 2021; Government of Japan 2021). It underscores the importance of the previously excluded humanities and social sciences, and stresses interdisciplinary cooperation. For the first time in Japan's S&T legal framework it explicitly outlines the two pillars of 'policy for science' and 'science for policy'.

To implement the objectives of the 2020 STI Basic Law, the government approved the Sixth STI Basic Plan covering the period 2021–2025. The latter sets out three major goals: 'S&T for social transformation', 'promotion of S&T', and 'development and securing diverse human resources for S&T'. It ambitiously aims to realize a society that is sustainable, resilient, diverse, inclusive and focuses on well-being. It introduces an approach known as 'convergence of knowledge', emphasizing the integration of social sciences and humanities with natural sciences and engineering. This marks a deliberate effort to bridge traditionally separate domains, fostering a more holistic and collaborative perspective in the pursuit of scientific and technological advancements and transition to a sustainable and inclusive society (Figure 2).

These legislative and strategic shifts underscore Japan's commitment to adapting to evolving global challenges and embracing a more inclusive and interdisciplinary approach to STI. This is aligned with Japan's 'Society 5.0' vision, introduced in the 5th STI Basic Plan (2016 to 2021). The overarching objective of Society 5.0 is to address societal challenges in areas such as environment and energy, health, food, and disaster prevention. This ambitious vision revolves around the integration of cyberspace and physical space through the application of advanced technologies, as illustrated in Figure 3.

The seamless transition from the 5th Basic STI Plan to the subsequent plan is noteworthy. The continuity underscores a commitment to long-term objectives and signifies the enduring nature of strategic STI initiatives. Furthermore, the 'Society 5.0' concept is instrumental in contributing to the achievement of the United Nations Sustainable

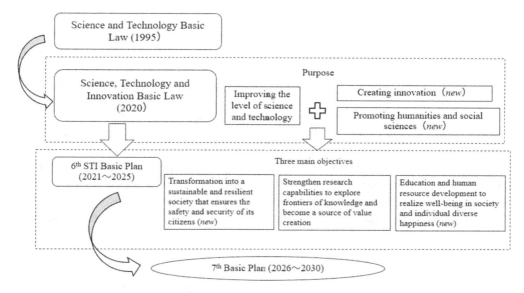

Figure 2. Japan's science and technology basic law system. Source: Author

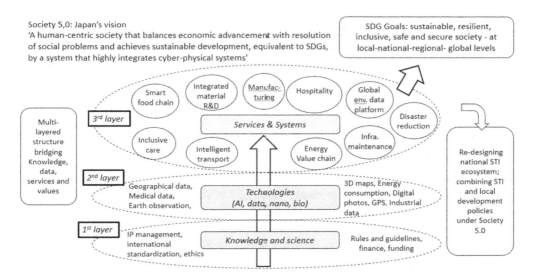

Figure 3. Concept of society 5.0. Source: Author, based on (Kyūma 2018).

Development Goals (SDGs), aligning Japan's scientific and technological endeavours with global sustainability targets (Kyūma 2018; Nakamura et al. 2021). This interconnectedness emphasizes the role of science and technology in addressing not only domestic challenges but also contributing to broader international aspirations for sustainable development.

In a further departure from economic value as the supreme priority of public policies including STI policy in the past three decades governed by neoliberalism, the Japanese government is embarking on a strategic shift, championing 'new (form of) capitalism' as the cornerstone of the country's socio-economic and political vision. The Grand Design and Action Plan for a New Form of Capitalism drawn up by the Kishida's cabinet emphasizes four pillars: people; STI; startups; and GX (green transformation) and DX (digital transformation) (Government of Japan 2023). This paradigmatic transition underscores a collaborative effort among ministries, cities, universities, and start-ups, working collectively towards the realization of a people-centred, globally connected, innovative, sustainable, resilient, and inclusive society. S&T are strategically positioned as powerful driving forces in the pursuit of these goals.

As a precursor to advancing S&T policies aligned with this overarching strategy, the Japanese government initiated the 'Strategic Innovation Programme' (SIP) in 2014 (described in more detail below), and the more recent 'Moonshot Programme' in 2020. Under the leadership of the Cabinet Office and in collaboration with various ministries, these programmes mark a departure from the traditional technology-push approach that has historically defined Japan's S&T policy (Sato 2020). Instead, they represent a pioneering foray into the realm of mission-oriented innovation policy (MOIP) characterized by a socio-economic problem-solving and needs-driven approach.[1] From formulation to the intricacies of implementation, they emphasize stakeholder engagement, effective leadership, robust management structures, comprehensive progress evaluation mechanisms, and the development of human resources attuned to the demands of a rapidly evolving technological landscape. This marks a significant departure from the status quo and underscores Japan's commitment to fostering innovation that is not only technologically cutting-edge but socially impactful.

Strategic balance in national STI policy: insights from Horizon Europe and implications for Japan

In STI policy, it is imperative to strike a balance in policy formulation, budget allocation, and management between 'policy for science' and 'science for policy' mission-oriented innovation policy. Horizon Europe (2021–2027), the European Union's current foundational plan for S&T, reveals a thoughtful allocation strategy. Roughly 30% of the total €920 billion budget is directed towards basic research, research infrastructure, and human resource development (Pillar 1: €250 billion), while twice that amount is allocated to STI Programs addressing global challenges and socio-economic problems (MOIP) (Pillar 2: €535 billion) (European Commission 2021).

This allocation model serves as a valuable lesson for Japan. A clear and committed allocation of the total budget to the two pillars at the initiation of Japan's new STI Basic Plan is crucial for long-term strategic planning. This commitment will play a pivotal role in shaping strategies, encompassing investment and management decisions, and human resource allocation by universities, funding agencies and companies. It will contribute to the establishment of stable research environments and provide incentives for individual researchers, fostering an ecosystem conducive to sustained scientific and technological advancement.

The SIP programme: a pioneering model of cross-ministerial mission-oriented innovation policy (MOIP) in Japan

The Strategic Innovation Programme (SIP) is an exemplar of Japan's foray into cross-ministerial Mission-Oriented Innovation Policy (MOIP), offering insights into both its distinctive characteristics and the challenges inherent in such initiatives. Drawing on my personal involvement as the sub-Project Director (subPD) for a decade, this section delves into the SIP Automated Driving Project to illuminate key aspects of MOIP (Cabinet Office 2023; CRDS/JST 2022).

Overview of the SIP programme

Initiated in FY2014 under the aegis of the Cabinet Office, the SIP represents a cross-ministry R&D programme that strategically addresses socio-economic challenges crucial to Japan's social fabric, economic landscape, and industrial competitiveness (Cabinet Office 2021a). The programme's modus operandi involves collaborative efforts among industry, academia and government to identify critical issues, followed by the allocation of budget and overall management responsibilities across relevant ministries and agencies. The scope spans basic technology development to the practical application and commercialization of outputs.

The Cabinet Office assumes a top-down approach in designating the Project Director (PD), entrusted with overarching responsibility for management and budget allocation within the project. The PD's role extends beyond R&D oversight, encompassing the formulation of roadmaps in collaboration with ministries and stakeholders to achieve mission objectives. This multifaceted mandate includes spearheading deregulation efforts for demonstration tests and societal implementation, as well as maintaining effective communication with society. To facilitate these objectives, a comprehensive implementation system is established, with a promotion committee chaired by the PD. The committee comprises representatives from relevant ministries, industries, and local governments. Critical to the programme's success is the establishment of a Governing Board by the Cabinet Office, comprised of experts tasked with evaluating and advising on the overall SIP programme and its constituent projects.[2] This institutional framework, driven by collaboration and oversight mechanisms, positions SIP as a pioneering model of MOIP, demonstrating Japan's commitment to addressing complex challenges through innovative and coordinated cross-sectoral efforts.

The SIP automated driving for universal services (SIP-adus) project

The SIP Automated Driving Project is designed to propel research and development in automated driving systems and facilitating their social implementation (Kuzumaki 2023). A distinctive feature lies in the emphasis placed on collaborative efforts among relevant government ministries and regional entities. Further, the project incorporates a proactive approach to legal system reform and the enhancement of social acceptance. A noteworthy initiative under the coordination of the PD is the delineation of 'areas of cooperation' and 'areas of competition' among concerned industries. During this phase, the 'Public-Private ITS (Intelligent Transportation System) Roadmap', of the Cabinet Secretariat plays a pivotal role in defining the awareness and roles of various stakeholders.

The Roadmap has a forward-looking orientation spanning the next 10 years. Developed through collaboration among ministries, agencies, companies, local governments, and universities, it plays a crucial role in aligning the efforts of stakeholders towards achieving the dual missions of the project: realizing a sustainable mobility society on a national or local scale, and enhancing the international competitiveness of companies. Beyond its role in research and development, the Roadmap serves as a comprehensive tool for understanding and analysing the progress of technology development, regulatory reform, and system and service development. This holistic approach has facilitated timely legal reform by ministries such as METI (Ministry of Economy and Industry), MIC (Ministry of Information and Communication), MLIT (Ministry of Land Management and Transportation) and NPA (National Police Agency), each having jurisdiction over specific aspects. Importantly, the Roadmap undergoes annual review and revisions that inform adjustments to both R&D plans and social implementation activities. The iterative process enables participating companies to mobilize resources consistently, ensuring stability in the provision of equipment and personnel. A crucial feature is the successful integration of public and private funds and human resources from companies.

General characteristics of MOIP

Effective promotion of MOIP hinges on strategic mission formulation with an appropriate scope and timeline (Larrue 2021a, 2021b). Analysing societal needs sets the groundwork for the mission, while assigning roles to stakeholders and constructing a comprehensive roadmap are also vital. Yet the SIP Automated Driving Project encountered constraints in local social implementation. Had the mission initially prioritized providing services to local residents and enhancing local well-being, collaboration with local stakeholders and citizens could have addressed specific needs beyond technological advancements. Considerations such as ageing and healthcare, energy, food, environment, and disaster prevention could have been seamlessly integrated. However, the SIP programme's initial emphasis on technology and system development inherently imposed limitations (Oyamada and Arimoto forthcoming).

Second, while inter-ministerial coordination has historically posed challenges in Japan, the collaborative process of mission setting and roadmap creation serves as an incentive for ministries to transcend silos, embodying a holistic government approach. The Cabinet Office and Project Director (PD) have pivotal roles in coordinating policy measures across various organizations, a task entailing significant coordination costs and time. Given the transient nature of administrative staff, establishing an organization for continuity and cultivating personnel becomes paramount to ensure the accumulation of technical knowledge and management expertise. Policy measures on the demand side, such as laws, regulations, and procurement are also vital, but these are often managed by different divisions, so strategic considerations about integration become imperative, underscoring the nuanced orchestration required for seamless MOIP implementation.

Third, the MOIP promotion structure, illustrated in Figure 4 using the Automated Driving Project as an example, has three overarching layers: strategic direction; policy

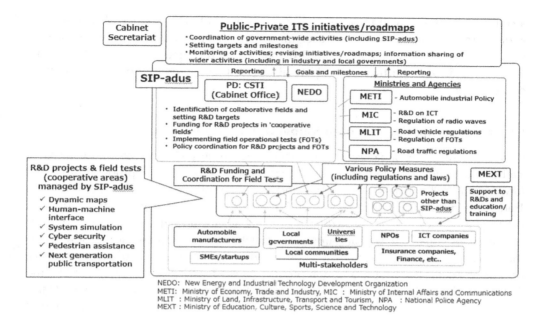

Figure 4. Multi-layered structure of the SIP automated driving project. Source: Author, based on (Arimoto 2023).

coordination; and policy implementation (Arimoto 2023). Coordination to share positions, roles, and responsibilities among ministries and stakeholders in each layer is needed. While Japan's STI policies have traditionally been technology-driven, the mission of social transformation necessitates a shift towards understanding and foreseeing social needs and problems. Flexible management has to take into account policy measures beyond STI policy and ensure social acceptability on the demand side.

Japan's conventional evaluation methods have historically focused on post-project summative evaluations (see Akai 2024, in this volume). However, in the case of MOIP, continuous learning and evaluation are called for. The system must constantly monitor project progress, assess social impacts, and facilitate real-time adjustments to improve and revise management during project implementation. Of course there is also a need for post-project evaluation to inform the design and management of subsequent programmes and projects. This adaptive approach not only aligns with the dynamic nature of MOIP but also ensures that the initiatives remain responsive to evolving social needs. It signifies a departure from static evaluation models. The continuous evaluation and learning system acts as a catalyst for informed decision-making, and enables effective adjustments and improvements throughout the project lifecycle and enhancement of future programmes.

Finally, missions with a long time horizon need a mechanism that encourages stakeholder participation and fosters sustained collaboration. Stakeholders need a sense of ownership and engage flexibly across multiple stages, in initial mission setting, budget allocation, role assignment, implementation, evaluation, and improvement. Drawing on Japan's historical experiences in addressing pollution issues during the 1960-80s, it is evident that overcoming complex societal problems requires a collaborative effort akin to MOIP. However, in the contemporary era, MOIP demands a more refined mechanism that accommodates the participation of more diverse stakeholders at the local, national and global levels. The mechanism should not only encourage broad participation but also instil a commitment to continued collaboration.

Expansion of mission-oriented innovation policy in Japan

In October 2020, the Japanese government unveiled an ambitious mission to achieve 'carbon neutrality' with zero greenhouse gas emissions by 2050. To propel this mission forward, a ¥2 trillion 'Green Innovation Fund' was established at the Ministry of Economy, Trade, and Industry (METI). Separately, in September 2021, the government inaugurated the Digital Agency, tasked with comprehensively advancing digital transformation (DX) for society at large. The 'Digital Garden City Initiative' aims to address local social issues through DX. Simultaneously, there is a burgeoning movement among local governments, private companies, startups, and non-profit organizations (NPOs) in initiatives like the Smart City Public-Private Partnership and SDGs Future City programme (Cabinet Office 2021b). These are tailored to local needs and future plans, fostering the proliferation of mission-oriented policies both locally and nationally. Some city activities have begun to transcend national boundaries and are being transferred to Asian cities. This potential for collective co-creation across national borders underscores the evolution of local and regional innovation ecosystems to address diverse needs and challenges.

In 2021, METI initiated a comprehensive 'Mission-oriented Economic and Industrial Policy' for the entire ministry, comprising eight missions to be achieved by 2023. The missions spanned carbon-neutral society, digital society, economic security, healthy society, disaster-resilient society, bio-manufacturing revolution, resource self-reliance, and inclusive local growth. Concurrently, METI is advocating agile governance for the realization of Society 5.0, in which technology seamlessly integrates with societal needs for a more human-centric and sustainable future (METI 2022).

Directions and challenges of Japan's STI policy for the next decade

As noted earlier, S&T is now at the centre of overall national power, featuring both soft power and hard power, as well as economic and national security dimensions amid escalating geopolitical tensions. As Japan strategically evaluates national and global interests, I believe that, from an STI policy perspective, it is imperative to establish and maintain Japan's basic research capability and research infrastructure, foster development of emerging technologies, promote mission-oriented innovation policy (MOIP), and bolster international activities.

Against the backdrop of the U.S.-China conflict in advanced technology and supply chains, Western and Asian countries have expressed a growing interest in expanding collaboration with Japan through a national leaders' summit (MOFA 2023a, 2023b; US Embassy 2023). This interest spans advanced technology development, supply chain resilience, the international circulation of researchers, and collaborative research to address social and security issues. Japan should capitalize on this opportunity by enhancing its capabilities in science and technology diplomacy.

The OECD has stated that 'continuous co-ordination between STI policy and other policy domains – trade and investment, foreign affairs and national security policy, and environment and energy – will be essential', and is advocating a paradigm shift in STI policy through the 3Ps of Promotion, Protection, and Projection (OECD 2023). For Japan to realize these 3Ps – promoting S&T, protecting S&T knowledge and researchers, and projecting international cooperation – in a dynamically evolving world, a fundamental change in STI policy is paramount. The forthcoming STI Basic Plan (7th Plan: 2026–2030), preparation of which will begin in early 2024, will serve as a linchpin for fostering a conducive research environment, motivating researchers, and enhancing research capabilities. The plan will play a pivotal role in positioning Japan as a key player in the evolving global landscape of science, technology, and innovation. By way of conclusion I note five key issues that need consideration.

(1) Recognition of the pillars of modern S&T policy: Recognizing the equal importance of the two pillars of modern S&T policy – 'policy for science' and 'science for policy', – needs a clear delineation of their budget allocation within the total budget framework (European Commission 2021). With the evolving objectives of STI policy, expanding beyond traditional economic values to include sustainability, resilience, quality of life, and security, a holistic transformation of the STI system into an new STI eco-system is essential. This holistic perspective should encompass policy-making and budget allocation, funding, management, R&D activities on the ground and evaluation systems.
(2) Addressing geopolitical tensions: We should acknowledge that geopolitical tensions have permeated university management and the research arena. Emphasized at forums such as the G7 Science and Technology Ministers' Meeting and the OECD, there is a need to strengthen research integrity and security not only in technology development but also in basic research. The OECD's messages regarding the 'securitization of S&T' (OECD 2023) and the need for research ministries and funding agencies to play a central role should guide future actions.
(3) Prioritizing international activities: International activities encompassing research collaboration, human resource circulation, funding, will be vital for the STI community and policy in the coming years, and for Japan's 7th STI Basic Plan. Japan's leadership in G-7 and G-20 discussions on S&T, security, international brain circulation, and the governance of emerging technologies underscores the importance of strengthening S&T diplomacy. Reinforcing the functions and human resources of S&T diplomacy has become essential for Japan.
(4) Strengthening intelligence and bridging functions: In a rapidly changing world, bolstering intelligence to collect, analyse, design and foresee information is essential to bridge science, politics/administration, and society with trust. Rebuilding policy planning and management capabilities within government, following the decades-long neoliberal outsourcing of administrative functions, is necessary. Simultaneously, establishing an independent organization outside the government to accumulate and transmit expertise, know-how, and experience in science, technology and management is needed. The organization should focus on securing and training expert personnel and strengthening its evaluation system. The

science-policy-society interface should become robust and sustainable to shape our common sustainable future.

(5) Promotion of mission-oriented innovation policy (MOIP): Finally, we must deepen the understanding that social problem-solving/needs-driven programmes and S&T-driven programmes differ significantly in terms of planning, management and evaluation. With the expanding objectives and scope of STI policy, there is a need for a coordinating mechanism with other public policies and instruments. MOIP must enhance management capacities and human development for boundary-crossing mobilization of resources and building a trustworthy science-policy-society interface (United Nations DESA 2021). Implementing a continuous learning and evaluation system is critical to monitor progress, assess social impact, and make agile improvements and revisions to MOIP project implementation.

These considerations will lay the groundwork for navigating the multifaceted challenges and opportunities that will define the future directions of Japan's STI policy.

Notes

1. Many countries have begun to embrace MOIP. The OECD (Larrue 2021a, 2021b) defines MOIP as 'a coordinated package of STI policy and regulatory instruments specifically tailored to address clearly defined goals related to social challenges'. Three common features are: 1) Strategic direction – direction of efforts of various stakeholders towards achievement of the mission in a time-bound manner; 2)Policy coordination – coordination among policy implementing agencies such as central ministries and funding agencies, universities and research institutions, local governments, businesses, and civil society organizations, and 3) Policy implementation – integration of a variety of policy instruments and initiatives.
2. SIP had two phases: Phase 1 (FY2014–2018) with 11 projects and a total budget of ¥158 billion, and Phase 2 (FY2018–2022) with 12 projects and a total budget of ¥144.5 billion.

Disclosure statement

No potential conflict of interest was reported by the author(s).

References

Akai, N. 2024. "Evidence-Based Policy Making in Japan's Public Expenditure: Compatibility of Fiscal Health and Investing for the Future." *Asia Pacific Business Review*. https://doi.org/10.1080/13602381.2024.2320543.

Arimoto, T. 2021. "Transforming Science and Technology Basic Law System from 1995 to 2020: Ideals, Realities and Implementation." *Gakujutsu no dōkō*, May, Japan Science Support Foundation.

Arimoto, T. 2023. "SIP-Adus and Mission Oriented STI Policy." *SIP 2nd Phase: Automated Driving for Universal Services – Final Results Report (2018–2022)*, 268–270. New Energy and Industrial Technology Development Organization. https://en.sip-adus.go.jp/file/rd_file/chapter8_s.pdf.

Biden, J., and R. Sunak. 2023. "The Atlantic Declaration: A Framework for a Twenty-First Century US-UK Economic Partnership."

Cabinet Office. 2021a. "Senryaku teki inobēsyon sōzō puroguramu 2021 [Cross-Ministerial Strategic Innovation Promotion Programme 2021]." Accessed February 10, 2024. https://www8.cao.go.jp/cstp/panhu/sip2021/sip2021.html.

Cabinet Office. 2021b. "Smart City Guidebook." Accessed January 29, 2024. https://www8.cao.go.jp/cstp/society5_0/smartcity/00_scguide_eng_ol.pdf.

Cabinet Office. 2021c. "Transition of Japan's Science, Technology and Innovation Policy." Accessed January 29, 2024. https://unctad.org/system/files/non-official-document/CSTD2021-22_c05_I_Japan_en.pdf.

Cabinet Office. 2023. "2nd Phase SIP-adus Final Results Report (2018–2022)." Accessed January 29, 2024. https://en.sip-adus.go.jp/rd/rd_page04.php.

CRDS (Centre for Research and Development Strategy). 2022. "Missyon shikōgata kagaku gijyutsu inobēsyon seisaku to kenkyū kaihatsu fandingu no suishin [Promotion of Mission-oriented Science, Technology and Innovation Policy, and Research and Development Funding in Japan]." Accessed January 29, 2024. https://www.jst.go.jp/crds/report/CRDS-FY2022-SP-01.html.

DESA (United Nations Department of Economic and Social Affairs). 2021. "CEPA Strategy Guidance Note on the Science-Policy Interface." New York: United Nations.

European Commission. 2021. "Horizon Europe – the EU Research and Innovation Programme 2021-2027." Accessed January 29, 2024. https://research-and-innovation.ec.europa.eu/system/files/2022-06/ec_rtd_he-investing-to-shape-our-future_0.pdf.

Government of Japan. 2021. "Science, Technology and Innovation Basic Plan." Accessed January 29, 2024. https://www8.cao.go.jp/cstp/english/sti_basic_plan.pdf.

Government of Japan. 2023. "Grand Design and Action Plan for a New Form of Capitalism – 2023 Revised Version." Tokyo.

Kuzumaki, S. 2023. "Looking Back Upon SIP-Adus History." *SIP 2nd Phase: Automated Driving for Universal Services – Final Results Report (2018–2022)*, 264–267. New Energy and Industrial Technology Development Organization.

Kyūma, K. 2018. Society 5.0 jitsugen ni mukete [Toward Implementing Society 5.0]." Accessed January 29, 2024. https://www.jates.or.jp/dcms_media/other/%E4%B9%85%E9%96%93%E5%92%8C%E7%94%9F%E6%B0%8F%E8%B3%87%E6%96%99.pdf.

Larrue, P. 2021a. "The Design and Implementation of Mission-Oriented Innovation Policies: A New Systemic Policy Approach to Address Societal Challenges." OECD Science, Technology and Industry Policy Papers No. 100. Paris: OECD.

Larrue, P. 2021b. "Mission-Oriented Innovation Policy in Japan: Challenges, Opportunities and Future Options." OECD Science, Technology and Industry Policy Papers No. 106. Paris: OECD.

METI (Ministry of Economy, Trade and Industry of Japan). 2022. "Agile Governance Update -How Governments, Businesses and Civil Society Can Create a Better World by Reimagining Governance." Accessed January 29, 2024. https://www.meti.go.jp/press/2022/08/20220808001/20220808001-b.pdf.

MOFA (Ministry of Foreign Affairs of Japan). 2023a. "The Commemorative Summit for the 50th Year of ASEAN-Japan Friendship and Cooperation." Accessed January 29, 2024. https://www.mofa.go.jp/a_o/rp/pageite_000001_00029.html.

MOFA (Ministry of Foreign Affairs of Japan). 2023b. "Japan-Australia-India-U.S. (Quad) Leaders' Meeting." Accessed January 29, 2024. https://www.mofa.go.jp/fp/nsp/page1e_000691.html.

Nakamura, M., T. Arimoto, H. Yamada, and R. Maruyama. 2021. "Transforming Science, Technology, and Innovation (STI) for a Sustainable and Resilient Society." *Science &*

Diplomacy. https://www.sciencediplomacy.org/article/2021/transforming-science-technology-and-innovation-sti-for-sustainable-and-resilient.

OECD. 2023. *Science, Technology and Innovation Outlook 2023 – Enabling Transitions in Times of Disruption.* Paris: OECD.

Oyamada, K., and T. Arimoto. Forthcoming. "Mission-Oriented Innovation Policy in Japan: Historical Development and Lessons from the Case of Automated Driving."

Sato, F. 2020. "Overview on Current Japanese R&I Policies." Cabinet Secretariat, Government of Japan.

US Embassy in Japan. 2023. "Fact Sheet: The Trilateral Leaders Summit at Camp David." Accessed January 29, 2024. https://jp.usembassy.gov/fact-sheet-trilateral-summit-at-camp-david/.

Japan's triple sustainability challenge

Tokutaro Nakai

ABSTRACT
Starting with a broad overview of the need for urgent action concerning climate change globally, this paper then reviews the evolution of environmental policy in Japan up to and including green transformation (GX) measures taken under the Kishida administration, and an assessment of the changes still needed to achieve sustainability in Japan. An integrated approach has been adopted in Japan, encompassing the environment, the economy, and society, to achieve three transitions: first, to a de-carbonized society; second, to a circular economy; and third, to a 'nature-positive', decentralized society which co-exists with nature. This approach was signalled in the Regional Circular and Ecological concept in the Fifth Environmental Basic Plan of 2018, building on extensive discussions within the Ministry of Environment and with other ministries from 2014, in the wake of the 2011 triple earthquake, tsunami and nuclear disasters.

Introduction

In this article I will argue that an integrated approach is needed for green transformation and sustainability in Japan, which encompasses the environment, the economy, and society. As well, three transitions are necessary: first, to a carbon-neutral, de-carbonized society; second, to a circular economy; and third, to a 'nature-positive', 'nature-revitalized', decentralized society which co-exists with nature instead of dominating it. These transitions need to be approached in an integrated way, beginning from a vision of where we want to be, and backcasting to adopt concrete policies and measures. This approach was signalled in the Regional Circular and Ecological concept in the Fifth Environmental Basic Plan of 2018; one objective of this paper is to assess progress towards its realization, and prospects for its implementation.

The paper consists of four sections in addition to the Introduction. It starts with a broad overview of the growing awareness of the need for urgent action concerning climate change and the environment globally. The second section reviews the evolution of environmental policy in Japan up to and including measures taken under the Kishida administration. The third section offers an assessment of recent policy measures, and the fourth considers policy implications, leading to an assessment of the changes still needed to achieve green transformation and sustainability in Japan.

Trends surrounding climate change in Japan and abroad

The Sixth Assessment Report Synthesis Report, published by the Intergovernmental Panel on Climate Change (IPCC) in 2023, states that the average global temperature has already risen by 1.1°C since before the industrial revolution, and that human influence has warmed the atmosphere, oceans and land areas. As a result, powerful hurricanes, typhoons, forest fires, etc. are occurring frequently in various parts of the world, putting many lives at risk and causing enormous socio-economic damage. The World Economic Forum's annual Global Risks Report has ranked extreme weather as the top global risk for seven consecutive years (World Economic Forum 2023). In Japan, the Ministry of the Environment (MoE) issued a 'climate crisis declaration' in June 2020, and the Diet also adopted a 'climate emergency declaration'.

In addition, infectious diseases transmitted by animals are increasing due to global deforestation and climate change. Globalization has seen an acceleration of zoonotic and other diseases spreading across national borders. And since 2020, the world has been facing a coronavirus pandemic. Japan's MoE has stated that the COVID-19 pandemic and the climate crisis are environmental problems that have a common root cause and require simultaneous solutions.

That the crisis of the global environment has been brought about by human activity, as stated in the IPCC report, is supported by the accumulation of scientific findings. Viewed from the point of view of the earth's limits, or boundaries (e.g. Steffen et al. 2015), if human beings stay within the range in which we can work safely to bring about change, human society can develop and prosper, but if the boundaries are crossed non-recoverable change will occur in natural resources required for the survival of humanity. Of the nine environmental factors considered in this study, the speed of extinction of species and physical circulation of nitrogen and phosphorus are in the zone of high risk beyond uncertainty, while climate change and land use change are areas of uncertainty, increasing risk.

Thus, according to Steffen et al. (2015), human activity is now exceeding the environmental capacity of the earth, and the stability of the environment or natural capital as a basis for our own survival is in crisis. To use a human body metaphor, the earth is a state of chronic, lifestyle-related diseases, and to survive we need a fundamental bodily transformation. To recover the sustainability of human society, we must solve structural problems of the economic and social systems, including culture and lifestyle. Based on this recognition, the Strategic Development Goals (SDGs) of 2016 to 2030, presented as a '2030 Agenda for sustainable development', were adopted at the UN General Assembly in September 2015 (United Nations 2015). The SDGs consist of 17 goals and 169 targets for implementing a sustainable world.

Already in 1992, the 'United Nations Framework Convention on Climate Change' was adopted in order to realize the ultimate goal of stabilizing the concentration of greenhouse gases (GHG) in the atmosphere, and there was international agreement to work towards containing global warming. Based on the Convention, a Conference of the Parties (COP) has been held every year since 1995. In December 2015, at the COP 21 in Paris, the Paris Agreement was adopted as a new international framework for reducing GHG emissions. With this agreement, 'all countries' efforts', which Japan has advocated for a long time, were accepted.

Member countries committed to reducing the average temperature rise of the planet to significantly lower than 2°C, and to make efforts to limit the rise to 1.5°C. To realize this, they would need to aim for Carbon Neutrality (net zero for amounts of human-based GHG emissions and absorption) later this century. The Paris Agreement of 2015 was a turning point in the quest for the construction of a decarbonized society throughout the world.

In 2018 the IPCC released its 1.5°C Special Report, noting that there are significant differences between 1.5°C and 2°C global warming in terms of extreme high temperatures, increase in intense precipitation events, as well as drought in some regions, and that it is in fact necessary for CO_2 emissions to reach net zero around 2050 in order to keep temperatures from exceeding 1.5°C (IPCC 2018). Since the publication of this report, there has been an international movement centred on European countries to upgrade the 1.5°C effort target to a global goal, and at COP26 in Glasgow in 2021 it was agreed that efforts to limit temperature rise to 1.5°C will continue, recognizing that the impact a 1.5°C increase in temperature will be much smaller than that of a 2°C increase.

There has been some progress towards these goals. The EU launched the European Green Deal in 2019 (European Commission 2019), with the goal of achieving 'climate neutrality' with virtually zero GHG emissions by 2050, raising the EU's climate targets towards 2030, and reviewing related regulations accordingly. As well as being an environmental policy, the European Green Deal is a comprehensive economic growth strategy that aims to transform the structure of Europe's socio-economy, targeting a wide range of policy fields such as energy, industry, transportation, biodiversity, and agriculture.

In the United States, although the Trump administration withdrew from the Paris Agreement, the Biden administration has advanced the Green New Deal, and returned to play a leading role in making carbon neutrality by 2050 a commitment of the international community. President Biden, who took office in January 2021, set a goal of reducing GHG emissions by 50 to 52 points compared to 2005 levels by 2030, and to net zero by 2050. Although the budget for the climate change legislation eventually passed was smaller than originally planned, it includes ambitious programmes and brings the U.S. closer to realizing a clean energy revolution that will surpass the Green New Deal. While the budget for the Green New Deal during the Obama administration was $150 billion over 10 years, Biden's budget for climate change countermeasures (the Inflation Reduction Act) is $390 billion, and while the two cannot be directly compared, this is a considerable increase.

China, now the world's largest emitter of greenhouse gases, has set a goal of becoming carbon neutral by 2060, if not 2050. China has set an interim 2030 goal of turning CO_2 emissions into a downward trend, and reducing CO_2 emissions per GDP unit by 65% or more compared to 2005. In fact, many countries and regions around the world − 158 as of May 2023 − have similarly announced the goal of achieving carbon neutrality with a fixed date such as 2050. These efforts notwithstanding, according to the IPCC Sixth Assessment Report Synthesis Report (IPCC 2023), global GHG emissions in 2030, based on Nationally Determined Contributions (NDCs) announced by October 2021, suggest that warming is likely to exceed 1.5°C during the 21st century. In order to limit global warming to 1.5°C, GHG emissions would need to be reduced by 43% by 2030 from 2019 levels, and the world needs to make deep, rapid and immediate emissions reductions, with a peak in global emissions by 2025. The G7 Hiroshima Leaders' Communiqué of May 2023 stated,

> Our goal of achieving net-zero GHG emissions by 2050 at the latest is unwavering and we emphasize the growing urgency of reducing global GHG emissions by approximately 43% compared to 2019 by 2030 and by approximately 60% by 2035.

Overview of Japanese environmental policy

The control tower of Japan's environmental policy – the (then) Environmental Agency – was established in 1971, originally to handle pollution problems such as Minamata disease and air pollution, which became a social problem in the 1950s and 1960s high-growth era. In 2001, the Environment Agency was reorganized into the Ministry of the Environment (MoE), which has developed environmental policies since in response to environmental issues. After tackling pollution problems, climate change, waste and circulation, and biodiversity and ecosystem protection became the three pillars of Japan's environmental policy.

The First Environment Basic Plan (1994), which defined the basic concept of environmental policy at that time, emphasized that socio-economic activities and lifestyles in pursuit of material richness, mass production, and mass consumption with large amounts of waste should be reconsidered. This is still a fundamental problem today. After the high economic growth period of the 1960s, internation-ally as well as domestically, it was generally thought that there was a trade-off between economic growth and environmental protection. In the Environmental Basic Act of 1993, however, the environment was defined as 'the foundation of humanity's survival', introducing the concept of sustainable development, and reflecting the discussion of UNCED in 1992. The either-or trade-off assumption was rejected in favour of economic development with a sustainable environmental impact. In particular, since the Third Environmental Basic Plan (2006) integrated improvement of the environment, economy and society were embedded in envir-onmental policy goals, although the trade-off stance persisted, especially in the business world in Japan.

In the wake of the 2011 Great East Japan Earthquake, with the Fukushima nuclear power plant accident, recovery and reconstruction became the most important policy challenge for the Japanese government. The MoE was responsible for tackling environ-mental pollution from radioactive substances released in the nuclear accident as a whole new policy area. Due to the need for a stable energy supply after the triple disaster and the demand for climate change measures, the Democratic Party of Japan (DPJ) adminis-tration at that time introduced a fixed price purchase system to promote the introduction of renewable energy, and a tax for global warming measures (on fossil fuels, which produced a ¥260 billion revenue effect, though the price signal effect was small). When the Liberal Democratic Party (LDP) returned to power in 2012, the Abe administration took over these policies, but the cessation of all nuclear power plant operations after the triple disaster resulted in a regression to coal-fired power generation. On the other hand, the triple disaster also called for a major rethink of the future. Regional social issues such

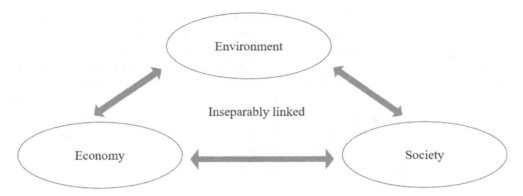

Figure 1. Integrated improvements of environment, economy and society. Source: Author.

as disaster prevention and revitalization by conversion to self-supporting, distributed social structures utilizing regional renewable energy, became widely discussed.

Against this background, building on extensive discussions within the Ministry of Environment and with other ministries from 2014, the Fifth Environmental Basic Plan (Ministry of the environment 2018) clearly proposed that future environmental policies should adopt an integrated approach that aims to improve the environment, economy, and society simultaneously (Figure 1). Through environmental policies, Japan will encourage innovation in all areas, including economic and social systems, lifestyle, and technology, achieving simultaneous solutions to economic and social issues. The aim of environmental policy will be 'new growth', that would create a high quality of life. Thus it can be said that we have reached a new stage, in which environmental policy aims to achieve 'new growth', rather than focusing on costs.

In particular, since the adoption of the SDGs and the Paris Agreement, recognition that economic and social activities are established on the foundation of natural capital (the environment), as in the so-called wedding cake model of the SDGs, and that damage to natural capital has a negative impact on economic and social activities, has become firmly established in Japan and elsewhere. As seen in the expansion of ESG (environment, social, governance) investments and the spread of initiatives such as the Task Force on Climate-Related Financial Disclosures (TCFD) and Task Force on Nature-Related Financial Disclosures (TNFD), there is a growing recognition that climate change is both a risk and an opportunity, with a movement to link the resolution of social issues, including environmental issues, to the creation of corporate value.

Declaration of 2050 carbon neutrality in 2020

In response to the 2015 Paris Agreement, the Abe administration set a GHG emission reduction target of 80% by 2050, in line with the 2°C target, and introduced policies to achieve this goal. Based on this target, in 2019 the Japanese government established a long-term strategy to reduce emissions by 26% by 2030 and carbon neutrality as early as possible in the second half of the 21st century. The Suga administration, which succeeded the Abe administration, subsequently announced in October 2020 that Japan would achieve carbon neutrality by 2050, taking into account the international situation regarding climate change since the publication of the IPCC 1.5°C Special Report in 2018. It further announced a target reduction of GHG emissions of 46% in FY2030 (compared to FY2013), and that it would take on the challenge of achieving an even higher goal of 50%.

The benchmark of GHG emissions is 1.408 billion tons, in FY2013, when all nuclear power plants were shut down, forcing Japan to rely on coal-fired power for its energy supply. Since this peak, Japan steadily reduced GHG emissions for seven consecutive years, the result of a combination of government policies and private sector reduction efforts. In FY2021, there was an increase compared to the previous year due to an economic rebound from the COVID-19 pandemic, but the reduction trend is generally in line with the reduction target of 46% by FY2030 target. During this post-2013 period, Japan's GDP has grown, thus achieving a decoupling between CO_2 emissions and economic growth.

Achieving carbon neutrality by 2050 will require innovation in technology, economic and social systems, and lifestyles, as well as huge decarbonization investments in various fields. Carbon neutrality should be pursued as a growth strategy, and the Japanese government has made it clear that it aims to create a virtuous cycle between the environment and the economy. In order to significantly reduce CO_2 emissions, innovation in the industrial and energy sectors that play a role in the supply side of economic activities is essential, so the Suga administration at first allocated ¥2 trillion yen of public financial support for this purpose, with the establishment of a Green Innovation Fund.

On the other hand, it is essential that the household sector and the demand side of economic activities, which account for approximately 60% of CO_2 emissions on a consumption basis, should shift towards decarbonization. In fact, this is gaining momentum, and it is noteworthy that over 900 municipal local governments – including Tokyo, Kyoto and Yokohama – where people live their daily lives, have committed to carbon neutrality by 2050. There is, however, a need for huge investment in the regions (outside the metropolitan centres) to achieve this. While Japan has been in a long-term economic stagnation since the 1990s – referred to by some as the lost three decades – there is now a possibility that a virtuous cycle of regional and domestic investment will begin, leveraging the realization of carbon neutrality.

Instead of waiting for innovation on the supply side, we should try to solve local issues by investing in existing technologies, such as introducing local renewable energy and microgrids. In 2021, the MoE took leadership within the government to formulate a Regional Decarbonization Roadmap (Cabinet Secretariat 2021), which aims to utilize existing technologies to create 100 leading decarbonization localities that will achieve carbon neutrality in the civil sector by 2030, and to use these as models to create a domino effect of decarbonization in local or regional areas of Japan. The roadmap includes intensive policy support over the next five years. The selection of advanced decarbonization localities, which began in FY2021, is having a major impact on the move towards carbon neutrality; after a three-stage selection process, 62 localities have already been selected.

Policy progress by the Kishida administration

In 2022 the Kishida administration, which replaced the Suga administration, made green transformation (GX) to achieve carbon neutrality by 2050 a pillar of its growth strategy, and promoted innovation and investment to achieve this through growth-oriented carbon pricing. A GX Implementation Council was established to formulate the 'Basic Policy for the Realizing of GX: Roadmap for the Next 10 years' (Cabinet Secretariat 2023). Through the realization of GX, the Japanese government aims to reduce greenhouse gas emissions by 46% in 2030 and achieve carbon neutrality by 2050, as well as realize a transformation of the energy supply and demand structure that will lead to a stable and inexpensive energy supply. It also aims to transform the industrial and social structures of Japan. The Basic Policy envisages huge investments states to realize GX, mainly on the supply side of industry. One estimate is that it will exceed 150 trillion yen over the next 10 years (cf. Figure 2). Through public-private collaboration, the council proposed 'pro-growth carbon pricing', consisting of the following three measures.

Up-front investment support utilizing 'GX economy transition bonds' etc
Introduction of a new 'GX Economy Transition Bond' totalling ¥20 trillion to support bold upfront investment by businesses to shift to non-fossil energy such as renewable energy and nuclear power; industrial structural transformation to integrate supply and demand in manufacturing industries such as steel and chemicals; and promotion of fundamental energy conservation, and investment in research and development for resource recycling and carbon capture technologies. The government thinks that the 'GX Economy Transition Bonds' will be issued in new formats that comply with international standards.

GX investment incentives through 'pro-growth carbon pricing'
Carbon pricing ultimately improves the added value of GX-related products and businesses by putting a price on carbon emissions. By introducing the system at a low cost initially and increasing it gradually, and by signalling that policy in advance, the government seeks to accelerate GX investment. Through the carbon pricing system design, it also aims to strengthen industrial competitiveness and reduce emissions efficiently and effectively based on ambitious reduction targets that take into account the circumstances

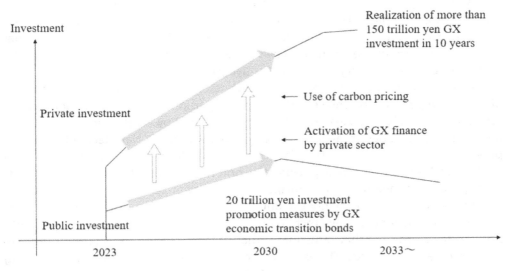

Figure 2. Future GX investment image. Source: Author.

of each company, mainly in high-emission industries. To do this the government will introduce an emissions trading scheme (ETS), as well as 'GX-surcharge' carbon pricing to promote GX more widely, not just in high-emission industries.

The ETS will begin on a trial basis from FY2023, with voluntary participation in the form of a 'GX League' of participating companies, with the aim of full-scale operation from FY2026. The 'GX-surcharge' will be introduced from FY2028. The government will encourage private companies to bring forward their GX investment by setting a low surcharge on fossil fuel importers and gradually raising it. And as with the EU the government will gradually introduce auctions for power generation from alternative methods such as renewable energy.

Utilization of new financial instruments

Achieving GX investments of over ¥150 trillion in the public and private sectors over the next 10 years will require active financing by private financial institutions and institutional investors, in addition to government support through GX Economy Transition Bonds. As well as expanding green finance, the former will need to provide funds for transition efforts by high-emission industries, which will require efforts to foster international understanding of transition finance. Some GX areas require large-scale, long-term funding, but in some cases technologies and demand are highly uncertain, and risks cannot be absorbed by private finance alone. In such cases, blended public and private finance is needed.

The government needs to create an environment to promote sustainable finance as a whole, including the disclosure of climate change information. Concretely, in 2023 it started a trial ETS with the same level of coverage as in Europe. Advance notice will be given as to the level of pricing. By issuing GX Economy Transition Bonds on the premise that future government carbon pricing revenues will be the source of redemption funds, and through investment promotion measures that utilize those revenues, companies will be able to accelerate their green transformation.

In sum, the government will (1) strengthen transition finance in high-emission industries, both domestically and internationally through issuance of the world's first 'transition bonds' issued by a government; (2) develop an ETS based on the experiences of other countries; and (3) implement concrete investment promotion measures worth ¥20 trillion. These new policies are designed comprehensively to achieve GX.

While it is important to utilize existing technologies for the early implementation of GX, it is impossible to achieve carbon neutrality using existing technologies alone. Japan has world-class GX-related technology seeds, and by accelerating research and development, it hopes to achieve early commercialization. New technologies may provide emissions reduction benefits, but they are likely to be more costly than existing technologies. Carbon pricing that bridges the cost difference, and investment promotion measures that anticipate the effects of carbon pricing, are needed. In other words, Japan will clarify the outlook for future carbon pricing introduction/increase, and introduce new technologies at an early date through investment promotion measures that anticipate the carbon pricing effects utilizing GX Economy Transition Bonds. This is the essence of Japan's 'pro-growth carbon pricing concept'.

Evaluation of the Kishida administration's GX policies

When making policies to achieve carbon neutrality by 2050, as well as economic growth and stronger industrial competitiveness, it is important to take into account the energy environment and economic security situation, which differs from country to country. Globally, there are two major policy responses, namely carbon pricing and investment promotion measures. The former, effective in reducing emissions, encourages decarbonizing investment on the supply side and decarbonization purchasing behaviour on the demand side through the price signal effect. Europe leads the way with its ETS, with individual countries setting emissions reduction targets, while recognizing some excess distribution of free quota to industries with high emissions. In the United States, carbon pricing has only been introduced at the state level.

Investment promotion measures, on the other hand, boost economic growth. Here the United States is implementing large-scale support of roughly ¥50 trillion over multiple years through the Inflation Reduction Act. Policy support is proportional to production, and not just initial investment. Europe, too, is considering concrete public-private investments of approximately ¥140 trillion through Green Deal industrial policy and other initiatives.

Despite Japan's severe financial situation, the Kishida administration has formulated the above measures, which will hopefully be a model for countries where Carbon Neutral policies must be newly developed. The use of the ¥20 trillion GX Economy Transition Bonds will require international certification and reporting based on analysis of GHG emission reduction potential. The government should consider allocating the finance to sectors with large emissions; in addition to the energy conversion sector (power generation, etc.), it should target industrial sectors (such as steel and chemicals), and sectors closely related to people's lives (such as households, transportation, and educational facilities). Investment should be promoted in sectors that can strengthen industrial competitiveness and economic growth.

The concept of carbon pricing was thoroughly debated within the government, with the MoE taking the lead, based on examples in the EU and other countries. It was taken up as a central issue of the GX Implementation Council. The Ministry of Economy, Trade and Industry (METI), as the main secretariat of the GX Implementation Council, has actively promoted the study of carbon pricing, including both an ETS and a surcharge on carbon. As someone deeply involved in this policy issue, it is gratifying that pro-growth carbon pricing, incorporating both investment promotion and carbon pricing, was quickly formulated, with Cabinet approval of the Basic Policy for Realization of GX and the subsequent enactment of relevant legislation. The mechanism for securing governmental financial resources for GX by imposing a price on carbon emissions has been legally established. However, the detailed design of the GX-surcharge and the ETS paid auction for the power generation sector is expected to be set out in a new law within the next two years; details of the system such as the specific price level and exemptions from carbon pricing have not been decided yet. No doubt there will be many twists and turns, and the adjustment of interests between affected industrial sectors.

As noted, carbon pricing aims to promote decarbonizing investment on the supply side and decarbonizing purchasing on the demand side through the price signal effect. The government plans to introduce carbon pricing without increasing the public burden, that is, to reduce the public burden through the current feed-in tariff system and increasing oil and coal taxes. At present, it is not clear whether it is possible to set a carbon price that fully produces the price signal effect that carbon pricing aims for. Furthermore, although the government anticipates the scale of public-private GX investment in the next 10 years to be ¥150 trillion, investment to reach the 2050 Carbon Neutral target will be huge, and the scale of both private and public sector investment is not yet known. Further work is needed in this area, and to understand the nature and scale of accompanying structural transformation. From this point of view, in addition to policies aiming to realize a carbon neutral socio-economy, further policies that aim to bring about integrated improvement of the environment, economic and society, based on backcasting from 2050, will be necessary.

The Kishida administration has made considerable progress in the former – environmental- area, but to realize sustainability, policies for integrated improvement proposed in the Fifth Environmental Basic Plan are needed. The Sixth Environmental Basic Plan, which will be decided by the Cabinet during 2024, will consider the following proposals, which have been discussed within the MoE.

Further development of Japan's policies for sustainability

An integrated approach and redesign of society through three transitions

Many of the environmental, economic and social challenges that Japan currently faces are complex, and are influenced by trends in a variety of policy fields, as noted by (Arimoto 2024) in this work. Climate change is a perfect example. Such complex issues must be addressed in an integrated way, in which specific measures can also address multiple different issues, taking into account perspectives such as 'new growth'. Indeed, in the 2023 G7 Hiroshima Summit Leaders' Communiqué, the G7 countries pledged to ensure sustainable and inclusive economic growth and development, increase economic resilience, work towards carbon-neutral, circular, climate-resilient, pollution-free and nature-positive socio-economies, and to halt and reverse biodiversity loss by 2030 in an integrated manner (G7 2023). This integrated approach is crucial. Many people around the world live below the minimum standard for essential human social needs, such as access to water, food, health care, shelter, energy, and education. *Doughnut Economics* (Raworth 2017) likewise depicts a safe activity space for humans, in combination with the planetary boundary, which is the limit of the earth's environmental capacity, pointing to the need to consider issues of the environment, distribution, and inequality in an integrated manner.

In brief, we must aim to simultaneously solve economic and social issues through environmental policy and contribute to the achievement of the SDGs. Among the SDG goals, as the 'wedding cake' metaphor suggests, the environment is the foundation, and on top of that, sustainable economic and social activities exist. Trade-offs among goals should be modified to find win-win solutions. 'Backcasting', which looks back from the ideal society and considers what needs to be done now, is helpful for this. Based on backcasting, we can conceptualize the total redesign of the economy and society through *three transitions*.

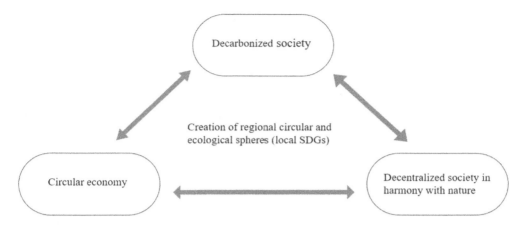

Figure 3. Redesign of economic society with 'three transitions'. Source: Author.

The first is the transition to a carbon-neutral, decarbonized society, from the perspective of energy. We hitherto relied on underground resources and fossil fuels, but with urbanization and deforestation, this puts a burden on the planet while impairing its ability to absorb CO_2. The goal is to have an energy procurement structure that is carbon neutral, and puts no burden on the earth.

The second is the transition to a circular economy. According to some estimates, by 2050 the cumulative amount of plastic waste entering the ocean will exceed the amount of fish, surely indicating that the linear economy of mass production, mass consumption and mass disposal has reached its limits. This transition is based on an understanding that all things are connected and circulated. In addition to conventional 3 R (reduce, reuse, recycle) initiatives, we need to reduce resource inputs and consumption, effectively utilize stock, and switch to economic activity based on services.

The third is a transition to a 'nature-positive', nature-revitalized, decentralized society that coexists with nature. Our economic and social lives are based on the biodiversity-rich ecosystem of the Earth. 'Nature-positive' calls for a socio-economy that is in harmony with a healthy ecosystem. This idea is presented by the International Union for the Conservation of Nature (IUCN) as nature-based solutions – solving social problems using the forces of nature. These three approaches to transition have traditionally been developed as independent policy fields in environmental policy, but they need to be developed in an integrated manner in order to realize a sustainable socio-economy (Figure 3).

Creation of a local circular and ecological sphere

The ultimate goal of environmental policy is the realization of a sustainable socio-economy, which requires an integrated approach. By aiming for an integrated improvement of the environment, economy, and society, and for the three transitions of carbon neutrality, circular economy and nature positivity in environmental policies, and by promoting the integration of these two, we should be able to completely redesign our socio-economy. The result will be a 'local/regional circular and ecological sphere'

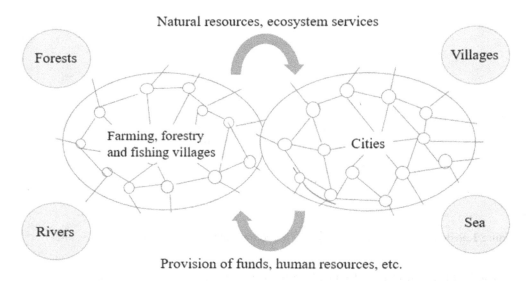

Figure 4. Local circular and ecological sphere. Source: Author.

proposed in the Fifth Basic Environmental Plan of 2018, and the realization of SDGs locally by sustainably utilizing local resources such as food and renewable energy. In other words, an *autonomous and decentralized society*, in which local communities form networks that support each other by leveraging the uniqueness of each locality.

Circulation and symbiosis will lead the transformation, in combination with the use of digital transformation (DX). Reducing dependence on other countries' natural resources such as food and energy will help to mitigate global climate change, pollution and the biodiversity crisis, and will contribute to national security. In this cyclical and life-based symbiotic society, knowledge from biology and the life sciences can be utilized in environmental policies. The 37 trillion cells of the human body function autonomously but also together to at a higher level; likewise local/regional ecosystems would ideally interact in a global ecosystem, with resources suitable for a small area circulating at the community or municipal level, and resources suitable for wide area circulating beyond. Individual well-being with the earth's ecosystem as a whole should be nurtured. This life-oriented, biologically-based conceptualization is built into a 'local/regional circular and ecological sphere' (Figure 4).

Setting higher-level objectives for integrated improvement of the environment, economy and society

To harmonize individual well-being with a global ecosystem, peoples' economic and social activities need to be based on a healthy natural environment. Economic growth or social infrastructure should not increase environmental burden, but instead improve it, with incentives to do this, creating demand (markets) for environmental conservation, for new jobs and a fair transition, and conversely disincentives to polluters based on the polluter pays principle, and internalizing externalities. Environmental education, education for sustainable development, developing human resources for local environmental conservation efforts, and partnership building and participation of diverse actors, are all called for.

The First Environmental Basic Plan saw problems such as climate change as largely due to structural problems in the economy and society. Conversely, we can combine and solve various economic and social issues by starting from environmental policy. As structural problems have continued for many years – for example Japan's 'lost decades' – we must change our viewpoint for solving them, by 'changing the way we change', so to speak. 'New growth' aiming for high quality of life for all current and future citizens should be the top priority of integrated policy efforts. It will be created by market value and non-market value, cognizant of the following:

(1) For well-being/high quality of life, not only the 'flow' represented by GDP is enriched, but also the 'stock', based on the vision of a future state, including stock of the future.

(2) Structural problems are addressed for the long-term. In an era of 100-year lifespans, we must act from a long-term perspective, such as proactive investment for the future, as many 100-year-old companies in Japan have done. A perspective which encompasses future generations – and one's future self – ensures sustainability, and intergenerational equity.

(3) Rather than over-emphasizing the seeds and strengths of suppliers, as in so-called 'path dependence' and the 'innovation dilemma', focus is on the desired future state, using the latest and best science. Disruptive innovation addresses structural socio-economic problems.

(4) People place more importance on spiritual wealth. In the economy, this means focusing on quality rather than physical quantity, creating value through intangible assets, including environmental value, and developing environmental human resources.

(5) Social capital improves well-being. This means enriching the community, achieving a balance among the state, market and community, gaining the participation of citizens, and building an inclusive society that includes the weak. Non-market values are incorporated into market values.

(6) From the perspective of well-being/high quality of life, shifting from a socio-economic system centred on Tokyo, to a socio-economic system that includes an autonomously and horizontally decentralized national structure.

Maintaining, restoring, and enriching natural capital as stock, and well-being/high quality of life

The foundation of 'new growth' is to maintain, restore, and enrich natural capital as a stock (Figure 5). If natural capital falls below a critical level – in other words economic and social activities exceed the carrying capacity of the environment – there is a risk that humanity will lose the basis of its very survival. The need is to not just reduce the environmental burden, but to maintain, restore, and enhance natural capital, for which we need supportive man-made capital and systems, both tangible (equipment, infrastructure, etc.) and intangible (human capital). This will contribute to well-being and quality of life. In other words, well-being or high quality of life, which includes the

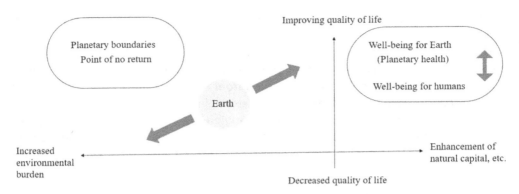

Figure 5. Relationship between natural capital/environmental load and well-being/quality of life. Source: Author.

subjectivity of people, and natural capital and the systems that maintain, restore, and enhance it, are mutually influential, each building the other in a co-evolutionary relationship.

For such co-evolution, from a long-term perspective, huge investments are needed domestically, with the public and private sectors working together. In light of the crisis we are already facing, the people of Japan must clearly share what they want as goals, including carbon neutrality by 2050. The path to achieving this goal is by no means easy, and will require both ingenuity and effort from the entire nation over a long period of time, but this will lead to a high quality of life.

Disclosure statement

No potential conflict of interest was reported by the author(s).

References

Arimoto, T. 2024. "The Transformation of Science, Technology and Innovation (STI) Policy in Japan." *Asia Pacific Business Review*. https://doi.org/10.1080/13602381.2024.2320539.
Cabinet Secretariat. 2021. *Chiiki datsu-tanso rōdo mappu [Regional decarbonization roadmap]*. Tokyo.
Cabinet Secretariat. 2023. *GX jitsugen ni muketa kihon hōshin: kongo 10 nen wo misueta rōdo mappu [Basic policy for the realizing of GX: Roadmap for the next 10 years]*. Tokyo.
European Commission. 2019. *The European Green Deal*. Brussels: EC.
G7. 2023. *Hiroshima Leaders' Communiqué*.
IPCC (Intergovernmental Panel on Climate Change). 2018. *Special Report on Global Warming of 1.5°C*. Geneva: IPCC.

IPCC (Intergovernmental Panel on Climate Change). 2023. *Sixth Assessment Report: Synthesis Report.* Geneva: IPCC.

Ministry of the Environment. 1994. *Dai ichiji kankyō kihon keikaku* [First environmental basic plan]. Tokyo.

Ministry of the Environment. 2006. *Dai sanji kankyō kihon keikaku* [Third environmental basic plan]. Tokyo.

Ministry of the Environment. 2018. *Dai goji kankyō kihon keikaku* [Fifth environmental basic plan]. Tokyo.

Raworth, K. 2017. *Doughnut Economics: Seven Ways to Think Like a 21st-Century Economist.* London: Random House Business.

Steffen, W., K. Richardson, J. Rockström, S. E. Cornell, I. Fetzer, E. M. Bennett, R. Biggs, et al. 2015. "Planetary Boundaries: Guiding Human Development on a Changing Planet." *Science* 347 (6223). https://doi.org/10.1126/science.1259855.

United Nations. 2015. *Transforming Our World: The 2030 Sustainable Development Agenda.* New York: UN.

World Economic Forum. 2023. *Global Risks Report 2023.* Cologny: WEF.

Evidence-based policy making in Japan's public expenditure: compatibility of fiscal health and investing for the future

Nobuo Akai

ABSTRACT

This article focuses on the introduction of evidence-based policy making (EBPM) in Japan, especially in the context of the Kishida administration's Grand Design and Action Plan for a New Form of Capitalism. First, the introduction and current situation of EBPM in Japan is summarized. It, consists of three allows: key performance indicators (KPIs), policy evaluation, and administrative project review. These are evaluated and briefly compared to EBPM in the US and UK. Next, investment and expenditure for green transformation proposed in the Grand Design is assessed from the perspective of EBPM, pointing to potential pitfalls and what must be done to ensure wise use of public resources for economic growth and sustainability in the future in Japan. This may serve as a reference for other countries.

Introduction

The Kishida administration issued its 'Grand Design and Action Plan for a New Form of Capitalism' (Cabinet Office 2023) in June 2022, and is currently (as of January 2024) implementing associated policies. According to this Plan, in order for Japan to begin a new growth trajectory, it must accelerate efforts to address slowing investment in people and capital investment, against a background of structural problems in the economy which include the curtailment of the domestic market due to the low birth rate and ageing society, management which emphasizes existing market share, and inflexibilities in the labour market and corporate organization.

To address these problems, four pillars were proposed: investment in people; boosting science, technology, and innovation; boosting startups; and green transformation (GX) and digital transformation (DX). The Plan also envisages that fields in which there tends to be too little investment if left to the market – such as investment in people, promoting domestic industry locations that leverage Japan's advantages in resilience, and investment to realize GX – will need goal-focused public expenditure, which will serve as a stimulus to expand private investment. This plan also proposed the public and private sectors to collaborate in order to transform social issues into an engine of growth, thus creating a virtuous cycle of growth and distribution in which economic added value is increased as companies distribute higher earnings to workers, consumption and corporate investment expands, and further economic growth is created; this will restore a broader middle class.

In order to achieve these objectives of the 'new form of capitalism', bold public investment and public expenditure are envisaged. While Japan is facing the problem of a declining birthrate and ageing population and sluggish economic growth, public spending continues to exceed tax revenue, and public debt is piling up. There are limits to the expansion of public spending. In order to achieve the Plan's objectives without compromising fiscal soundness, wise spending, that is, efficient and effective public spending is required.

This article focuses on the public governance system called EBPM (Evidence Based Policy making) that the Kishida administration is working on in order to achieve efficient and effective public spending. I examine whether the current system is robust enough to achieve efficient and effective public spending. In particular, I will discuss how the governance system works for GX, which is one of the four pillars of this new form of capitalism in which large-scale public spending is planned, and whether the system needs to become more sophisticated in terms of governance.

The article is structured as follows. The first section explains EBPM as a public governance structure to improve the efficiency of public expenditure. In section 2, I critically examine how EBPM is evolving. Section 3 explains the use of EBPM to improve GX policy in the Grand Design and Action Plan for a New Form of Capitalism, and section 4 concludes.

EBPM as a governance structure to improve the efficiency of public expenditure

The Kishida administration emphasizes EBPM as a public governance mechanism for efficiently and effectively implementing policies, including public spending, and achieving policy goals. EBPM attempts to clarify the following three points.[1]

(1) Policy objectives
(2) Effective administrative measures
(3) Logic and evidence

First, the objectives of the policy need to be clear. Next, the administrative methods that can most efficiently achieve those objectives need to be decided. For this, the logic (logic model) to concisely express the relationships among inputs (input resources), activities, outputs (products of activities), and outcomes (policy effects) must be clarified. Evidence with data needs to be shown. This series of efforts constitutes EBPM, which also attempts to improve transparency and accountability in policy.

Position of EBPM in the PDCA cycle

The PDCA cycle of Plan, Do, Check and Act is used for each government project. By repeating the cycle, the content of the policy can be implemented more efficiently and effectively, where *efficiency* means that the cost is minimized for given benefits, and *effectiveness* means that the benefits are maximized for the given cost. PDCA stages can be summarized as follows.

(1) Plan: Planning
Plan (P) is the stage of clarifying the purpose of the policy and planning how to solve social issues through policy means. Policy planned at this stage should be efficient and effective from an ex-ante viewpoint.

(2) Do: Executing
Do (D) is the stage of implementing the plan made at the P stage. The premise is that the plan is in a form that is executable.

(3) Check: Evaluation
Check (C) is checking and evaluating whether the expected results have been obtained as a result of executing the plan. Through evaluation, we can judge whether the results are as expected or not, and whether the results are efficient and effective.

(4) Action: Improvement
Act (A) re-examines P based on the evaluation results and utilizes this in the formulation of the next plan. If the method of improvement is identified, a new plan will be formulated again at stage P, and a new PDCA cycle will commence.

Regarding the connection between EBPM and PDCA, Stage C is where the effects produced by the implemented policy are evaluated, to show whether the administrative methods are used most efficiently and achieve the objective, and access its logic and evidence based on data. In other words, EBPM is an effort to make stage C more meaningful.

EBPM in Cabinet Office policy

The first description of EBPM in government economic policy appeared in the Council on Economic and Fiscal Policy (CEFP 2017a), which proposed the 'promotion of Evidence-Based Policy Making through the preparation of data platforms'. In addition, it stated that 'the Council on Economic and Fiscal Policy will strengthen progress management, check and assess the reforms and further proceed with collecting more evidence, based on the perspective of Evidence Based Policy Making (EBPM), bringing the results of discussions and examinations into the budget formulation'. This move can be summarized as a reorganization of the policy evaluation efforts that have been carried out since the enactment of the Act on Policy Evaluation by Administrative Organs (2001), using the EBPM framework developed overseas.

CEFP (2018a) requested each ministry to implement a thorough review of administrative operations in all fields of expenditure, as well as promote EBPM while securing and training human resources, and to collect the necessary data for this, in order to improve budget quality and verify its results. CEFP (2018a) also requested the government to develop a range of indicators of satisfaction and quality of life and incorporate these into related KPIs in each field, to realize improvements in the satisfaction and quality of life of people.

CEFP (2020) added steps for the government to prioritize budget allocation according to effective measures which are supported by evidence and data collection, and promote wise spending by strengthening EBPM structures, budget prioritization and the connection between multiple-year-measures and the budget formulation process. To promote EBPM, CEFP (2021) again urged the Government to prioritize the budget allocation through measures which are supported by evidence and the data collection, to build evidence and to establish a mechanism to verify policy outcomes with data by utilizing data held by administrative organs and the private sector.

Finally, to put EBPM into practice, CEFP (2022b) urged the government to revamp administrative project review sheets one by one, to utilize them as a platform in the budgeting process, to rationalize government evaluation-related tasks to secure resources for policy making and implementation, to prioritize budget allocation for measures which are supported by evidence, and to use the data collection to build evidence. Multifaceted governance is expected to be complementary and to increase effectiveness The EBPM movement is accelerating further under the Kishida administration (CEFP 2023).

The three arrows of EBPM and recent progress

There are three EBPM initiatives currently being carried out, dubbed the 'three arrows', namely:

(1) Key Performance Indicators (KPIs) in economic and fiscal revitalization plans, etc., conducted by the administrative office of the CEFP and the Committee for the Promotion of Integrated Economic and Fiscal Reforms;
(2) Policy evaluation based on the Government Policy Evaluations Act (No. 86 of 2001) conducted by the Administrative Evaluation Bureau of the Ministry of Internal Affairs and Communications;
(3) Administrative project review conducted by the Cabinet Secretariat Administrative Reform Promotion Office (ARPO).

A characteristic of EBPM in Japan is to execute EBPM comprehensively using these three arrows, which correspond to three categories of policies (Table 1). The first arrow relates

Table 1. Policy (broad sense) segmentation for the three arrows of EBPM.

Policy segmentation	Contents	EBPM (Three Arrows)
Policy (narrow sense)	A large grouping of administrative activities aimed at realizing a basic policy to address a specific administrative issue.	Key Performance Indicators (KPIs) in the economic and fiscal revitalization plan
Concrete measure	A grouping of administrative activities aimed at realizing specific policies based on the 'basic policy' described above, which can be regarded as specific measures and countermeasures to realize 'policy (narrow sense)'.	Evaluation based on the Government Policy Evaluations Act
Project	Administrative work and projects as individual administrative means to realize the above 'concrete measures and policies'. Projects are the basic units of administrative activities.	Administrative project review

Source: National Diet Library (2020): 21.

to policy-level initiatives, and is an evaluation of the basic policy. The second is an initiative at the measure level, and is an evaluation of specific policies and measures to achieve the basic policy. The third is a project-level initiative, and is an evaluation of individual projects (the most basic unit of administrative activities) to realize specific policies and measures.

Let us consider the first arrow: The KPIs are part of the Economic and Fiscal Revitalization Plan, which is a plan for fiscal consolidation, and was first included in CEFP (2015). In addition, the Plan's 'Reform Roadmap' summarizes the progress status and future approaches for individual policies. EBPM was first incorporated in the 2017 Reform Roadmap (CEFP 2017b), and a trial analysis was conducted in two areas, namely 'empirical analysis of diverse educational policies' and 'employment support for welfare recipients'. CEFP (2018b) reviewed the KPIs so that results could be more quantitatively understood, values could be updated, and connections with policy goals clarified (Cabinet Office 2019).

The Cabinet Office (2020a) considered how to proceed with EBPM for multi-year projects, and established an EBPM advisory board under the Committee for the Promotion of Integrated Economic and Fiscal Reforms to strengthen the EBPM framework and ensure wise spending (Cabinet Office 2020b). It further proposed that the government utilize data held by administrative agencies and the private sector, and make an evidence development plan for integrated economic and fiscal reform, with the aim of building a system to verify policy effects using data (Cabinet Office 2021). In 2022, this evidence development plan was presented by the EBPM advisory board under the above Committee. It sought to explain the efforts and processes for 1) verifying the connections (logic) between policy goals, KPIs, etc. in the reform roadmap, and 2) build the necessary evidence, in order to improve the New Economic and Fiscal Revitalization Plan reform roadmap. The relevant ministries thus report the progress of each initiative to the Committee, and the results of the evidence created are expected to be reflected in revision of the reform roadmap, which in turn informs revision of the development plan, thereby building a system for verifying policy effects using data, and improving the government's policy-making by utilizing data held by administrative agencies and the private sector.

Turning to the *second arrow*, policy evaluation by the Administrative Evaluation Bureau of the Ministry of Internal Affairs and Communications (MIC) is conducted based on the Government Policy Evaluations Act (No. 86 of 2001). A basic plan is formulated for each three to five year period based on the government's basic policy, stipulating matters related to policy evaluation of each administrative agency. In addition, an implementation plan is formulated every year, setting out the policies to be implemented that year and their methods. The policies are evaluated quantitatively as much as possible, with self-evaluation from the perspectives of necessity, efficiency, effectiveness, and so on. Policy evaluation is done both before and after a policy is implemented, evaluation reports are prepared and reflected in policy, and a report on the implementation status and reflection of policy evaluation is submitted to the Diet every year. The Administrative Evaluation Bureau of MIC, which is responsible for designing these policy evaluation systems, explicitly introduced EBPM in 2017.

The Bureau gave instructions to promote the use of statistics and other data in evaluation and to create a trial logic model in 2017. For the first time, data utilization and EBPM methods were incorporated into the policy evaluation reports of each government agency (AEB 2017). To further promote EBPM, in 2019 the Bureau requested each ministry to evaluate policy effectiveness using objective statistical data and facts (AEB 2019). It presented leading cases of EBPM by conducting joint empirical research with ministries and academic experts, and extended this to each administrative agency in 2020 (AEB 2020). The knowledge obtained through joint empirical research would be accumulated and organized, and used to support the practice of evidence-based policy planning in each administrative agency. Further measures were taken in 2022 (AEB 2022).

The *third arrow*, administrative project review, is a process in which each ministry, in principle: 1) ascertains the actual status of budget expenditures and uses for all administrative projects (approximately 5,000 projects); 2) makes them public; 3) inspects the contents and effects of the projects; and then 4) reflects the results in budget requests and execution. There are some differences from policy evaluation described above. First, although policy evaluation is based on the Policy Evaluation Act, there is no law that serves as the basis for administrative *project* reviews. Second, for some projects that are deemed important, a 'public process' is implemented in which outside experts participate in evaluation of the projects. Finally, the subject of administrative project reviews is administrative work (the basic units of administrative activities), while the subject of policy evaluation is measures. Since the administrative project review focuses on projects, it is easy to relate to discussions on selecting desirable projects and improving budget efficiency, such as whether to continue or abolish a project.

Administrative project review has the following four characteristics. The first is *autonomy*. The heads of the ministries are responsible for all projects. Every year, all 5000 or so administrative projects are comprehensively inspected to reduce inefficiencies and implement projects efficiently and effectively. Second, *transparency* is necessary to make the inspection process visible. A uniform review sheet is issued each September, making the process of project execution, results, flow of funds, and self-inspections transparent. Third, *openness* means utilizing outside perspectives for the inspection process. All projects are inspected by external experts once every five years. Additionally, for some 'public process' inspections are held in June. After completion, the Cabinet Secretariat Administrative Reform Promotion Office conducts an 'Autumn Review' in November to publicly verify whether government agencies' self-inspections are sufficient. Fourth, *policy reflection* means inspection results are reflected in the following year's budget and project execution, including the results of the 'Autumn Review'.

EBPM in administrative project reviews[2]

In 2017–18, the following three measures were implemented as new EBPM initiatives (ARPO 2017).

(1) Clarification of evidence in ministries' review sheets:
Ministries were required to state the sources of statistics and data that serve as the basis for setting performance targets.
(2) Public verification under ARPO:
Case studies are taken up in the 'Autumn Review' and verification by external experts will be attempted from an EBPM perspective.

(3) Full-scale self-inspection in the 'public process': Using the results of the 'Autumn Review', each ministry must carry out full-scale inspections from an EBPM perspective during the 'public process'.

Additionally, the following points were reportedly stressed.

(1) Validity of logic model

After setting the purpose of the project clearly and concretely, establishing the validity of:

- the causal relationship from the budget input (input) at the project stage to the project content (activity), activity results (output), and performance goals (outcome);
- the explanation of the causal relationship leading to the outcome goals (impact) at the higher-level policy/measure stage (verification of logic model);
- the setting of performance goals (outcomes) in respective stages (setting initial, mid-term, and long-term outcomes in line with the progress of the project and the realization of results).

(2) Collection and analysis of statistics and data

- Evidence, such as statistics and data, that proves the validity of the causal relationships shown in the logic model;
- Evidence that shows the rationality and effectiveness of the activity content as a means to achieve the objective
- Accuracy of statistics and data used as evidence for setting performance goals (outcomes);
- Statistics and data necessary to follow up on the degree of achievement of outcome goals.

Under this initiative, verification from an EBPM perspective was set using logic models, etc. in 2018 and 2019 (ARPO 2018; AEB 2019). In 2020, the government sought to raise the level of effort of the entire government, moving from the previous 'creation of episodes' to a broader range of EBPM practical activities, including integration with various policy-making processes (ARPO 2020). In 2021 the government sought to further promote the dissemination and penetration of EBPM in a series of policy processes (policy planning, evaluation, and review), and to improve the quality by focusing on evidence that supports the logical connection between policy instruments and objectives (ARPO 2021).

Evaluation and future direction of EBPM

In 2023, the EBPM movement accelerated further. As stated by CEFP (2023), in order to strengthen EBPM efforts, it is important to set KPIs ex ante in a way that can be verified ex post, and to request the submission of evidence and results for verifying policy effects. This promotes visualization of policy priorities. In particular, by actively utilizing the administrative project review sheets, the effects of EBPM are expected to be made explicit for all budget projects. It is also important, however, to further expand data collection and development to create policies whose effectiveness is supported by evidence.

Let us now consider the future of EBPM through each of the three arrows. Regarding the first arrow ('KPIs in the Economic and Fiscal Revitalization Plan'), progress is being made in compiling a plan to prepare evidence for integrated economic and fiscal reform. Up until now, KPI settings have been difficult because 1) the connection (logic) between the first and second KPI tiers was not clear; 2) quantitative goals were not set, making it difficult to evaluate progress; and 3) there were issues such as a lack of conceptualization regarding output (first layer) and outcome (second layer). The evidence development plan calls for verifying the connections (logic) between the 'policy goals' and 'KPIs' in the 'reform roadmap', and evidence is necessary for this purpose. Evidence that truly verifies policy effects (i.e. the quality of the evidence) should be discussed in a transparent manner.

Regarding the second arrow (policy evaluation based on the Government Policy Evaluations Act), currently there is a problem that evaluation itself is the objective, i.e. the purpose is the creation of evaluation reports. In future, it will be necessary to create a system that leads to policy improvements, including the decision-making process, by actually utilizing policy evaluation. With regard to empirical joint research, there is a related problem that just researching has become a goal, whereas it is necessary to check how research results are being used to improve policies and create a system that runs the PDCA cycle effectively. With the 'level of evidence' required for analysis and analytical methods, focus should be on analysis that can be done in practice by taking into account the cost required for analysis. The government now aims to provide technical guidelines and aims to establish a PDCA cycle for policy evaluation systems that will improve the quality of the ministries' efforts (AEB 2023).

Policy evaluation based on the Government Policy Evaluations Act is similar to that based on the Evidence-Based Policymaking Act (also referred to as the Evidence Act) of 2018 in the United States, and the guidelines for policy evaluation such as Green Book, Magenta Book and Aqua book in the United Kingdom. The Evidence Act in the United States requires changes to how the federal government manages and uses the information it collects, emphasizing strong agency coordination for the strategic use of data (ASPE 2018). The Memorandum on Restoring Trust in Government Through Scientific Integrity and Evidence-Based Policymaking (2022) notes that scientific and technological information, data, and evidence are central to the development and iterative improvement of sound policies, and to the delivery of equitable programmes, across every area of government (White House 2021).

The United Kingdom Green Book provides guidance on how to appraise policies, programmes and projects, and on the design and use of monitoring and evaluation before, during and after implementation (HM Treasury 2013–2023). The Magenta Book provides guidance on evaluation in government: its scoping, design, conduct, use and dissemination as well as the capabilities required of government evaluators (HM Treasury, 2011–2020). The Aqua Book provides guidance for producing quality analysis for government (Government Analysis Function and HM Treasury 2015–2023). In addition, to support policy evaluation based on the guidelines, institutions such as the Government Analysis Function,[3] Office for Budget Responsibility (OBR)[4] and What Works Network (WWN)[5] have been established.

Considering the examples of the United States and the United Kingdom, the following lessons can be learned for Japan. In the United States, laws regarding EBPM have been established, and efforts to utilize EBPM are proceeding. In the UK, in addition to multiple guidelines, a mechanism for incorporating expert opinion and a network between ministries have also been established. The level of awareness of evidence generation and the need for evidence in both countries is higher than in Japan. In Japan, the use of evidence is being promoted under the initiative of the government, but it is also necessary to understand the value of evidence and further heighten the need for it. The cases of both countries will serve as a reference point for deepening Japan's policy evaluation system, including EBPM.

Briefly regarding the third arrow – administrative project review – the review sheets that are constructed for all projects merely describe the implementation of policies without the logic behind them. Policymakers should have created this logic before implementing policies. What is needed is a system that clarifies the logic used to generate policy effects, and whether the policy adopted is the most efficient and effective. By giving policymakers the responsibility to explain their logic, governance effects can emerge through transparency. Finally, we should note that each of these three arrows is developing independently, but collaboratively. The division of roles, and a broadly designed system in which the arrows complement each other, are a work in progress. EBPM promotion teams have been created in each ministry, and the Cabinet Office is monitoring the teams, confirming progress, and providing governance. Hopefully this will achieve transparency and accountability.

Using EBPM to improve GX policy in the 'Grand Design and action plan for a new form of capitalism'

The Council for Economic and Fiscal Policy (CEFP 2022b) describes the context of green transformation (GX) as follows. A rapidly increasing number of countries and regions around the world have announced carbon neutrality (CN) targets, and their combined GDP now accounts for approximately 90% of the world total. In addition to the EU, countries such as China and South Korea have introduced carbon pricing, including emissions trading systems. The EU has also decided on support measures with the goal of realizing investment of approximately ¥40 trillion over 10 years through public-private cooperation, and some member countries have also decided on measures worth several trillion yen. In the United States, in addition to the bipartisan Infrastructure Investment Act, the Inflation Reduction Act of approximately ¥50 trillion over 10 years was approved in August 2022. We are now in an era in which the success or failure of GX initiatives directly affects the competitiveness of companies and countries. With this context in mind, let us consider the GX strategy advocated by the Kishida administration in its Grand Design and Action Plan for a New Form of Capitalism.

The Cabinet Office 'Grand Design and Action Plan for a New Form of Capitalism, 2023 Revised Version', encompasses GX policy and measures. Specifically, in order to invest more than ¥150 trillion in GX over 10 years through public-private efforts, the government must offer long-term multi-year support programmes to ensure predictability for private businesses. To this end, new GX Economy Transition Bonds programme amounting to ¥20 trillion will be launched, which can be leveraged for up-front investment. This programme for promoting investment will be implemented together with regulatory and structural initiatives designed to have a positive impact on the creation of new markets and demand (see Nakai 2024, in this collection). Investment coverage will be in areas where it is genuinely difficult for the private sector alone to make investment decisions, and in sectors that will simultaneously strengthen industrial competitiveness, and contribute to both economic growth and emissions reductions. It will facilitate adjustments of land use, and encourage more efficient and more resilient supply chains by digitalizing trade procedures.

From the perspective of EBPM, the most efficient and effective way to do all of this should be explored. EBPM can also be effective in determining whether investment decisions in the private sector are truly difficult and whether they will contribute to strengthening industrial competitiveness, economic growth, and reducing emissions. In December 2022, CEFP (2022a) formulated a new economic and fiscal revitalization plan 'reform roadmap' for policy issues that require expansion (GX, defence, and children). EBPM is proceeding under the following logic. In order to carry out efficient and effective policies, a clear logic regarding policy goals and policies, as well as the effects that those policies will produce, is needed. In other words, a logic model that expresses the logical relationships among inputs (input resources), activities, outputs (products of activities), and outcomes (policy effects) is required. It should also lead to improved transparency and accountability in policy.

The policy goal is to fulfil international commitments such as carbon neutrality by 2050 and simultaneously strengthen industrial competitiveness and economic growth, leveraging the ¥150 trillion of public and private GX investment noted above over the next ten years. First, as a logic, the government has to be responsible for setting out transparent explanations as to how this GX investment will actually achieve these multiple goals of meeting international emissions reduction commitments while strengthening competitiveness and economic growth. Although we must recognize some uncertainty, the government's public funds will be used effectively only when this logic can be persuasively explained to the public.

GX investment policy has four pillars: (1) a 'growth-oriented carbon pricing initiative', (2) integrated regulatory and support investment promotion measures, (3) use of new financial means, and (4) international strategy. Several policies will be implemented for each pillar. The first pillar involves issuing GX Economic Transition Bonds and making public investments, which must be shown to be efficient and effective through data and evidence.

To achieve over ¥150 trillion of public and private GX investment over the next ten years, KPIs for evaluating policy impacts are the most important step in EBPM and PDCA processes. In general, two types of KPI are set for measuring policy impacts; Tier 1 KPIs and Tier 2 KPIs. The latter measure impact closer to the goal. Examining this KPI evidence, EBPM performs ex-ante evaluation to see whether outcomes and impacts will be realized efficiently and effectively as policy effects, and ex-post evaluation to see if they are actually being realized. CEFP (2022a) sets KPI Tier 2 as 'Realizing public-private investment of over 150 trillion yen over the next ten years'.

Taking Tier 2 KPIs first, although CEFP (2022a) stipulates that 'over the next 10 years, public and private sectors will achieve over 150 trillion yen in investment', this KPI cannot be used to evaluate whether or not the goal has been reached. This still means input of policies. If the government invests heavily through subsidies, private investment will also increase, but this does not mean that the goal towards green environments will be achieved. The key for Tier 2 KPIs is to be able to assess how green is implemented through public policy and private investment. Furthermore, in order to make further progress, it is necessary to utilize public funds efficiently and effectively, and this is the role of Tier 1 KPIs.

There are three types of Tier 1 KPIs. The first is to realize investment in renewable energy, stationary storage batteries, and promotion of adoption of hydrogen and ammonia, the size of which are expected to be over ¥60 trillion over the next 10 years. The second is to realize investments which will promote energy conservation and fuel switching in the manufacturing sector, promote DX for decarbonization, establish a storage battery industry, invest in changing the structure of the aircraft industry, promote next-generation automobiles, and improve the thermal insulation performance of homes and buildings. The size of these investments is expected to be over ¥80 trillion over 10 years. The third is to realize investments in biomanufacturing, and carbon capture and storage (CCS) technology development. Investment is expected to be over ¥10 trillion yen over 10 years. However, it is not clear how new technologies which are expected to contribute to the achievement of green environment will be realized, given all the investments described above. Evidence based policy should be made. Cost-effectiveness is also important because the public funds are from citizens' tax payments. All policies above should be evaluated transparently through EBPM and PDCA processes.

Regarding KPIs in EBPM and PDCA processes, since it is highly likely that private investment will be enhanced with higher government subsidies, KPIs that focus on cost-effectiveness are also necessary in order to achieve efficient and effective government spending. In other words, it is necessary to have KPIs for how effectively government spending increases incentives for private investment. Second we must evaluate how public and private GX investment contribute to final goals such as carbon neutrality by 2050 and simultaneously realize Japan's industrial competitiveness and economic growth. Even if ¥150 trillion of public and private GX investment is achieved, Japan's industrial competitiveness and economic growth will not necessarily be improved.

Finally, a new special account and a new public institution for GX policies will be established as an executive agency. If the objective becomes to continue and expand this organization, there is a possibility that budget will be wasted. To efficiently increase industrial competitiveness and economic growth, it is important to continue to evaluate the effectiveness of public and private GX investment from the perspective of EBPM with transparent discussions, including third party involvement outside the government.

Conclusion

In this short article, I have described the three arrows of EBPM in Japan and how they will be utilized in GX policy. By clearly specifying logic models and KPIs, the outcome and impacts of GX policies which involve large amounts of public investment will be made transparent based on evidence, and GX policies will be implemented responsibly. Transparency and responsibility through EBPM will make the self-creation of *efficient* and *effective* GX policy inside governments possible, in turn contributing to Japan's industrial competitiveness and economic growth. Based on the EBPM governance system, inefficient GX policies should always be re-evaluated, and policies evolved. Then public resources will be used efficiently, and contribute to productivity and economic growth.

This challenge may serve as a reference for other countries where policy change is needed.

Notes

1. For a comprehensive survey, see Ohtake et al. (2023).
2. For details of administrative project reviews, including the annual schedule, see: https://www.gyoukaku.go.jp/review/review.html accessed 29 October 2023.
3. See: https://analysisfunction.civilservice.gov.uk/ accessed 1 February 2024.
4. The aim of The Office for Budget Responsibility is to provide independent and authoritative analysis of the UK's public finances: https://obr.uk/ accessed 1 February 2024.
5. The aim of WWN is to ensure that spending and practice in public services is informed by the best available evidence: https://www.gov.uk/guidance/what-works-network accessed 1 February 2024.

Disclosure statement

No potential conflict of interest was reported by the author(s).

References

AEB (Administrative Evaluation Bureau). 2017. "EBPM suishin ni kakaru gyōsei kaikaku kyoku no torikumi ni tsuite [Regarding the Efforts of the Administrative Evaluation Bureau related to EBPM promotion]." 1st EBPM Promotion Committee, Material 7, Ministry of Internal Affairs and Communications. August 1. https://warp.ndl.go.jp/info:ndljp/pid/11987457/www.kantei.go.jp/jp/singi/it2/ebpm/dai1/siryou7.pdf.
AEB (Administrative Evaluation Bureau). 2019. "Gyōsei hyōka tō puroguramu [Administrative Evaluation Program 2019]." Ministry of Internal Affairs and Communications. Accessed February 1, 2024. https://www.soumu.go.jp/main_content/000610649.pdf.
AEB (Administrative Evaluation Bureau). 2020. "Gyōsei hyōka tō puroguramu [Administrative Evaluation Program 2020]." Ministry of Internal Affairs and Communications. Accessed February 1, 2024. https://www.soumu.go.jp/menu_news/s-news/hyouka_200331-1.html.
AEB (Administrative Evaluation Bureau). 2022. "Gyōsei hyōka tō puroguramu [Administrative Evaluation Program 2022]." Ministry of Internal Affairs and Communications. Accessed February 1, 2024. https://www.soumu.go.jp/menu_news/s-news/hyouka_22033100156246.html.
AEB (Administrative Evaluation Bureau). 2023. "Gyōsei hyōka tō puroguramu [Administrative Evaluation Program 2023]." Ministry of Internal Affairs and Communications. Accessed February 1, 2024. https://www.soumu.go.jp/menu_news/s-ews/hyouka_230508000165410.html.
ARPO (Administrative Reform Promotion Office). 2017. "EBPM suishin no tameno gyōsei jigyō rebyū no torikumi ni tsuite [Regarding the Initiatives of 'Administrative Business Review' to Promote EBPM]." 1st EBPM Promotion Committee, Material 6, Cabinet Secretariat. August 1. https://warp.ndl.go.jp/info:ndljp/pid/11987457/www.kantei.go.jp/jp/singi/it2/ebpm/dai1/siryou6.pdf.
ARPO (Administrative Reform Promotion Office). 2018. "2018 nendo gyōsei jigyō rebyū kōkai purosesu ni okeru EBPM no shikōteki jissen [Trial Implementation of EBPM in 2018 Administrative Business Review Public Process]." 3rd EBPM Promotion Committee, Material 2-1,

Cabinet Secretariat. August 28. https://warp.ndl.go.jp/info:ndljp/pid/11987457/www.kantei.go.jp/jp/singi/it2/ebpm/dai3/siryou2_1.pdf.

ARPO (Administrative Reform Promotion Office). 2019. "Gyōsei jigyō rebyū kōkai purosesu wo katsuyō shita EBPM no torikumi [Initiative of EBPM Utilizing Administrative Business Review Public Process]." 4th EBPM Promotion Committee, Material 2-1, Cabinet Secretariat. Accessed February 1, 2024. https://warp.ndl.go.jp/info:ndljp/pid/11987457/www.kantei.go.jp/jp/singi/it2/ebpm/dai4/siryou2-1.pdf.

ARPO (Administrative Reform Promotion Office). 2020. "2020 ni okeru EBPM no torikumi ni tsuite [About Initiative of EBPM in 2020]." 5th EBPM Promotion Committee, Material 2, Cabinet Secretariat. Accessed February 1, 2024. https://warp.ndl.go.jp/info:ndljp/pid/11987457/www.kantei.go.jp/jp/singi/it2/ebpm/dai5/siryou2.pdf.

ARPO (Administrative Reform Promotion Office). 2021. "2021 ni okeru EBPM no torikumi [Initiative of EBPM in 2021]." 7th EBPM Promotion Committee, Material 1, Cabinet Secretariat. Accessed February 1, 2024. https://warp.ndl.go.jp/info:ndljp/pid/11987457/www.kantei.go.jp/jp/singi/it2/ebpm/dai7/sankou1.pdf.

ASPE (Assistant Secretary for Planning and Evaluation). 2018. "Implementing the Foundations for Evidence-Based Policymaking Act at the U.S." Department of Health & Human Services." Accessed February 1, 2024. https://aspe.hhs.gov/topics/data/evidence-act-0#:~:text=The%20Foundations%20for%20Evidence%2Dbased%20Policymaking%20Act%20of%202018%20(also,data%20and%20expanding%20evaluation%20capacity.

Cabinet Office. 2019. "Shin keizai zaisei saisei kaikaku kōteihyō ni okeru EBPM no suishin ni muketa torikumi ni tsuite [Efforts to Promote EBPM under the New Economic and Fiscal Revitalization Plan's Reform Roadmap]." Director-General for Policy Planning (Economic and Social Systems), Material 4. September 9. https://warp.ndl.go.jp/info:ndljp/pid/11987457/www.kantei.go.jp/jp/singi/it2/ebpm/dai4/siryou6.pdf.

Cabinet Office. 2020a. "Keizai zaisei ittai kaikaku ni okeru EBPM no wakugumi kyōka ni tsuite [Regarding Strengthening the EBPM Framework by the Committee for Promoting the Integrated Economic and Fiscal Reforms]." 6th EBPM Promotion Committee, Material 4, Director-General for Policy Planning (Economic and Social Systems). November 6. https://warp.ndl.go.jp/info:ndljp/pid/11987457/www.kantei.go.jp/jp/singi/it2/ebpm/dai6/siryou4.pdf.

Cabinet Office. 2020b. "Keizai zaisei ittai kakikaku suishin linkai ni okeru EBPM no torikumi ni tsuite [Regarding Efforts toward EBPM by the Committee for Promoting the Integrated Economic and Fiscal Reforms]." 5th EBPM Promotion Committee, Material 3-3, Director-General for Policy Planning (Economic and Social Systems). May 20. https://warp.ndl.go.jp/info:ndljp/pid/11987457/www.kantei.go.jp/jp/singi/it2/ebpm/dai5/siryou3-3.pdf.

Cabinet Office. 2021. "Keizai zaisei ittai kakikaku suishin linkai ni okeru EBPM no torikumi ni tsuite [Regarding Efforts toward EBPM by the Committee for Promoting the Integrated Economic and Fiscal Reforms]." 7th EBPM Promotion Committee, Material 3, Director-General for Policy Planning (Economic and Social Systems). June 30. https://warp.ndl.go.jp/info:ndljp/pid/11987457/www.kantei.go.jp/jp/singi/it2/ebpm/dai7/siryou3.pdf.

Cabinet Office. 2023. "Grand Design and Action Plan for a New Form of Capitalism 2023 Revised Version." June 16. https://www.cas.go.jp/jp/seisaku/atarashii_sihonsyugi/pdf/ap2023en.pdf.

CEFP (The Council on Economic and Fiscal Policy). 2015. "Keizai zaisei saisei keikaku kaikaku kōteihyō [New Economic and Fiscal Revitalization Plan, Revision of Reform Timetable 2015]." December 24. https://www5.cao.go.jp/keizai-shimon/kaigi/special/reform/report_271224_2.pdf.

CEFP (The Council on Economic and Fiscal Policy). 2017a. "Basic Policy on Economic and Fiscal Management and Reform 2017." Accessed February 1, 2024. https://www5.cao.go.jp/keizai-shimon/kaigi/cabinet/honebuto/2017/2017_basicpolicies_en.pdf.

CEFP (The Council on Economic and Fiscal Policy). 2017b. "Keizai zaisei saisei keikaku kaikaku kōteihyō [New Economic and Fiscal Revitalization Plan, Revision of Reform Timetable 2017]." December 21. https://www5.cao.go.jp/keizai-shimon/kaigi/special/reform/report_291221_1.pdf.

CEFP (The Council on Economic and Fiscal Policy). 2018a. "Basic Policy on Economic and Fiscal Management and Reform 2018." June 15. https://www5.cao.go.jp/keizai-shimon/kaigi/cabinet/honebuto/2018/2018_basicpolicies_en.pdf.

CEFP (The Council on Economic and Fiscal Policy). 2018b. "Keizai zaisei saisei keikaku kaikaku kōteihyō [New Economic and Fiscal Revitalization Plan, Revision of Reform Timetable 2018]." December 20. https://www5.cao.go.jp/keizai-shimon/kaigi/special/reform/kouteihyou2018/report_310325.pdf.

CEFP (The Council on Economic and Fiscal Policy). 2020. "Basic Policy on Economic and Fiscal Management and Reform 2020." July 17. https://www5.cao.go.jp/keizai-shimon/kaigi/cabinet/honebuto/2020/2020_basicpolicies_en.pdf.

CEFP (The Council on Economic and Fiscal Policy). 2021. "Basic Policy on Economic and Fiscal Management and Reform 2021." June 18. https://www5.cao.go.jp/keizai-shimon/kaigi/cabinet/honebuto/2021/2021_basicpolicies_en.pdf.

CEFP (The Council on Economic and Fiscal Policy). 2022a. "Aratana kakujū wo yōsuru seisaku kadai (bōei, GX, kodomo) no kaikaku kōteihyō [New Economic and Fiscal Revitalization Plan for Policy issues that require new expansion (defense, GX, children), Revision of Reform Timetable]." December 22. https://www5.cao.go.jp/keizai-shimon/kaigi/special/reform/report_221222_4.pdf.

CEFP (The Council on Economic and Fiscal Policy). 2022b. "Basic Policy on Economic and Fiscal Management and Reform 2022." June 7. https://www5.cao.go.jp/keizai-shimon/kaigi/cabinet/honebuto/2022/2022_basicpolicies_en.pdf.

CEFP (The Council on Economic and Fiscal Policy). 2023. "Basic Policy on Economic and Fiscal Management and Reform 2023." Accessed February 1, 2024. https://www5.cao.go.jp/keizai-shimon/kaigi/cabinet/honebuto/2023/summary_en.pdf.

Government Analysis Function and HM Treasury. 2015–2023. "The Aqua Book: Guidance on Producing Quality Analysis." U.K. Accessed February 1, 2024. https://www.gov.uk/government/publications/the-aqua-book-guidance-on-producing-quality-analysis-for-government.

HM Treasury and Evaluation Task Force. 2011–2020. "The Magenta Book." U.K. Accessed February 1, 2024. https://www.gov.uk/government/publications/the-magenta-book.

HM Treasury and Government Finance Function. 2013–2023. "The Green Book: appraisal and evaluation in central government." U.K. Accessed February 1, 2024. https://www.gov.uk/government/publications/the-green-book-appraisal-and-evaluation-in-central-government.

Nakai, T. 2024. "Japan's Triple Sustainability Challenge." *Asia Pacific Business Review.* https://doi.org/10.1080/13602381.2024.2320541.

National Diet Library. 2020. "EBPM no torikumi to kadai [Initiatives and Challenges of EBPM]." Accessed February 1, 2024. https://www.ndl.go.jp/jp/diet/publication/document/2020/index.html#rm1230577.

Ohtake, F., Y. Uchiyama, and Y. Kobayashi. 2023. EBPM: Ebidensu Ni Motozuku Seisaku Keisei No dōnyū to Jissen *(EBPM: Introduction and Practice of Evidence-Based Policy Making)*. Tokyo: Nihon Keizai Shimbun Publishing.

The White House. 2021. "Memorandum on Restoring Trust in Government Through Scientific Integrity and Evidence-Based Policymaking." January 27. https://www.whitehouse.gov/briefing-room/presidential-actions/2021/01/27/memorandum-on-restoring-trust-in-government-through-scientific-integrity-and-evidence-based-policymaking/.

WWN (What Works Network). 2018. "The What Works Network Five Years on." Accessed February 1, 2024. https://assets.publishing.service.gov.uk/government/uploads/system/uploads/attachment_data/file/677478/6.4154_What_works_report_Final.pdf.

Much to be done in Japan's family and gender equality policies

Nobuko Nagase

ABSTRACT

Prime Minister Kishida's 'unprecedented' measures to counter declining births in Japan include increasing youth incomes, extending childcare leave entitlement and employee social insurance entitlement to precarious workers, and targeting 50% of fathers to take childcare leave by 2025 by increasing the childcare allowance to 80% of salary. He also proposed reskilling opportunities, and mandating firms to disclose their gender wage gap and gender managerial gap. However, reform should also make fundamental changes to Japanese employment practices and the Employee Social Insurance Scheme which is based on a breadwinner-housewife model. Unless the government explicitly moves towards a worker-carer model, the gender wage gap will stay high, and hinder marriage and births, since double income is seen as a must among younger generation. Fundamental change should be in line with the new attitudes of young non-married males and females.

Introduction

The Kishida government sees the challenge of Japan's low birth as well as the large gender wage gap as two top issues to be addressed. Japan's total fertility rate (TFR) dropped from 1.57 in 1989 to 1.26 in 2005, then showed slight increase to over 1.4 from 2012 to 2018 when the use of childcare leave and childcare places expanded. However, having a second child requires a higher contribution of fathers when both parents work, but this has not been achieved. The TFR again dropped below 1.4 starting in 2019 and reached another low of 1.26 in 2022. The drop was partly due to the COVID-19 pandemic, but only partly. We see a change in attitude among the young in different surveys, in that more of them expect to stay single.

Facing a shrinking labour force and prolonged low birth rate, Prime Minister Kishida's 'new capitalism' emphasizes human capital investment and the increased role of women in the economy, as well as the increased role of men in family care. The Kishida government claimed that it would tackle declining births as never before. It plans to re-construct social policy to support child-rearing, change work culture to allow fathers take an increased role, and to encourage the increase of women in management. The government also seeks to extend stronger protection for non-standard employees by increasing social security coverage. However, to allow more equal involvement of men and women, the implicit contract inherent in Japanese long-term employment should be reformed, along with a change in the social protection for dependent wives. How much the Kishida government can reform employment practice and increase paternal involvement in child-rearing is yet to be seen. Whether Kishida can make a pathway to change social policy from a breadwinner model to a worker-carer model is very important for the coming years for the Japanese economy, which is experiencing both ageing and declining births.

In this paper, I will first compare family policy and gender wage gap policies in Japan with OECD countries. I will then look at Kishida's new policies on family and on gender. Second, I will present statistics on the yet stubbornly strong gender division of labour within couples, showing that former policies have not provided much change in the strong gender division of labour. The third section argues that such gendered division of labour within households is embedded in the Japanese employment system. I will discuss the 'membership/non-membership' and *unlimited contract* concepts. In the fourth section, I will argue that the social insurance rules that favour breadwinner-carer model actually give incentives to married women to stay below the earning threshold and/or stay at low income. In the fifth section, I will look at changes of youth attitudes, which are not supporting the gendered division of labour. Lastly, I will show that many policies are still under discussion, and consider what additional policies might be added to bring about a stronger impact for Kishida's policies, since fundamental change of Japanese employment system and social security rules must accompany 'unprecedented' measures to address declining births.

Japan's family and gender equality policies in comparative perspective

In this section, policies for children and policies for gender equality in labour market in Japan will be compared with other OECD countries.

Policies for children

Figure 1 shows public spending on family benefits from the OECD Social Expenditure database of 2019. It gives a general overview of the scale of Japanese expenditure on family benefits. Benefits in cash include single families, which may not be included in the data from other countries which do the transfer through tax system. Despite this, benefits in cash to families are as low as 0.66% of GDP in Japan, and declined from 0.74 in 2011 when the Liberal Democratic Party (LDP) regained power from the Democratic Party of Japan (DPJ) and child benefits in cash again became means tested. Benefits in services such as day care started to rise from around 0.45% of GDP to the 1.08% of GDP in 2019, reflecting the large increase of childcare places. Support for childcare provision was reformed in 2012 to include not only day care centres but also nursery schools. Prime Minister Abe, who came into office in late 2012, made a rapid increase of childcare places. Tax breaks for families stayed around 0.20% of GDP. In total, the expenditure for families was 1.95% of GDP in 2019, which is below the OECD average of 2.29%. The Kishida government furthers plan to increase expenditures for families, especially child allowances, and childcare leave allowance.

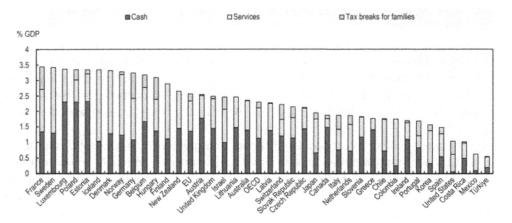

Figure 1. Public spending on family benefits by type of expenditure. (% GDP, and latest available) Source: OECD Social Expenditure Database. Accessed 19 November. https://www.oecd.org/els/soc/PF1_1_Public_spending_on_family_benefits.pdf

Policies for closing the gender wage gap

The gender wage gap in Japan is large among the OECD countries. The *Equal Employment Opportunity Law* was enacted in 1986, strengthened in 1997 and 2007, but its power is weak as this policy only mandates firms to equally treat both men and women if hired in the same work category. However, firms hire much fewer women than men in implicit long-term employment contract, associated with high wage increases and long working hours. More women tend to be employed in a different and slower promotion work category and in non-standard work employment. The Japanese public pension still holds 'model insured workers' as 'full-time salaried working males' who have 'dependent housewives'. Spouses married to salaried workers are given beneficial treatment as dependent housewives under the Japanese social security system, as we shall see below.

Kishida's new family and gender equality policies

Proposed changes in family policy

Kishida's 'new capitalism' proposes to put more focus on the younger generation and the child-rearing life stage as it recognizes the declining births as one of its most important challenges. The Cabinet Office announced in April 2023 that the priority is to increase income level of youth, abolish means-test for child allowance, increase the age limit, and double the allowance for the third child from late 2024. It will also encourage non-standard workers to become regular workers and encourage workers to move into fields with high labour demand by offering re-skilling opportunities (see Zou 2024).

Second, it proposes to take various measures to change the social climate so that the child-rearing burden should be born not only young women, but also by men, and by society. The government set a target for men's child-care leave take-up of 50% in 2025, and 85% in 2030. In order to accelerate the use, Kishida decided to promote disclosure of take-up by companies, and also to provide support for small and medium-sized companies. It also proposed to increase the childcare leave allowance to 80% of income for 28 days from the present 67% if both parents take the leave for more than 14 days within 8 weeks after the birth of the child, hoping that the higher replacement rate will allow more fathers to take the leave. This is planned to be implemented from 2025. The government will also extend the child-care leave allowance to non-standard workers and self-employed workers if they are not otherwise entitled to receive it.

Third, the government plans to increase the income of non-standard employees, firstly by increasing the minimum wage, and secondly by changing social security policy so that they will be covered by the employee social security scheme. At the same time, the government will take measures so that housewives do not adjust their working hours to keep their income below the tax and social security thresholds. It will offer subsidies to companies in the coming three years so that increased social security payments for the companies and also the employees will be off set by pay increases. The government is also discussing including even shorter working week employees in the social insurance scheme.

The fourth point is to encourage women in management. The Kishida government newly mandated disclosure of the gender wage gap at companies over 300 regular employees by the Law for the Promotion of Women's Activities from 2022. Some statistics were already mandated to be disclosed but companies previously could choose what data to disclose among options. It also mandated that companies listed on the Prime section of the Tokyo Stock Exchange disclose female board members and make a Female Executive Information website in which companies' appointments of women to executive positions is shown. Government policy on women is to achieve women's economic independence, and to progress the Fifth Basic Plan for Gender Equality.

Trends in annual income distribution and domestic work hours of males and females

Unchanging gender income gap among ever-married males and females

The policies that aim to increase women's employment and promotion were already introduced from late 2012 by the Abe administration, called *Womenomics* policy. The policy did result in more women who keep ong-term employment, or *seishain* status, at their first birth using childcare leave, especially among university graduate females. The percentage of mothers with young children who keep their long-term job rose to nearly 50% of university graduates, whereas the comparable number was only around 30% in the early 2000s (Nagase 2018a). The rate should be even higher today. Working hours of part-time workers also increased during *Womenomics*.

However, Figure 2 shows that the gender income gap today is still surprisingly large. Even though we see an impressive increase in the labour force participation of married women in Employment Status Surveys, their income continues to stay low, unless they keep long-term employment during child-rearing years. The left side of Figure 2 shows the income gap of ever-married males and females. Ninety five percent of ever-married males earn more than 2 million, while for ever-married females, it was only 53% as many quit work and return to non-standard

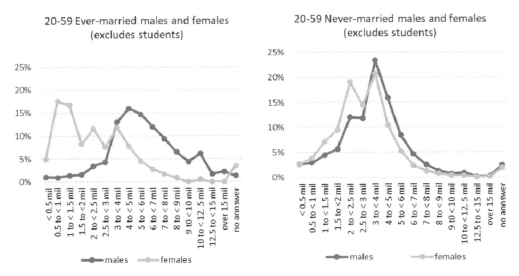

Figure 2. Annual income distribution of ever-married and never-married workers. Note: The figure excludes non-workers. Figures for 'ever-married' include those who are married, divorced or widowed. Source: Statistics Bureau. Employment Status Survey 2022.

employment. Should the statistics include married women out of the labour force, the percentage would be even much smaller, presumably around 35%. On the other hand, income gap between gender is small for never-marrieds, as shown on the right side of Figure 2.

Large domestic work hour gap within couples

We also see that when married, women do much of home production. *The White Paper on Gender Equality 2023* (Cabinet Office 2023) provides an international comparison of the difference between men and women in paid and unpaid work, that Japanese men's daily paid work time is the longest among OECD countries and Japanese men's unpaid work the shortest.

Table 1 shows time use of parents living with children over years using data from the Statistics Bureau's Survey on Time Use and Leisure Activities. We do see some closing of gender gap compared with 1991, such as a slight increase of domestic work by husbands, especially when families have new born babies as can be seen in the third panel: domestic work of fathers increased from 4.4 hours per week in 1996 to 15.4 hours in 2021. Yet as also shown in the table, in 2021, average weekly domestic work hours was 7.6 hours for husbands and 39.2 for wives, while average work hours were 44.1 for husbands and 19.0 hours for wives, showing a large disparity. Even for double income couples with children, average weekly work hours of husbands in 2021 was 50.4 while wives was 28.5, and average weekly domestic work hour of husbands was 7.1 while that of wives was 34.8. It is hard to see any strong signs of closing of the gender gap in the time series.

MUCH TO BE DONE IN JAPAN'S FAMILY AND GENDER EQUALITY POLICIES

Table 1. Weekly work and domestic work hour average of husbands and wives living with children.

		1996	2006	2016	2021
All married couples with children					
Work	husband	48.5	47.4	46.4	44.1
	wife	17.2	16.5	18.1	19.0
Domestic work	husband	3.0	4.8	6.1	7.6
	wife	40.7	41.0	40.4	39.2
Married couples with children, both in labour force					
Work	husband	52.0	52.6	52.6	50.4
	wife	31.5	29.9	28.7	28.5
Domestic work	husband	2.3	3.9	5.4	7.1
	wife	31.9	33.3	34.3	34.8
Married couples with youngest child 1–2					
Work	husband	53.2	54.1	53.1	51.8
	wife	11.8	14.6	20.8	22.6
Domestic work	husband	4.4	7.5	11.4	15.4
	wife	46.2	43.5	42.8	42.1

Note: Husbands and wives with child(ren) living in the household. Data were reported by minutes of an average day of a week. The author converted to weekly hours. Domestic Work includes household chores, child care, elderly care and shopping.
Source: Statistics Bureau. Survey on Time Use and Leisure Activities, Long time Series, various years.

Large gender gap in promotion

Due to requirement of long working hours and difference in employment category, women have been much less likely than men to be promoted to managerial positions. The female ratio of section heads was around 12% in 2021 according to the Basic Wage Structure Survey. Using the micro data of the same survey, Nagase (2021) found that women were promoted much later and much less compared with men. For younger cohorts, the difference in promotion timing between genders became smaller, yet women were only about half as likely to be promoted as men.

Japanese labour practices that reward high commitment and long-term employment

'Membership' and 'non-membership'

Why is the gender income gap and gender domestic work gap so stubborn when the government has introduced policies to close it? As early as 2003 the Gender Equality Bureau made a national target of 30% of leadership positions to be held by women by 2020, but it was far from reached. I presume that the strong division of labour within households that we see comes not only from culture and tradition, but also from Japanese employment practices that inherently reward long-term dedication of workers to companies, implicitly expecting the workers' spouses to take care of family and children, and also from social security insurance that gives comparably high benefits to spouses that earn below the income threshold so as to be identified as 'dependent'.

In his report to the Industrial Competitiveness Council, Employment and Human Resources Subcommittee hearing, Hamaguchi (2013) described Japanese employment practices as 'membership type employment' and 'non-membership type of employment'.

To be a member, one typically enters a firm at graduation, and is expected to follow a seniority-based wage path in a lifetime employment contract. In return, employers typically can order overtime work, and allocate employees to different departments and jobs for human resource development in the long term. On the other hand, some long-term contracts are regionally based, and are offered more to females. When the place of employment is pre-determined, wages rises are expected to be much less. As for 'non-membership work', described by Hamaguchi, or non-long-term contract work such as hourly part-time employment and fixed-term contract work, where the work hours, job content, and place of work are defined, wages are typically much lower than long-term employees. Such 'non-membership' employees are typically seen as outsiders by company-based labour unions.

Since it is not easy for workers to raise children under 'membership contracts', many companies have given a spousal allowance to add to the husband's salary, expecting that the employees have a low-earning dependent spouse to care of children and the elderly. Such spousal allowance is not only added to the monthly salary, but also to the annual bonus payment, and to retirement lump sum payment, and even to the public pension payment after retirement.

Unlimited contract regular employees and limited contract employees

Sato (2012) categories long-term employees as 'unlimited contract regular employees' (*mugentei shain*), and employees whose work location and job type as limited 'limited contract regular employees' (*gentei shain*). He defines the former as a work contract where companies can order job content, work relocation and also overtime work. This naming does indicate the difficulties of balancing work and family, and may be another way to look at Hamaguchi's description of 'membership work'. In Europe and the U.S., transfers and changes of job content, even within the same company, are typically only realized after an individual applies for the position and is hired for the position. Such is not the case under Japanese long-term employment.

The Ministry of Health, Labour and Welfare (MHLW 2012) 'Study Group Report on Various Forms of Regular Employees' for which Sato was the chair, identified the number of the 'so-called regular employees' (or unlimited contract regular employees), in a survey conducted at companies with over 300 employees. In this survey, according to his classification, Sato found that among the long-term employees, more than 40% were 'unlimited contract regular employees', and less than 30% were 'limited contract regular employees', from the viewpoint of work hours and work location, while the rest cannot be classified as such. If classified by gender, the survey found that more than 70% of unlimited contract regular employees were men, 45% of limited contract regular employees were men. On the other hand, the survey found that 70% of non-standard workers who are not 'long-term employees' were women.

The ratio of female employees clearly increased as work location, job, and working hours become more well defined. At the same time, their annual income decreased. While more than 70% of unlimited contract regular employees earned annual incomes of ¥4 million or more, this figure was less than 50% for *limited contract regular employees*. For non-standard employees, the figure was only just over 10%. This shows that wages in

Japan are defined not so much by occupation but more by whether one has an unlimited regular employee contract and also on whether one is long-term employee or not.

This survey found that the disadvantages of the work style felt by limited contract regular employees were 'low salary' (nearly 50%) and 'lack of prospects for promotion and advancement' (25%). On the other hand, 'Worries about relocation' (35%) was the most common disadvantage felt by unlimited contract regular employees. As many as 60% of them replied that they wished to convert to a contract with limited work location, but 60% of them hoped that this would not result in lowering their wages or promotion prospects. In other words, 'unlimited contract regular employees' are dissatisfied with company-ordered transfers, but don't want lower wages or promotion. The Abe administration's *Work Style Reform* policies enacted in 2019 put clear overtime hour cap on all employees for the first time, and introduced the 'equal pay for equal work' principle, but Japanese courts seem to define 'equal work' as not only pertaining to occupation and work content, but also to how much the work contract expects company-initiated job rotation and re-location.

Job descriptions not clearly defined in Japanese-style employment

Ono (2016) points to 'overtime work as norm' (*tsukiai zangyō*) as a phenomenon unique to Japan under strong group ties and hierarchical relationships. He also notes that job descriptions are not clearly defined, so that job rotation can be flexibly handled. Furthermore, the spousal tax deduction given to the household head reflects the socially accepted notion that wives are to work so long as it does not impact on their housework duties, which strengthens the traditional division of labour. Since Japanese employment practices are based on the complementarity of various systems, he says there will be pain and resistance on the part of both individuals and companies before a new equilibrium can be achieved to remedy long working hours.

In sum, while there has been much discussion about the need to reform Japanese-style employment, it is still not easy for employees to achieve work and life balance. While there has been a significant increase in the use of childcare leave, it is mainly women who take childcare leave and work shorter hours for the sake of childcare.

Social insurance regulation favouring a gendered division of labour

Social insurance premium exemption of low-earning spouses

In addition to employment practices, social insurance has also given explicit and special consideration for dependent spouses of salaried workers. Dependent housewives of salaried workers do not have to pay their social insurance premiums on medical insurance but are nonetheless given the full entitlement of medical insurance as dependents. As to the old-age public pension for employees, dependent housewives are given even more special consideration called 'category 3' – they are exempted from social insurance payment but are given the full *Basic Pension Entitlement*.

This reform to give *Basic Pension Entitlement* to housewives without their payment came about in 1985. The reform was brought about to settle different challenges then, but the concept of 'Japanese-style welfare society' advocated from around the end of the

1970s by the LDP might have given it support. Hori (1981) characterized the 'Japanese-style social welfare concept' of the time as denying the Western-style social welfare state, emphasizing self-help efforts, welfare by families, mutual assistance in local communities, and corporate welfare. As for corporate welfare, he cites lifetime employment and seniority-based wages as providing life income security, retirement benefits, corporate pensions, health insurance unions, and unemployment insurance benefits. As for welfare by families, he points out that the 1978 White Paper on Health and Welfare extolled the extended family as an 'informal asset of welfare'. Osawa (1993), on the other hand, described the 1986 and 1987 White Papers on Welfare as 'family-oriented, big business-oriented, and male-oriented', noting that it was men who were to be the model insured workers, and not women.

The spouses of salaried workers were seen at the time of the reform as the ones who would take care of housework, childcare, and elderly care. Thus, the reform of 1985 indeed encouraged women to stay as low-earning housewives. This social security system continues to this day as discussed in Ochiai (2015). It is not in line with the changing consciousness of today's youth and the economic demands for women's employment. It is also not in line with the changing Japanese family. In 1985, among households with family members 65 years old or older, 44.8% lived in three generation households and 13.1% were single-person households. In 2022, three generation households constituted only 7.1%, and single-person households 31.8%. In 1985, only 1.25 million elderly lived alone, but the number in 2022 was 8.9 million. Women are no longer an 'informal asset of welfare' where they stay at home to take care of the elderly.

The system favouring dependent spouses was questioned in 2000–2001 when a 'Changing Lifestyle of Women and Pension Committee' was organized at the Ministry of Health and Welfare, for which the author was one of the committee members. At the time, all those aged 20 to 59 who were not covered by employee insurance were mandated to pay the pension premium to the Peoples' Pension, including students and unemployed, while low-earning housewives were exempted but given the same *Basic Pension Entitlement* since the employee pension was paying the premium for them. The committee gathered a considerable audience, and was given widespread media coverage, signifying high public interest. Six options to change the Category 3 were proposed (Ministry of Labour Health and Welfare 2001), but the Commission did not reach an agreement, and the Ministry did not implement any of the options, except in 2004, when pension splitting upon divorce was introduced based on the discussion.

Annual income targeting of married women that keeps part-time wages low, and proposed changes

According to Statistics Bureau's Employment Status Survey of 2022, among 29 million women in the labour force, around 14 million were non-standard female workers, and two out of three of them, that is, 9.3 million females, earned below ¥1.5 million, or roughly $10,000 a year, which is not enough to make one's own living. Of these, 70% were housewives. The remaining one third are singles, but as shown in Figure 3, they mostly earned below ¥2.5 million a year, which is not enough for single living, so many such singles often share housing with their parents. According to the same statistics, as shown in Figure 3, 58.3% and 58.6% of married non-standard workers who earned ¥0.5 to

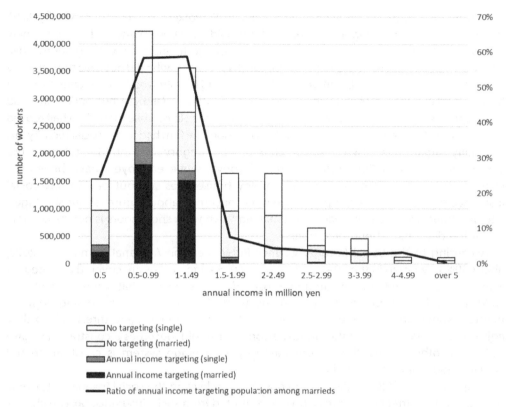

Figure 3. Income targeting among non-standard female employees. Source: Statistics Office. *Employment Status Survey 2022.*

1.0 million and ¥1.0–1.5 million respectively replied that they intentionally adjust their work hours so that their annual income is below a certain income threshold to take advantage of tax and social security tax exemption rules. Non-marrieds can also become dependent on their parents and can be exempted from medical insurance, but they are not given entitlement to the public pension as dependent wives unless they pay their own premium. Therefore, such work adjustment and income targeting are smaller for non-married women as shown in Figure 3.

Companies were not required to include non-standard workers in employee social insurance if their work hours were below 75% of regular employees. Many were housewives who got their social security entitlement as 'dependents' through their spouse. Both companies and wives took advantage of this rule, so that they were both exempted from social security fees. Today, however, MHLW is trying to include more part-time workers in employee social insurance, to collect social security tax from housewives but also to extend social protection to different workers. Starting from larger firms in 2016, workers with more than 20 hours over the 1.06 million yen threshold were mandated to be included in employee insurance. The company size will be lowered to firms with more than 50 employees in October 2024. The Kishida government is now trying to further include more employees by mandating smaller-sized firms, and to extend to even shorter work-week workers. However, a survey by JILPT showed that 48.1% of Category 3 workers who should have been mandated under the new law avoided the social security levy reform of 2022 by shortening their working hours, while such work hour adjustment was about half as much for workers who did not have the Category 3 benefit (JILPT 2023). A similar survey on the reform of 2016 showed that about one third of firms replied that they changed human resource management. Of these, two out of three had tried to shorten work hours to avoid the social insurance tax levy, while more than half replied that they tried to extend work hours of workers to whom the firm had to pay social security tax.

Finally, again, the discussion for change of Category 3 is on the table of the Government Pension Committee. As noted above, while employers have benefitted from the current system as they can employ housewives without paying any social insurance premium, more companies are now concerned about future labour shortages. Keeping housewives on low wages and making them work short hours is not sustainable under the declining labour force trend.

According to the Social Security Council Public Pension Actuarial Committee, 2023, about 30% of women in the 40–44, 45–49, and 50–54 age groups are covered by Category 3, and account for 70% of the Category 3 insured. Analysis shows that when the youngest child gets older – from under 6 to 6–9 and to 10–12 years old – the working hours of married women increase and more women hit the income targeting threshold, so they adjust their work hours and the 'annual income threshold' becomes a constraint (Nagase 2018b). In other words, the current Category 3 coverage system is constraining the working hours of middle-aged wives.

Kenjō and Kenjō (2022), discuss the possibility of levying the social insurance tax only on employers so that housewives who are exempted from social insurance tax can choose whether to have additional pension for themselves or not. Koreeda (2023a, 2023b) discuss levying the social insurance tax for short working week workers to both employers and employees, while retaining some benefit to housewives who had been exempted from all these taxes. Both Kenjō and Koreeda propose reforms while keeping Category 3 insurance for housewives. Nagase (2023) on the other hand advocates increasing coverage to short hour workers, but taking steps to abolish Category 3, creating support and credit for those who are out of work or low paid due to child care (the proposal extends the benefit not only to dependents of salaried workers, but also to single mothers and wives of self-employed), and also re-defining what 'equal work' is in the government's 'equal pay for equal work' principle. The present definition of 'equal work' in Japanese law not only looks at actual work content, but also to the implicit employment contract of overtime work and job rotation (Kanki 2018), as noted above, meaning that two workers doing the same tasks are not necessarily deemed to be doing 'equal work'. Unless more weight is given to what women – often working under 'limited work contract' and on 'non-standard work contract' – actually do, the gender wage gap will not be easily narrowed.

Changing attitudes and gender role choice among youth

The younger generation no longer supports a strong gender-role division of labour within the family. The 'Marriage and Family in the Era of 100 Years of Life Survey' (2022) was commissioned by the Gender Equality Bureau of the Cabinet Office for the 2022 *White Paper on Gender Equality*, shows an interesting change of attitudes.

First, the desire to marry is found to be lower among singles: more than 60% of women and nearly 60% of men in their 20s would like to get married, but the desire declines with age. Even lower is the ideal number of children for singles. Twenty four percent of women and 31% of men in their 20s said they wish to have no children, and an additional 14% of women and 15% of men said they don't know. Considering that society cannot sustain itself without nurturing the next generation, we should reflect on why 40% of young people responded like this.

We also see a rapid change in the ideal way to take care of infants aged 2 or 3. For the age group in their 20s, more than 50% of males and over 40% of females answered that their ideal is to use childcare leave and work return so that both husband and wife can have long-term employment. On the other hand, for those in their 60s, the comparable ratio thought that husbands working full-time and wives staying at home was ideal.

The working styles and family formation of the younger generation are changing in response to these attitudes, yet changes are slow; family formation has actually stagnated, and childbearing has continued to decline.

How can we change the gender-role division of labour in the family?

Looking back at men and women now in their 60s who entered the labour market in the 1980s, 'Japanese-style employment' was in full swing. It was taken for granted that women would quit work after marriage or childbirth, and even if they remained in the company, the wage gap between men and women was assumed to be exceptionally large. In 1985, the Equal Employment Opportunity Law was enacted, but it only resulted in the renaming of female jobs as 'slow-track jobs (*ippanshoku*)' and male jobs as 'career-track jobs (*sogoshoku*)', and did not change Japanese employment practices by seriously considering the recruitment and training of women who would have children to fully build their human capital. Although the Equal Employment Opportunity Law was strengthened, many women were not hired for career-track positions in the same way as men, and even those women who were hired for career-track positions often left the workforce for family reasons and also by questioning the high commitment to company in the male dominated community. What followed was a shift to non-regular employment, including among single people and young people, and since 2000 the number of non-standard workers has increased substantially without any major changes in the rules for regular employees.

It was after 2007 to 2010 that women returning to work after taking childcare leave increased and then accelerated. However, this was mainly for regular employees of large companies, and the increasing number of non-regular employees were not subject to support and training, even at large companies. Since then an increasing number of companies have consciously increased the number of women in career-track positions. However, it is difficult to say that the system has changed sufficiently when it comes to how employers incorporate child rearing, which is an important part of human life, while also building their own human capital. In addition, the preferential treatment for households with dependent spouses does not provide sufficient support for family formation, but this point has not yet been seriously reviewed.

In post-COVID society, economic support for households with children and social support in the form of flexible working hours and childcare time should be provided to both male and female employees, including part-time workers, and in addition, low-income households should receive economic support. The same is true for households that need to provide full-time care. Systems that encourage women to remain as dependents should be abolished, but at the same time, more flexibility in work hours should be introduced, as well as support to re-enter the labour market and better childcare support.

Conclusion: proposal for additional change

Sato et al. (2022) point out that unless the work style of unlimited contract regular employees is reformed, the increase of limited contract regular workers will only increase the stratification of regular employees. Although new employment styles are emerging, so far stratification is undeniable.

There are still 7.5 million Category 3 females who are exempted from any social security premium payment and are given premium payment from the employee group as a whole. These women do work when their children grow older, but they often are poorly paid, and they even try to adjust their work hours so that they can keep their income below the 1 to 1.3 million yen thresholds. This system has to be fundamentally changed. I propose to expand childcare leave entilement and at the same time reduce beneficial treatment of housewives on social insurance when their youngest child is over certain age, such as age 9 so that fewer women make working hour adjustments to obtain social security premium exemption when they indeed can work more hours. I also propose to implement policies to increase the hourly wages of non-standard workers, and to include them in employee insurance. At the same time, we should change the understanding of the 'equal pay for equal work' principle, so that 'Equal Work' is what one does at the time of comparison, instead of being in a 'membership' employment relationship or not. 'Unlimited contract' employment itself should be changed if the government truly seeks higher involvement of fathers in childrearing.

Overall, the government is trying to change social policy and family policy from a breadwinner model to an earner-and-carer model. However, the change proposed still lacks ambition. Large change needs coordination of different interests. The government should take stronger leadership to bring about this change.

Disclosure statement

No potential conflict of interest was reported by the author(s).

Funding

This work was supported by the The Research Institute of Science and Technology for Society (RISTEX) of the Japan Science and Technology Agency (JST) (grant number JPMJRX19H4; PI Nobuko Nagase); Grants-in-Aid for Scientific Research Fund for the Promotion of Joint International Research (Fostering Joint International Research (B)) (grant number 19KK0042; PI Nobuko Nagase).

References

Cabinet Office Commissioned Survey. 2023. *Reiwa 4 nendo atarashii raifu sutairu, atarashii hatarakikata wo fumaeta danjo kyōdō sankaku suisin ni kansuru chōsa hōkokusho* [Fiscal 2022, Gender Equality Promotion Taking Into Account New Life Styles and New Ways of Work]. Osaka: Marketing Communications.

Hamaguchi, K. November 5, 2013. *""Kongo no rōdō hōsei no arikata"* (Labour Law From Now). *Sangyō kyōsōryoku kaigi koyō/jinzai bunkakai hiaringu shiryō* (Industrial Competitiveness Council Labour and Human Resource Sub Group Hearing)." February 11, 2024. https://www.kantei.go.jp/jp/singi/keizaisaisei/bunka/koyou_hearing/dai1/siryou2.pdf.

Hori, K. 1981. ""Nihon Gata Fukushi Shakai Ron" (Concept of Japanese Type of Welfare Society)." *Kikan Shakai hoshō kenkyū (The Quarterly of Social Security Research)* 17 (1): 37–50.

Japan Institute for Labour Policy and Training. 2023. "Shakai hoken no tekiyō kakudai heno taiou jōkyō ni kansuru chōsa oyobi hatarakikata heno anketto chōsa" [How Firms Responded to the Expansion of Social Insurance to Part-time Workers; Survey on Work Style of Employees]. *JILPT Research Series No.* 243.

Kanki, C. 2018. "Rōdōhō niokeru seiki/hiseiki 'kakusa' to sono 'kyūsai': pāto taimu rōdōhō to rōdō keiyakuhō 20 jou no kaishaku wo sozai ni" [Interpretation of Unreasonable Disparities and Remedies Based on Article 20 of the Labour Contract Act]. *Nihon Rōdō Kenkyū Zasshi (The Japanese Journal of Labour Studies)* 60 (1): 65–75.

Kenjō, Z., and E. Kenjō. 2022. *Motto Kininaru Shakai Hoshō* [Thinking about Social Security]. Tokyo: Keiso Shobo.

Koreeda, S. August 25, 2023a. Shūnyū no kabe repōto 1, dai 3 gou hihokensha seido no minaoshi ha kokumin nenkin no zaisei akka no fukusayō wo motarasu [Report on Income Threshold 1, Remedy on Category 3 Will Harm People's Pension Budget]. *Daiwa Sōken Repōto (Daiwa Researh Institute Report)*.

Koreeda, S. August 25, 2023b. Shūnyū no kabe repōto 2, dai 3 gou hihokensha minaoshi go no ukezara toshiteno 1.5 gō/2.5 gō hihokehshaseido sōsetsu no teian [Report on Income Threshold 2, Proposal to make 1.5 or 2.5 Category for the Remedy of Category 3]. *Daiwa Sōken Repōto (Daiwa Research Institute Report)*.

Ministry of Labour Health and Welfare. 2001. "Josei no raifu sutairu no henkatō ni taiō shita nenkin no arikata ni kansuru kentōkai: josei jishin no kōken ga minoru nenkin seido" [Report on the Review of Women and Public Pension in View of Changing Life Style of Women: Public Pension System Where Women's Contribution Pays Off]. February 11, 2024. https://www.mhlw.go.jp/shingi/0112/dl/s1214-3a.pdf.

Ministry of Labour Health and Welfare. 2012. *"Tayōna keitai ni yoru seishain ni kansuru kenkyūkai hōkokusho* (Report on the Study of Different Types of Long-Term Employees)." Tokyo. February 11, 2024. https://www.mhlw.go.jp/stf/houdou/2r985200000260c2.html.

Nagase, N. 2018a. "Has Abe's WOMENOMICS Worked?" *Asian Economic Policy Review* 13 (1): 68–101. https://doi.org/10.1111/aepr.12202.

Nagase, N. 2018b. "Seiki koyō to hiseiki koyō no kakusa: josei, jakunen no jinteki shihon kakujū notameno shisaku ni tsuite" [Measures to Close the Wage Gap of Standard and Non-standard Workers]. *Nihon Rōdō Kenkyū Zasshi (The Japanese Journal of Labour Studies)* 60:19–38.

Nagase, N. 2021. "Abe's Womenomics Policy: Did It Reduce the Gender Gap in Management?" In *The Political Economy of the Abe Government and Abenomics Reforms*, edited by T. Hoshi and P. Lipscy, 310–356. Cambridge: Cambridge University Press.

Nagase, N. 2023. "Nihonteki koyō shisutemu ni okeru dansei shūrō to kea wo meguru jirenma: 'mugentei na hatarakikata' to dai 3 gō hihokensha seido wo tegakarini" [Dilemma Japanese Male Workers Face in Maintaining Income for Family and Taking Time for Family: Japanese Employment Rules of "Fast Track Course" and Social Insurance Protection Rules that Favour Breadwinner and Dependent-Housewife Couples]. *Shakai Hosho Kenkyu [Journal of Social Security Research]* 8 (3): 270–294.

Ochiai, E. 2015. "Nihongata fukushi rejīmu ha naze kazoku shugi no mama nanoka—4 houkoku heno komento" [Why the Japanese Welfare Regime is Still Family Based: Comment on Four Presentations]. *Kazoku Shakaigaku Kenkyū (Japanese Journal of Family Sociology)* 27 (1): 61–68. https://doi.org/10.4234/jjoffamilysociology.27.61.

Ono, H. 2016. "Why Do the Japanese Work Long Hours? Sociological Perspectives on Long Working Hours in Japan." *Nihon Rōdō Kenkyū Zasshi (The Japanese Journal of Labour Studies)* 58 (12): 15–27.

Osawa, M. 1993. *Kigyō chūshin shakai wo koete: gendai nihon wo 'jendā' de yomu* [Looking at Present Day Japan from a Gender Perspective: Going Beyond Corporate-centred Society]. Tokyo: Jijitsushinsha.

Sato, H. 2012. "Seishain no genteika to hiseishain no mugenteika: jinji kanri no atarashii kadai" [Making Long-Term Employees Limited Contract, and Making Non-Standard Employees Unlimited Contract Workers: The New Challenge of Human Resource Management]. *Nihon rōmu gakkai zenkoku taikai kenkyū hōkokushū (Japan Society of Human Resource Management National Conference Report)*, Wakayama University, 42: 201–208.

Sato, H., E. Takeishi, and H. Sakazume. 2022. *Tayō na jinzai manejimento* [Managing Diversified Employees]. Tokyo: Chuo Keizai.

Zou, F. 2024. "The 'New Trinity' Reform of Labour Markets in Japan." *Asia Pacific Business Review.* https://doi.org/10.1080/13602381.2024.2320550.

∂ OPEN ACCESS

Can affirmative action overcome STEM gender inequality in Japan? Expectations and concerns

Hiromi M. Yokoyama (iD), Yuko Ikkatai (iD), Euan McKay (iD), Atsushi Inoue (iD), Azusa Minamizaki (iD) and Kei Kano (iD)

ABSTRACT
Compounding skill shortages from Japan's shrinking and ageing workforce is low female participation in research and science-related areas. Why do so few women choose to work in science, technology, engineering and mathematics (STEM)? Previous research suggests the influence of gendered images of STEM fields, but do these apply to Japan, and if so, how? We introduce multiple studies that shed light on gendered images and elucidate the roles of those who affect women's choices and women's own attitudes. Our findings further suggest that a social climate of inequality affects the gendered images of STEM fields. Finally, we offer a critique of recent quota-based systems for increasing women's STEM participation in Japan.

Introduction

The current Japanese government is calling for the creation of a new form of capitalism in Japan, in part through digital and green transformation (DX and GX). This builds on former government policy to realize Society 5.0, a form of super smart society exploiting the possibilities of artificial intelligence and other new technologies and that is fundamentally human centric in nature. Such a society will require a technologically savvy workforce, yet Japan faces a rapidly ageing and shrinking population. Achieving gender equality and mobilizing female labour in both the economy and research will prove essential, yet Japan faces falling research output and lack of researchers. Further, it faces the risk of contraction, casting a pall over the sector's future (Normile 2022). All this suggests that the human may not be as central to government policy as is claimed, and makes it highly important to understand the position of women in Japan's labour force and in science, technology, engineering and mathematics (STEM) fields in particular.

Japan has the lowest proportion of women at the undergraduate level in STEM among Organisation for Economic Co-operation and Development (OECD) countries. The first half

---

This is an Open Access article distributed under the terms of the Creative Commons Attribution-NonCommercial-NoDerivatives License (http://creativecommons.org/licenses/by-nc-nd/4.0/), which permits non-commercial re-use, distribution, and reproduction in any medium, provided the original work is properly cited, and is not altered, transformed, or built upon in any way. The terms on which this article has been published allow the posting of the Accepted Manuscript in a repository by the author(s) or with their consent.

of this paper reviews recent Japanese research that focuses on gender perceptions of STEM among multiple groups and the social climate of equality. In Japan, gendered occupational and competence stereotypes are deeply linked to STEM gender images, and they have a similar impact in England, where we conducted surveys of the gendered image of multiple fields. A social climate of inequality, in which gendered differences are socially accepted, also affects the STEM gender image. The second half of the paper discusses affirmative action for gender inequalities through a women's quota in STEM faculties, which some Japanese universities began implementing in 2023. Although there is some criticism, affirmative action has been generally accepted not for social justice but to secure human resources for a modern capitalist society, i.e. Japan. The paper explores potential strategies for Japan to achieve genuine gender equality and remove barriers for women who wish to opt for STEM.

The research environment and social climate in Japan

Japan's scientific research capacity has stagnated in recent years. This is primarily due to the instability of positions for young researchers as a result of university reforms in 2004. At the same time, the percentage of women STEM researchers in Japan is among the lowest in the OECD, and while there has been a slight increase, no significant improvement has occurred.

The proportion of undergraduate women in STEM in Japan is 27% in the natural sciences and 16% in engineering. Fields such as mathematics and physics have fewer than 20%, and mechanical engineering and electrical and electronic engineering have even lower rates. Globally, there are far fewer women than men majoring in mathematics-based fields, such as mathematics, physics, earth sciences, engineering, computer science and economics (Ceci et al. 2014; Kahn and Ginther 2018; OECD 2015).

This century, university enrolment rates for women have increased significantly in developed countries, surpassing those of men in many countries (Goldin, Katz, and Kuziemko 2006; OECD 2015). However, in Japan the proportion of women entering university is lower than that of men, with a 15% lower proportion of women at the undergraduate level, 40% at the master's level and 50% at the doctoral level. Especially at prestigious universities, such as the University of Tokyo, female student enrolment has long hovered around 20%, despite various efforts to increase the proportion. Regional disparities in university enrolment rates are also significant, with higher female participation rates in urban centres and extremely low rates in certain regions. Japan has a strong historical social climate that views women in higher education and the sciences negatively.

The gender gap is further evidenced by Japan's low ranking in the gender gap index published by the World Economic Forum. In 2023, Japan ranked 125th out of 156 countries, with a score of 0.647. (In 2022, Japan ranked 116th out of 156 countries, with a score of 0.650). The gender gap is particularly pronounced in political and economic representation. Given STEM's role in driving the economy, the gender gap is likely to affect the economy in multiple ways.

The Japanese government, led by the Cabinet Office and the Ministry of Education, Culture, Sports, Science and Technology (MEXT), has supported numerous activities aimed at developing female STEM professionals, but these efforts have not yielded significant change, due to the lack of a clear, evidence-based strategy. Furthermore, the government's top science and technology policy body, the Japan Council for Science, Technology and Innovation (CSTI), has noted a bias towards the humanities in university specializations compared to overseas universities and urges the expansion of science faculties. There are concerns that the population of 18-year-olds is rapidly declining in Japan, a society with a decreasing birth rate, and that the number of science and engineering graduates is also decreasing. In this complex environment the underrepresentation of women in STEM in Japan is a serious issue, and the reasons for this warrant further investigation, which we will now proceed to.

Reasons for the low proportion of women in STEM

Factors reported around the world

The reasons for the under-representation of women in STEM have long been studied worldwide. It is generally believed that STEM requires mathematical competence. In the field of biology, some studies have suggested an innate gender gap in mathematics (Wilder and Powell 1989), but comprehensive reviews have cast doubt on this notion (Ceci, Williams, and Barnett 2009). Many scholars now assert that STEM competence is not attributable to gender but to individual differences.

The (false) perception that female students are less proficient in mathematics than their male peers, commonly referred to as the 'mathematics stereotype', prevails globally. In Japan, an analysis using academic tracking data in one Japanese city (Isa and Chinen 2014) found no differences between boys and girls in primary school, but girls reported lower scores than boys in junior high school. In the TIMSS (Trends in International Mathematics and Science Study) test, Japanese primary and junior high school girls scored slightly better than boys on average, but no statistically meaningful differences have been found since 2003. In the Program for International Student Assessment (PISA), taken by 15-year-olds, Japan consistently ranks highly, and scores between boys and girls show minimal differences, with girls' scores among the highest in the world. Despite their excellent maths skills, however, girls are less likely to pursue science compared to their counterparts in other countries.

In the US, studies have shown that mathematics stereotyping begins as early as 5–6 years old, with girls internalizing this stereotype and therefore underachieving in maths (Spencer, Logel, and Davies 2016; Spencer, Steele, and Quinn 1999). However, mathematics stereotyping can be ameliorated, as Spencer, Steele and Quinn (1999) have shown that reading statements affirming women's ability to achieve the same grades as men improved the performance of female students. In Japan, utterances such as 'even though you are a girl, it's amazing that you can do maths' affect grades (Morinaga, Furukawa, and Fukudome 2017).

Yet career choices cannot be explained by mathematics scores alone (Turner and Bowen 1999). Social factors, including the influence of teachers (Bettinger and Long 2005; Carrell, Page, and West 2010; Lim and Meer 2020) – particularly maths and science teachers (Carrell, Page, and West 2010); friends (Brenoe and Zölitz 2020; Fischer 2017); and single-sex schools (Park, Behrman, and Choi 2018) – have also been noted. The influence of mothers is particularly strong. In the US, it has been reported that only when mothers rated their daughters' mathematical abilities highly, daughters went on to physics courses at the same rate as sons (Bleeker and Jacobs 2004).

Disciplines and scientists are often associated with particular images. Mathematics, for example, is often perceived as a 'number, objective, abstract, inhuman subject' (Sam and Ernest 2000). In Japan, there are strong gender orientations within professions, with physics often perceived as a male field (Adachi 2014). Furthermore, one educational psychology study found that female Japanese junior high school students may 'pretend' to dislike mathematics and science (Uchida and Mori 2018). Even when they like maths and science, statements such as 'I can do maths' or 'I like science' by adolescent girls could be labelled unusual, and lead to difficulties in forming girls' group friendships because Japanese people dislike being different from others. Changing this cultural environment could make it easier for girls to enter STEM fields.

What is happening in Japan

Gender images such as 'STEM is for men' may be a barrier for women to enter STEM. To understand the situation in Japan, it is necessary to focus on the social climate, including university enrolment rates and the less-than-welcoming atmosphere for highly educated women. In recent years, web surveys have made data collection more accessible. As a result, we collected and analysed relevant data for the Research Institute of Science and Technology for Society (Ristex) project, supported by the Japan Science and Technology Agency (JST) from October 2017 to March 2021. Here we present ten studies, based on a series of surveys, and subsequently offer a comprehensive overview of the challenges involved in increasing the number of women in STEM in Japan.[1]

The first study examines brilliance, an individual characteristic often associated with and seen as a required ability to excel in science subjects. Next, we introduce two studies looking at gendered images of fields or disciplines in society, as some are seen as masculine while others are seen as feminine, which may affect women's choice of field. This is followed by two studies that aim to understand how women's subject choices are affected by their personal views of gender equality. Since decisions are not made in a vacuum, three more studies examine the influences of parents and teachers on female students' choice of field. A further study extends this research to elucidate the social climate surrounding female students' choice of field. The final study provides egalitarian information to participants to see whether motivation towards STEM fields can be influenced.

'Brilliance'

'Brilliance' is a special ability related to intelligence that is exceptional and innate. Among the STEM disciplines, mathematics and physics, in particular, have a strong image of 'Brilliance', or special talent as if bestowed from above. It seems that the stronger the image of 'Brilliance' in a field, the lower the percentage of female PhDs in that field (Leslie et al. 2015). That said, the specific abilities associated with 'Brilliance', and what constitutes their gendered images, remain unclear.

Based on multiple intelligence theory and dual process theory, we organized the abilities required for STEM into seven categories: logical thinking, calculation, memory, abundant knowledge, ability to judge things quickly, ability to think deeply about things, and ability to grasp the needs of society. We conducted a survey through an Internet research company in Japan and England to determine whether these skills are perceived as male-oriented or female-oriented, and to what extent they are seen as necessary in six STEM fields (Y. Ikkatai, K. Inoue, et al. 2021).[2] Men and women (1177 in Japan and 1082 in England) between the ages of 20 and 69 were surveyed.

The results showed that in both Japan and England, 'ability for logical thinking' and 'mathematical ability' were strongly associated with masculinity, while 'ability to understand the needs of society' was strongly associated with femininity. Physics and mathematics students were strongly associated with excellence in 'mathematical ability' and 'ability for logical thinking', and those in information science and engineering with excellence in 'logical thinking' in both countries.

On the other hand, mechanical engineering students were strongly associated with 'mathematical ability' in Japan, but with 'ability for logical thinking' in England. There were also differences in perceptions of chemistry and biology students. Breaking down the concept of brilliance into component abilities, we showed that while there are commonalities between Japanese and English in whether fields are seen as masculine or feminine, there are also culturally specific associations.

Nursing for girls?

Next, we conducted an Internet survey to examine Japanese gender images in 18 fields, including STEM.[3] A total of 1086 men and women (541 men and 545 women, aged 20–69) were surveyed concerning gender images from the three viewpoints of (a) 'gender appropriateness', (b) 'employability', and (c) 'marriage appropriateness'. We also measured egalitarian attitudes using the Shortened Egalitarian Sex Role Attitude Scale (SESRA-S), which consists of a set of 15 questions developed in the field of psychology to measure egalitarian attitudes.

Nursing was selected by the highest number of respondents as a field suitable for women, and mechanical engineering the lowest. In general, STEM was considered more suited for males than females. Employability was associated with nursing for women and medicine for men. Overall, the results indicate that there is a strong gender image of the fields in Japan, which accords with the actual gender distribution, and that this stereotypical image may be a barrier to girls entering 'male-oriented' fields, especially physics, mathematics, and mechanical engineering (Ikkatai et al. 2020a). People with stronger stereotypical gender images had stronger preferences.

Academic field keywords and gender image

We have seen that different fields of academia have different gender images. What keywords, then, are associated with STEM fields in Japan? Are there gender images for those keywords as well? We extracted representative images for physics, chemistry, mechanical engineering, information science, mathematics, and biology using keywords and examined the gender image of each field and the gender image (masculine or feminine) of the keywords (Ikkatai et al. 2020b).

First, an online survey asked 210 men and women (105 men and 105 women, aged 20–69) to write three words that they associated with each field. 15–20 keywords in each field were then extracted by four independent raters. Names of physicists such as

'Galileo' and 'Einstein' were extracted for physics, and 'covered in oil' and 'welding' for mechanical engineering. Next, we asked 791 men and women (397 men and 394 women, aged 20–69) to rate the gender level for each field and for the keywords extracted on a 5-point scale, and also measured the egalitarian attitude of the respondents using the SESRA-S.

Of the six fields, the one with the most masculine image was mechanical engineering, and the one with the least masculine image was biology, although it still had a masculine image. There was a statistically significant difference between the gender degree of physics, chemistry and biology, and the egalitarian gender role attitudes of the respondents. These results indicate that those with low egalitarian attitudes had a more masculine image of these fields than those with high egalitarian attitudes. As well, women had a more masculine image of these fields than men.

Regarding keywords, respondents with more masculine attitudes towards 'welding', 'making machines', 'tools', and 'machine design' had more masculine attitudes towards mechanical engineering, and those with masculine attitudes towards 'Einstein', 'electro-magnetic field', 'relativity', 'thermodynamics', 'principle' and 'theory' in physics had more masculine attitudes towards physics. In other words, masculine images of various fields of science are strong in Japan, and individual (less) egalitarian attitudes may be related to the formation of these masculine images. But there are also strong images that transcend national stereotypes, as noted above.

Women in general science majors dislike physics in junior high school

In Japan, pupils must select physics in university entrance examinations in order to enter engineering and physics departments. However, very few girls choose physics in high school. Therefore, we investigated factors related to selection of physics in university entrance examinations through an Internet survey of 1101 male and female science university graduates (554 males and 547 females aged 20–69).

Both male and female university graduates who chose physics for their university entrance examinations reported that they liked physics in junior high school or in the first year of high school. Women with a college degree in science who liked biology in junior high school or in the first year of high school tended not to choose physics when they took the university entrance examination.

We also examined what kind of activities college-graduate science males and females who reported liking physics in junior high school liked as children. Males with a college degree in science liked 'to play outdoors' in elementary school, while their female counterparts liked, for example, 'reading novels and history books', 'solving difficult maths problems', and 'visiting museums, science museums, and planetariums' in elementary school, and thought that learning physics and arithmetic would be useful in the future in junior high school.

For physicists, the same survey was conducted through the Physical Society of Japan, and responses were obtained from 495 researchers (423 males, 71 females, and 1 other) affiliated with the society. Significantly, while physicists of both sexes were more likely to report that they liked physics in elementary, junior high, and high school, fewer female college graduates of other sciences liked physics in junior high school. As well, physicists tended to have more sex-role egalitarian attitudes than college graduates of other sciences; female physicists particularly had a weaker maths stereotype than other science graduates. This suggests that reducing the number of women who dislike physics in middle school and having a variety of experiences at an early age may lead to future physics choices for both men and women (Ikkatai, Inoue, et al. 2021B).

Girls with traditional views do not go into STEM

The gender difference in the choice of subject major is thought to be largely due to environmental factors, including parents. Does the environment of Japanese female high school students affect their career choices?

Using data from the 2012 Survey of High School Students and Their Mothers, we compared female students who affirmed the fixed gender role stereotype (e.g. 'men should work outside the home and women should stay at home') with those who neither affirmed nor denied it. The latter were more likely to choose STEM, but we did not find a statistically meaningful relationship between the stereotype of 'males are more capable of using mathematics and specialised skills' and the desire to pursue a STEM career for either males and females, which was surprising, and requires further study. We also confirmed that family environment, such as parental educational background, and household income, had a statistically meaningful relationship with the desire to pursue a career in STEM (Inoue et al. 2021).

Daughters of mothers without stereotypes go into STEM

Using the same data, we examined the relationship between parental gender stereotypes in mathematics and daughters' subject majors. We found that daughters of mothers who disagreed with the statement 'women are less mathematically competent than men' went into STEM fields more than daughters of mothers who agreed with it. The probability of majoring in natural sciences (science, engineering, agriculture, and health) was higher for the daughters of mothers who answered, 'I disagree completely' and 'I disagree somewhat' than for the daughters of mothers who answered, 'I agree completely' and 'I agree somewhat'. On the other hand, this trend was not observed in the relationship between fathers and daughters. This suggests that mothers' gender stereotypes of mathematics may be transmitted to their daughters and may be related to their daughters' choice of field of study (Inoue 2019).

Non egalitarian parents oppose higher education in general

In another internet survey we focused on the possibility that parents' gender equality and gender role attitudes influence girls' career choices, measuring the gender equality and gender role attitudes of 1236 parents (618 mothers and 618 fathers) of daughters and sons (of any age) with college degrees or higher, through the SESRA-S. Parents with higher SESRA-S scores (more gender-equal and less gender-role-oriented) were more positive about female students' university study, while parents with lower scores (more gender-unequal and more gender-role-oriented) were more negative about female students' university study, in *any* field.

More than 40% of all parents surveyed were in favour of female students going on to higher education if they wished to do so, 'Because they won't have trouble finding a job' in science fields and 'Because it is suitable for women' in humanities fields. The field in which parents were most in favour of science education for female students was pharmacy. Reasons given by parents opposed to female students entering the sciences included 'It is not suitable for women' for engineering in general, 'Because it is hard work' for veterinary medicine, animal science, and nursing, and 'Because the tuition fees are high' for pharmacy, medicine, dentistry, and information science, biology, mathematics, and physics. Parents in favour of these fields chose 'Because they won't have trouble finding a job' (Ikkatai et al. 2019).

Teachers only recommend physics over biology to male students

The percentage of girls who choose physics as a science subject in high school is very low in Japan. We focused on the influence of high school teachers as one external factor. An online experiment was conducted with 316 high school teachers (257 males and 59 females) through an internet research company. Teachers were asked to read seven scenarios describing situations in which a high school teacher advises high school students who are struggling to choose between physics and biology, and to indicate to what extent they agree with the advice of the high school teachers in the scenarios. For each scenario, the high school students were given a female name, a male name, and an alphabetical name.

The relationship between the degree of agreement with the high school teacher's advice and the gender of the high school students was examined. We found that the participants recommended physics more strongly than biology when the student had a male name, under certain circumstances. In Scenario F, for example, 'I think physics offers more department options' was often selected as the reason for agreeing with the teacher's advice, and applied to male students. Overall, the results indicate that there may still be a gender bias that strongly associates boys with a wide range of future options (Minamizaki et al. under review).

Social climate in Japan and England

Cheryan et al. (2017) proposed a model to explain the low number of women studying computer science, engineering and physics in the United States using three groups of questions (masculine culture of the fields, insufficient early experience, and gender gaps in self-efficacy). We considered it necessary to add a fourth group – social climate of inequality, to explain the masculine image of mathematics and physics in Japan.

Responses from 1177 men and women (594 men and 583 women, 20–69) living in Japan and 1082 men and women (529 men and 553 women, aged 20 to 69) in England were compared. In Japan both mathematics and physics had statistically significant effects on 'employment', 'maths stereotype' and 'image of being smart'. In other words, people who viewed mathematics or physics as masculine were also more likely to think that the occupation in which they would find a job after studying mathematics or physics was male-oriented, that women had less mathematical ability than men, and that people who entered a mathematics or physics departments were generally smart. The effect of 'views of intelligent women' was statistically significant only for mathematics; i.e. those who disagreed with the statement that 'women should be intelligent' tended to view mathematics as more masculine.

Similarly, in England there were statistically significant effects on 'employment' and 'math stereotypes', for both maths and physics, and a statistically significant effect of 'female role models' in physics. Those who had been told or heard that they would not be popular with the opposite sex if they entered a certain department tended to regard mathematics as masculine. These results suggest commonalities between Japan and England regarding what influences the formation of masculine images of objects (Ikkatai et al. 2021b). Despite the similarities in gendered attitudes towards STEM fields, however, the fact remains that women's participation in STEM fields is higher in England than Japan. It may be that attitudes towards intelligent women may be a factor. This factor was only significant in Japan and suggests a cultural context in which intelligent women are not appreciated, in contrast to England.

Equality views related to STEM motivation

Finally, we examined whether providing egalitarian information, such as the fact that STEM offers better employment opportunities for both men and women, that a movement is taking place towards a gender equal society, and that no gender difference exists in mathematical ability, would change children's willingness to go STEM schools and parents' willingness to support STEM schools.

An online experiment was conducted with 1,089 first-grade junior high school children (544 boys and 545 girls) and their parents (534 men and 555 women) through an internet research company. The children and parents were asked to read specific information, and to answer the same questions before and after reading the information. The information was categorized into four types – (a) employment in STEM, (b) egalitarian society, (c) absence of a gender difference in maths ability, and (d) irrelevant information – and provided to the participants in one of four combinations: (a) only, (a) and (b), (a) and (c), and (d) only. We anticipated that information on (a) STEM employment would have been provided at the many events held to support women's entry into STEM, so this was used as the basis for providing information in (b) and (c) in combination.

We found that the children who received information about both (a) and (b), and those who received information about both (a) and (c), were more likely to be motivated to enter STEM fields. Parents who were given information on both (a) and (c) also showed an increase in their willingness to support their children's STEM education. The results indicate that the provision of information, especially egalitarian information in conjunction with employment information, may be effective in motivating children and their parents to pursue STEM education in the short term (Ikkatai et al. 2021a).

The future of STEM gender in Japan

The above ten studies revealed that gender image in academic fields is associated with the level of equality. However, as revealed in the final study, this could be rectified to some extent by providing factual information that contradicts existing perceptions.

On the other hand, some results were unexpected. For example, the results in the fifth study above showed that female students do not go on to study science due to gender stereotypes, that is, gender role consciousness matters rather than mathematics stereotypes. The results in the ninth study also showed that attitudes towards intelligent women in Japan may be a barrier to women's participation in STEM. These results suggest that resolving women's low STEM participation rate may require changes to Japanese social attitudes rather than simple interventions.

Accelerated gender affirmative action in STEM, 2023

In 2023, a decision was taken in Japan to establish a 'women's quota', a recommendation system exclusively for female students, in several Japanese university engineering departments, with leadership taken by the presidents of the respective universities. The universities were Nagoya University, the University of Toyama, Shimane University, the Tokyo Institute of Technology (to be merged with Tokyo Medical and Dental University) and the Tokyo University of Science, while Shibaura Institute of Technology has done so since 2018. Tokyo Institute of Technology is particularly popular as a high-level university in Tokyo, and attracts considerable attention due to the scale of its quota for women: in 2024, for a total of 143 students, or 14% of the bachelor's degree programmes each year.[4]

Different requirements are set for women under these recommended quotas, and they differ from the general admission requirements for which women can also apply. For engineering entrance examinations, applicants must normally study high-level mathematics, known as Mathematics 3, in their third year of high school, and they are often required to choose physics from among the science subjects. Under the quota for women, however, female applicants can receive a recommendation even if they have not studied these subjects. Moreover, Ochanomizu University and Nara Women's University have announced the establishment of engineering faculties. These women's universities have long histories, and admission is restricted to female students from the outset. (Since 2020, Ochanomizu University has allowed transgender students whose gender identity is female to enrol.) While the public mood is generally in favour of the establishment of engineering departments in women's universities, some argue that affirmative action is a form of reverse discrimination. The next sub-section discusses issues of affirmative action aimed at increasing the proportion of women in STEM fields in Japan.

Background to Japanese-style gender affirmative action

Affirmative action, especially a women's quota in university admissions, has not been common in Japan until now, and sufficient social discussion has also been lacking. The Japanese entrance examination system is generally a score-based system. Students are accepted or rejected by private universities mainly on the basis of their scores in their respective university examinations, and by national universities on the basis of their scores in the common examinations and the examinations of the respective universities. Going to a 'good' university is considered a shortcut to a stable job, and competition in university entrance examinations and secondary school entrance examinations that lead to them is fierce. To some extent, universities accept a diverse range of people, such as those with comprehensive selection examinations based on essays and interviews. The University of Tokyo, for example, has had an entrance examination quota for school recommendations since 2016. These students, however, are accepted based on excellence in some area of activity. Overall, however, the entrance examination system in Japan is based on scores.

Against this backdrop, Kyushu University's announcement that it would provide a women's quota in the Department of Mathematics in the Faculty of Science from 2012, but this was subsequently withdrawn due to public criticism that it was reverse discrimination. It was also argued that a women's quota is problematic because it 'stigmatises' women who are accepted because they are female (Tsujimura 2011). Ten years later in 2023, when many universities, including the Tokyo Institute of Technology, simultaneously proposed quotas for women in engineering departments, similar criticism arose, but not as intensely. These quotas appear to be based purely on students' interest in the field and feature lower hurdles to entry.

Japan's gender gap index (GGI) score has not changed significantly since it was first published in 2006, but its global ranking has declined; from 80th in 2006, to 125th out of 146 countries in 2023, which is the lowest among developed countries. These annual rankings have been widely reported over the past few years, which is stimulating discussion in society.

Universities are also expected to make the necessary reforms, and the University of Tokyo, for example, made headlines by making five of its nine presidents and board members (i.e. the majority) women by 2021. It has further set a target to hire 300 female professors and associate professors by 2027 fiscal year and to increase the percentage of female faculty members from 16% to 25%. However, to achieve this goal, the number of women entering Ph.D programmes and obtaining Ph.Ds needs to increase.

The representation of women in senior positions is also a major challenge in industry. In April 2013, the government made the modest request that one board member in each company should be a woman, but in 2023, the percentage of female board members was still low at 15.5% versus the OECD average of 29.6%, and the government is calling for a further increase. In particular, STEM companies have expressed a strong desire for female STEM personnel. While some companies are promoting activities to support women's recruitment and there are some changes appearing, such as Japan Airlines' recent appointment of a former cabin attendant as the company's first female president and the Nissan Foundation's award for activities that promote women's choice of STEM, there remains little change overall, despite this need.

The Japanese government has made efforts to promote female STEM personnel. These were initially aimed at increasing the number of female students, as the number of STEM personnel is decreasing due to the super-ageing society and declining birth rate. Gradually, however, the concept of diversity has been updated. One representative activity is *Rikochare*, or STEM challenge, which takes the form of role model introduction events organized by the Cabinet Office in collaboration with industry. This long-running activity introduces women working in STEM companies to junior and senior high school students. The Cabinet Office also funds these activities for universities. However, the proportion of women in engineering has only increased slightly. In other words, for a long time efforts to increase the number of female students, both at the initiative of the government and various universities, have failed to produce significant change.

Given these circumstances, the proposed quotas for women in STEM by the respective universities have not been met with much opposition from society, although they have been criticized on social network service (SNS, e.g. X) as a form of reverse discrimination against men. Some were also angered by the inference that universities considered women to have inferior abilities.

Positive and negative aspects of the women's quotas: is that social justice?

The positive message to female students with the establishment of quotas for women in engineering may be significant. More than ever, it shows that universities and society are serious about wanting women in STEM. This may help female students to consider pursuing a science major, and encourage parents and teachers to support this. On the other hand, there are concerns. First, there is concern that the message conveyed is that universities believe female students are not as capable in mathematics and physics as their male counterparts, and that interest alone is sufficient for entry to the field. The academic achievements of Japanese female students in science-related fields are top-notch, and many exceptionally talented female students tend to aspire to enter medical schools. The important thing is to increase girls' interest in STEM and help them find jobs, reduce their dislike of maths and physics, and encourage them by repeatedly sending the message that they are capable.

Second, the question of whether women can keep up with regular lectures has arisen. The quota is a recommendation, and there may be some difference in academic ability between these women and students who pass the regular entrance examinations. Third, these students may be subjected to the stigma that they were only admitted because they are female, and this may also affect female students admitted under the regular entrance system, who will receive the same lectures in mixed classroom situations. Other students will not know which entrance examination they have passed unless they declare this themselves. Fourth, even if a university offers places for women, the programme may fail to attract sufficient applications from female students. Kanazawa Institute of Technology, which introduced a quota for women in 2008, only had 12 applicants out of a capacity of 40, and in 2009 the programme was cancelled after it received only 13 applicants.

Generally, affirmative action is carried out as a social justice measure to correct inequalities. Japan's establishment of quotas for women was driven by a labour shortage as a result of an ageing society and a social drive to promote gender equality, which calls for universities to develop female human resources in the sciences. However, even with this background in mind, can Japan's affirmative action be called social justice? Rather, imposing quotas for female students suggests that women's abilities as being unreasonably undervalued, and this appears to be the result of a strong gender bias regarding abilities. Another factor may be that there are not enough women in the executive departments of universities that have promoted affirmative action. Our research revealed that, the masculine culture of STEM and a social climate of gender inequality in Japan strengthen the image of STEM as masculine. Universities' executive branches should be the first to understand this situation. Increasing the number of female students will lead to a higher evaluation of the university, and the quota for women may be an easy goal to achieve. But we are concerned that there has not been sufficient discussion of the matter.

Assuming that affirmative action in the form of quotas for women in STEM continues for some time in Japan, flexible university management is needed to deal with possible problems. In particular, it is important that universities fulfil their responsibility for: a) supporting the studies of students admitted under the female quota. Follow-up surveys should be conducted to confirm whether there are any changes in graduation rates, etc; b) paying attention to whether female students suffer from stigma; and c) fostering social discussion, and the content of the discussion should be made open.

The quotas for women in engineering face many challenges. They appear to be supported in the current atmosphere in 2023, but they may not last into the future. Careful and continuous explanations and commitment from universities are important. Rather than implementing women's student intake quotas, universities need to change the university and social climate by eliminating mathematics stereotypes in society. And they need to explain the employment advantages and the benefits of increasing gender equality so that women can choose career paths they want to study without women's quota. Finally, while some women who choose STEM fields go on to become researchers, an essential human resource needed by Japan, as we have seen, implementing undergraduate quotas may negatively impact the position of women in STEM fields by undermining trust in women's ability.

Discussion: extending diversity in STEM in Japan

This paper has reviewed gender image and equality issues in STEM in Japan. It has also discussed recent affirmative action 'women's quota' initiatives. It is important to disseminate information that introduces children to professions they are interested in, and to promote gender equality and reject stereotypes about mathematics. While broadcasting and newspapers have recently disseminated valuable information, further enhancement on platforms such as YouTube and SNS which are popular among children is needed. It is vital for various stakeholders to create a multi-layered information environment with a focus on gender equality.

What distinguishes Japan from other developed countries is its accelerated ageing and need for change at a time when the use of ChatGPT and AI is being promoted and job insecurity is increasing. Occupations such as bank tellers, traditionally dominated by women, are expected to disappear *en masse*, and more students are expected to choose science-related professions. Programming education became compulsory in elementary schools in Japan in 2020. Programming and simple tasks will be carried out by ChatGPT, which will require highly skilled personnel who can use AI and provide instructions.

In our parent survey, computer science was the second most popular field supported by parents for women pursuing higher education. Historically, the representation of women in computer science has been exceedingly low, but a breakthrough may arise in Japan where job demands, educational opportunities and parental support are aligned. Children with programming education will enter university in 2032. We hope a full-fledged era of STEM gender equality and a society that believes in and supports the talents of female students will follow. The main reason for the recent scarcity of STEM women in Japan is seen to be the substantial gender disparity in academic backgrounds (Yamaguchi 2023). We hope that the increase in STEM women will contribute to closing the gender gap and create the human resources to maintain Japan's research output into the future.

Notes

1. The following survey overviews were originally published in Japanese as a report for the JST-Ristex project and are here translated into English by the authors with additional information.

2. The STEM fields were physics, mathematics, biology, information science and engineering, mechanical engineering, and chemistry. The reason for limiting it to England rather than to the entire UK is that the education system in England is unified.
3. The fields were mathematics, chemistry, physics, mechanical engineering, information science, biology, agriculture, geology, medicine, dentistry, pharmacy, nursing, law, economics, social sciences, humanities, music, and fine arts.
4. https://www.titech.ac.jp/english/news/2022/065243 accessed 9 February 2024.

Acknowledgments

This work was supported by the World Premier International Research Centre Initiative (WPI), MEXT, Japan.

Disclosure statement

No potential conflict of interest was reported by the author(s).

Funding

This work was supported by the Ministry of Education, Culture, Sports, Science and Technology [23H01018].

ORCID

Hiromi M. Yokoyama ⓘ http://orcid.org/0000-0003-4760-762X
Yuko Ikkatai ⓘ http://orcid.org/0000-0001-5418-6726
Euan McKay ⓘ http://orcid.org/0000-0001-8533-3573
Atsushi Inoue ⓘ http://orcid.org/0000-0002-5971-7802
Azusa Minamizaki ⓘ http://orcid.org/0000-0003-4700-4829
Kei Kano ⓘ http://orcid.org/0000-0002-4536-5869

References

Adachi, T. 2014. "Occupational Gender Stereotypes Among University Students: Their Relationships with Self-Efficacy and Gender Role Attitudes." *Japanese Association of Industrial/Organizational Psychology Journal* 27 (2): 87–100. https://doi.org/10.32222/jaiop.27.2_87.
Bettinger, E. P., and B. T. Long. 2005. "Do Faculty Serve as Role Models? The Impact of Instructor Gender on Female Students." *American Economic Review* 95 (2): 152–157. https://doi.org/10.1257/000282805774670149.
Bleeker, M. M., and J. E. Jacobs. 2004. "Achievement in Math and Science: Do mothers' Beliefs Matter 12 Years Later?" *Journal of Educational Psychology* 96 (1): 97–109. https://doi.org/10.1037/0022-0663.96.1.97.
Brenoe, A. A., and U. Zölitz. 2020. "Exposure to More Female Peers Widens the Gender Gap in STEM Participation." *Journal of Labor Economics* 38 (4): 1009–1054. https://doi.org/10.1086/706646.
Carrell, S. E., M. E. Page, and J. E. West. 2010. "Sex and Science: How Professor Gender Perpetuates the Gender Gap." *The Quarterly Journal of Economics* 125 (3): 1101–1144. https://doi.org/10.1162/qjec.2010.125.3.1101.

Ceci, S. J., D. K. Ginther, S. Kahn, and W. M. Williams. 2014. "Women in Academic Science: A changing landscape." *Psychological Science in the Public Interest* 15 (3): 75–141. https://doi.org/10.1177/1529100614541236.

Ceci, S. J., W. M. Williams, and S. M. Barnett. 2009. "Women's Underrepresentation in Science: Sociocultural and Biological Considerations." *Psychological Bulletin* 135 (2): 218–261. https://doi.org/10.1037/a0014412.

Cheryan, S., S. A. Ziegler, A. K. Montoya, and L. Jiang. 2017. "Why are Some STEM Fields More Gender Balanced Than Others?" *Psychological Bulletin* 143 (1): 1–35. https://doi.org/10.1037/bul0000052.

Fischer, S. 2017. "The Downside of Good Peers: How Classroom Composition Differentially Affects Men's and Women's STEM Persistence." *Labour Economics* 46:211–226. https://doi.org/10.1016/j.labeco.2017.02.003.

Goldin, C., L. Katz, and L. Kuziemko. 2006. "The Homecoming of American College Women: The Reversal of the College Gender Gap." *Journal of Economic Perspectives* 20 (4): 133–156. https://doi.org/10.1257/jep.20.4.133.

Ikkatai, Y., A. Inoue, K. Kano, A. Minamizaki, E. McKay, and H. M. Yokoyama. 2019. "Parental Egalitarian Attitudes Towards Gender Roles Affect Agreement on Girls Taking STEM Fields at University in Japan." *International Journal of Science Education* 41 (16): 2254–2270. https://doi.org/10.1080/09500693.2019.1671635.

Ikkatai, Y., A. Inoue, K. Kano, A. Minamizaki, E. McKay, and H. M. Yokoyama. 2021. "Factors Related to girls' Choice of Physics for University Entrance Exams in Japan." *Physical Review Physics Education Research* 17 (1): 010141. https://doi.org/10.1103/PhysRevPhysEducRes.17.010141.

Ikkatai, Y., A. Inoue, A. Minamizaki, K. Kano, E. McKay, and H. M. Yokoyama. 2021a. "Effect of Providing Gender Equality Information on students' Motivations to Choose STEM." *Public Library of Science ONE* 16 (6): e0252710. https://doi.org/10.1371/journal.pone.0252710.

Ikkatai, Y., A. Inoue, A. Minamizaki, K. Kano, E. McKay, and H. M. Yokoyama. 2021b. "Masculinity in the Public Image of Physics and Mathematics: A New Model Comparing Japan and England." *Public Understanding of Science* 30 (7): 810–826. https://doi.org/10.1177/096366252110023.

Ikkatai, Y., K. Inoue, A. Minamizaki, A. Kano, M. Euan, and H. Yokoyama. 2021. "Gendered Image of STEM Competencies: A Comparative Study Between Japan and the UK (Text in Japanese)." *Journal of Science, Technology and Society* 19 (6): 79–95. https://doi.org/10.24646/jnlsts.19.0_79.

Ikkatai, Y., A. Minamizaki, K. Kano, A. Inoue, E. McKay, and H. M. Yokoyama. 2020a. "Gender-Biased Public Perception of STEM Fields, Focusing on the Influence of Egalitarian Attitudes Toward Gender Roles." *Journal of Science Communication* 19 (1): A08. https://doi.org/10.22323/2.19010208.

Ikkatai, Y., A. Minamizaki, K. Kano, A. Inoue, E. McKay, and H. M. Yokoyama. 2020b. "Masculine Public Image of Six Scientific Fields in Japan: Physics, Chemistry, Mechanical Engineering, Information Science, Mathematics, and Biology." *Journal of Science Communication* 19 (6): A02. https://doi.org/10.22323/2.19060202.

Inoue, A. 2019. "The Association Between Parents' Math-Gendered Stereotypes and Daughters' Major Choices in Natural Science (Text in Japanese)." *Proceedings of the 43rd Annual Meeting of the Japanese Society for Science Education*, 9–12. https://doi.org/10.14935/jssep.43.0_9

Inoue, A., Y. Ikkatai, A. Minamizaki, K. Kano, M. Euan, and H. Yokoyama. 2021. "Gender Stereotypes and Career Aspirations for Science Among High School Students (Text in Japanese)." *Journal of Science, Technology and Society* 19 (1): 64–78. https://doi.org/10.24646/jnlsts.19.0_64.

Isa, N., and W. Chinen. 2014. "Gender Gaps of Achievement and Aspirations in Mathematics. (In Japanese)." *Japanese Journal of Labor Studies* 648:84–93. https://www.jil.go.jp/institute/zassi/backnumber/2014/07/index.html.

Kahn, S., and D. Ginther. 2018. "Women and Science, Technology, Engineering, and Mathematics (STEM): Are Differences in Education Ad Careers Due to Stereotypes, Interests, or Family." In *The Oxford Handbook of Women and the Economy*, edited by S. L. Averett, L. M. Argys, and S. D. Hoffman, 767–798. Oxford, UK: Oxford University Press.

Leslie, S. J., A. Cimpian, M. Meyer, and E. Freeland. 2015. "Expectations of Brilliance Underlie Gender Distributions Across Academic Disciplines." *Science* 347 (6219): 262–265. https://doi.org/10.1126/science.1261375.

Lim, J., and J. Meer. 2020. "Persistent Effects of Teacher–Student Gender Matches." *Journal of Human Resources* 55 (3): 809–835. https://doi.org/10.3368/jhr.55.3.0218-9314R4.

Minamizaki, A., Y. Ikkatai, K. Kano, A. Inoue, E. McKay, and H. M. Yokoyama. under review. "Exploratory Research on High School Teachers' Unconscious Gender Bias in Guidance Counselling for Physics Classes."

Morinaga, Y., Y. Furukawa, and K. Fukudome. 2017. "女子中?生の数学に対する意欲とステレオタイプ." *Japanese Journal of Educational Psychology* 65 (3): 375–387. https://doi.org/10.5926/jjep.65.375.

Normile, D. July 6, 2022. "Mass Layoff Looms for Japanese Researchers". *Science* 377 (6602): 141–141. https://www.science.org/content/article/mass-layoff-looms-japanese-researchers.

OECD. 2015. Share of Women Graduates by Field of Education. Accessed February 10, 2024. http://www.oecd.org/gender/data/shareofwomengraduatesbyfieldofeducation.htm.

Park, H., J. R. Behrman, and J. Choi. 2018. "Do Single-Sex Schools Enhance Students' STEM (Science, Technology, Engineering, and Mathematics) Outcomes?" *Economics of Education Review* 62:35–47. https://doi.org/10.1016/j.econedurev.2017.10.007.

Sam, L. C., and P. Ernest. 2000. "A Survey of Public Images of Mathematics." *Research in Mathematics Education* 2 (1): 193–206. https://doi.org/10.1080/14794800008520076.

Spencer, S. J., C. Logel, and P. G. Davies. 2016. "Stereotype Threat." *Annual Review of Psychology* 67 (1): 415–437. https://doi.org/10.1146/annurev-psych-073115-103235.

Spencer, S. J., C. M. Steele, and D. M. Quinn. 1999. "Stereotype Threat and Women's Math Performance." *Journal of Experimental Social Psychology* 35 (1): 4–28. https://doi.org/10.1006/jesp.1998.1373.

Tsujimura, M. 2011. Pojitivu-akusyon: 'Hō ni yoru byōdō' no gihō (*Positive Action: Techniques for 'Equality by Law'*). Tokyo: Iwanami Shinsho.

Turner, S. E., and W. G. Bowen. 1999. "Choice of Major: The Changing (Unchanging) Gender Gap." *ILR Review* 52 (2): 289–313. https://doi.org/10.1177/001979399905200208.

Uchida, A., and K. Mori. 2018. "Detection and Treatment of Fake Math-Dislikes among Japanese Junior High School Students." *International Journal of Science and Mathematics Education* 16:1115–1126. https://doi.org/10.1007/s10763-017-9825-3.

Wilder, G. Z., and K. Powell. 1989. "Sex Differences in Test Performance: A Survey of Literature." *College Board Report* 1989 (1): 3. https://doi.org/10.1002/j.2330-8516.1989.tb00330.x.

Yamaguchi, K. 2023. "The Labor-Market Valuation of 'SK skill' and 'SS Skill' in Occupations, and Their Relationship with the Gender Wage Gap and an Underutilization of the Skills Among Irregular Employees (Text in Japanese)." *RIETI Discussion Papers* 23-J-033.

Remedying Japan's deficient investment in people

Yoshifumi Nakata

ABSTRACT

This paper asks if there is deficiency of investment in people in Japan. To answer this question we examine comparative and historical data, as well as the reasons behind the data. We then look at public policies of recent administrations, particularly the Kishida administration, since one of its core policy agendas is 'investment in people'. We find that there *is* a deficiency of investment in people, by governments, companies and people themselves, for a variety of reasons, and that the Kishida administration has to date only proposed temporary measures without long term solutions. The paper concludes with policy implications and some proposals for additional action.

Introduction

We often hear about Japan's meagre investment in people, but is this really true? Japan used to be called 'Japan as No.1', based on that reputation that 'Japan's only resources is its people'. For many students of Japan, the first reaction to this non-investment claim may be scepticism. So, the research question of this paper is whether or not there is a deficiency of investment in people in Japan. Indeed, Japan has just registered its highest October current account surplus since 1985, which looks contradictory to the claim. And even if the claim is true, a natural question to follow is why, and with what consequences. This is the agenda of this paper. We pay particular attention to the Kishida administration, as the Prime Minister is quoted as saying that investment in people is his number one policy priority.

The paper is structured as followed. First, it examines data on investment in people, both comparatively as well as historically, to find our answer to the research question. It then asks the reasons behind those numbers. If the investment is deficient, why is this so, and has it created any problems? Third, what public policies have been devised by recent administrations, particularly by the Kishida administration, since one of its core policy agendas is 'investment in people'. Lastly, we draw some policy implications and propose some additional actions.

The state of investment in people

Household investment in people

We start with household sector investment in people. The first data looks somewhat odd; it is the birth rate of Japan. The reason for doing so is simple – we cannot invest in people unless we have people to invest in. And it is a household sector activity. So, let us examine how many new babies Japanese household give birth to, in Figure 1.

The Japanese birth rate has registered the largest decline since World War II among major western nations. Among the US, France, Germany, Italy, Sweden, UK and Japan, the 2020 birth rate had dropped to less than half the 1951 figure only in Japan (Cabinet Office 2022, Figure 1-1-4). The rate fell below the sustainable level of 2.04 around the year 1975, and it continued falling in the 1980s, and 1990s until 2005, when it reached 1.26, albeit with a small bump in the middle. It has recovered marginally since then and has been hovering around 1.4. The drop of the number of births is conspicuous; it was more than 2.6 million in 1947 when the number was first recorded after the war. It declined in the following decade, but then rebounded from 1962 to 2.1 million in 1973, which is called the second baby boom. Since then, it has been declining without any sign of resurgence. The latest number in 2022 is 800,000, less than one third of that of 1947 and two fifth of 1971. The National Institute of Population and Social Security Research predicts it will continue declining into the next decade. So, according to this matrix the drop of the household's investment in people in the form of new babies is the biggest in Japan among comparative developed countries.

Second, let us examine the educational composition of the Japanese population in comparison with other countries, as the national educational composition measures the magnitude of educational investment per head of population. Table 1 shows the share of the population entering tertiary education. At BA and BSc levels, the Japanese share is slightly lower than the OECD average. But as for the share of population with higher degrees (masters and doctorate), the Japanese shares are far less. Those with a masters degree are just one third of the average, and those with a doctorate are less than a half of the average of those countries in the table. These numbers support the claim that Japan lags behind other western countries in terms of investment in high degree holders.

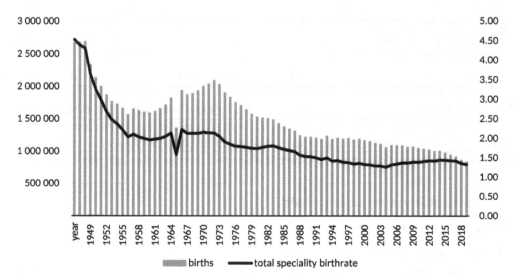

Figure 1. Births and birth rate: 1947–2020. Source: Ministry of Health, Labour and Welfare (2022). *Reiwa 4-nen Jinkō Dōtai Tōkei (Kakuteisū) no Gaikyō*. Accessed 6 February 2024. https://www.mhlw.go.jp/toukei/saikin/hw/jinkou/kakutei22/index.html.

REMEDYING JAPAN'S DEFICIENT INVESTMENT IN PEOPLE

Table 1. Entry rates to tertiary education by level of education: 2020%.

	Less than 25 yrs old		Less than 30 yrs old	
	Level 5	Level 6	Level 7	Level 8
ISCED2011 category	associate	BA, BS	Master	Doctor
Average	**11.3**	**52.4**	**21.6**	**1.8**
JPN	–	**50.8**	**7.4**	**0.7**
USA	29.2		9.4	0.8
CAN	26.3	44.2	9.2	1.1
UK	9.2	66.0	29.6	2.6
DEU	0.3	44.5	27.7	2.4
FRA	27.1	54.8	39.3	2.0
ITA	1.1	44.8	27.2	1.3
NLD	2.5	61.6	22.9	1.2
BEL	2.1	69.8	32.7	–
DNK	12.7	53.0	29.7	1.8
SWE	4.8	32.9	25.4	1.1
FIN	–	48.0	7.2	1.2
NOR	3.2	49.6	30.4	1.3
AUT	29.3	37.6	22.8	1.8
CHE	0.8	48.7	20.9	3.8
ESP	27.8	43.1	18.8	1.9
PRT	7.2	50.0	32.6	2.0
CZE	0.4	56.2	29.1	2.6
POL	0.0	61.6	33.1	0.7
KOR		66.0	7.7	7.7
AUS	24.7	72.8	22.9	1.3
NZL	13.4	50.6	7.0	1.1
MEX	4.0	45.6	3.6	0.2

*ISCED2011: International Standard Classification of Education; Level 5: Short-cycle tertiary education; Level 6: Bachelor's or equivalent level; Level 7: Master's or equivalent level; Level 8: Doctoral or equivalent level.
Source: JILPT (2023). *Databook of International Labour Statistics.*
https://www.jil.go.jp/english/estatis/databook/index2023.html. Accessed 6 February 2024.

Corporate sector investment in people

Next we move to corporate sector investment in people. Here statistics, particularly comparative perspective statistics, are hard to be found, but we can show the share of training costs in the total labour costs among four countries in years 2000 and 2020. Although the number of countries compared is limited, they do show the relative size of off-job training (off-JT) among those countries. The numbers show that Japanese firms

Table 2. Structure of labour costs as a percentage of total costs: manufacturing industries.

year	2000		2020	
cost type	Labour costs except pay	Training costs	Labour costs except pay	Training costs
Japan	19.7	*(0.3)*	19.2	*(0.1)*
UK	23.2	*(2.4)*	18.2	*(1.7)*
Germany	24.2	*(0.5)*	23.6	*(0.4)*
France	35.2	*(1.5)*	36.0	*(1.3)*

Japan's data in 2000 is actually 2002; US year 2000 data is actually 2004; UK year 2020 data is 2016.
Source: JILPT (2023). *Databook of International Labour Statistics*, Tables 6–11, 2006 and Tables 5–9, 2023.
https://www.jil.go.jp/english/estatis/databook/index2023.html. Accessed 6 February 2024.

142 REFORMING CAPITALISM, GOING DIGITAL AND GREEN

spent a far smaller portion of total labour cost on training relative to the other countries (Table 2).

Training costs comprised only 0.3% of pay-excluded labour costs in Japan in 2000, while the shares of other countries were at least two thirds larger. And the difference between Japan and other countries grew significantly in the next 20 years. In 2020, Germany spent four times, France 13 times, and the UK 17 times more as a share of their labour costs on employee training than Japan.

Workers learn from their daily work, which is called on-job training (OJT). Numerous studies have concluded that the quality of Japanese manufacturing goods depends on rich OJT on the shopfloor. Although there is no national data of OJT, we can share two illuminating surveys to show how it has changed in Japan, as well as how it fares compared to other countries.

The first data comes from a software engineer survey conducted in 5 countries in 2015 and 2016 (Table 3). Numbers in the table show that the OJT environment for software engineers in Japan is not good compared to the other economies. But this data pertains to software engineers, while most previous research on the Japanese OJT environment is for blue collar workers. Does the situation for software engineers pertain more widely? The answer is given in Table 3.

The Japanese Electrical Electronic & Information Union conducted a comprehensive survey on their members' life and work in 2015. Table 4 shows the evaluation of workplace environment by type of occupation. We can see that a majority of union workers in electrical, electronic and information industry, regardless of their occupation, think that OJT promoting environment is disappearing.

Public expenditure

Next, let us turn to Japanese public expenditure on education. Table 5 shows the proportion of government expenditure at different levels of education in total national public expenditure as well as their share of GDP. Even a casual look shows clearly that

Table 3. Software engineers 'too busy to learn while working' (%).

	No	Not really	Somewhat	Yes
China	10.2	48.4	35.8	5.6
France	10.7	30.9	47.4	11.0
Germany	24.8	40.	26.3	8.0
Japan	5.0	27.	49.3	18.0
US	23.6	41.4	27.8	7.2

Source: Table produced by the author from 5 country survey of software engineers, 2016, IPA.

Table 4. Groups reporting 'OJT-promoting environment is disappearing' (%).

	Yes	Somewhat	Not really	No	No response
Engineers	15.4	37.5	37.0	9.6	0.5
Blue collar workers	19.0	37.5	35.6	6.8	1.1
White collar workers	15.5	36.5	37.6	9.7	0.7

Source: *Denki Rengō (Japanese Electrical Electronic & Information Union) 2015. Kurashi to hatarakikata ni kansuru chōsa* (Survey on Life and Work), Q19B.

Table 5. Government expenditure on education as a percentage of total government expenditure (2020).

	Primary	All secondary	All tertiary	Early childhood education	Government expenditure on education as a percentage of GDP		
					Primary, secondary and post-secondary non-tertiary	All tertiary	Primary to tertiary
France	2.0	3.9	2.1	1.1	3.7	1.3	5.0
Germany	1.5	4.4	2.7	2.0	3.1	1.4	4.5
Italy	2.1	3.3	1.5	0.8	3.1	0.9	4.0
Japan	**2.6**	**2.9**	**1.6**	**0.3**	**2.5**	**0.7**	**3.2**
United Kingdom	3.5	4.1	3.1	0.5	3.8	1.5	5.3
United States	3.3	3.7	3.9		3.3	1.8	5.1
OECD average	3.2	4.1	2.7	1.6	3.4	1.3	4.7
EU25 average	2.6	3.8	2.3	1.6	3.1	1.2	4.3
G20 average	3.4	4.3	2.8		3.3	1.2	4.5

Source: OECD (2023). Table C4.1. Accessed 6 February 2024.
Permanent location of this file: https://stat.link/g2ostn.

Japan is a consistent underachiever at every level relative to western counterparts, OECD average, E25 average and G20 average. The Japanese government simply spends less on education than other governments.

Why investment in people in Japan is so low

Data presented so far points to a relative lack of investment in people. Let us consider possible causes for this lack. We do this by sector as we did in the previous section.

Household sector

Quantity side of human capital investment
Why have births decreased so systematically since the 1970s? Is there a particular reason for the decline in the Japanese context which distinguishes it from other countries? There seem to be two direct reasons. First, a larger portion of marriage-age Japanese people don't marry or marry late (Table 6). Compared to 1960, in 2020 the proportion of not-yet-married males aged 35 to 39 years increased almost 10 times to 34.5%, and female counterparts more than 4 times to 23.6%. Unlike some of other countries like France, few births happen outside marriage in Japan, therefore a significant decrease in marriage has a large impact on the number of births.

Second, married Japanese couples do not have as many babies as before. The completed fertility rate dropped by almost half from 3.60 in 1957 to 1.94 in 2015 (Cabinet Office 2022,

Table 6. Percent of non-married by age group.

Males age group	1960	2020	2020/1960	Females age group	1960	2020	2020/1960
25–29	46.1	72.9	1.58	25–29	21.7	62.4	2.88
30–34	9.9	47.4	4.79	30–34	9.4	35.2	3.74
35–39	3.6	34.5	9.58	35–39	5.5	23.6	4.29

Source: Cabinet Office (2022). *Shōshika shakai taisaku hakushō, Reiwa 4 nenban* (Annual Report on the Declining Birthrate 2022). Figure 1-1-9.

Figure 1-1-13). As for reasons behind this, the Cabinet Office conducted an extensive analysis in 2004 (Cabinet Office 2004) and concluded that: the value of marriage for Japanese young people has decreased; and the relative value of children, which is one of the purposes of marriage, to the cost of bearing and raising children for the Japanese parents has also declined. In fact, married couples have fewer children than they would ideally like, for the following reasons (Cabinet Office 2004):

(1) The psychological burden of bearing and raising children among married couples has increased;
(2) Financial costs of bearing and raising child has increased;
(3) Work and family balance among young married couples has changed towards work;
(4) Both family and community capability to raise children has declined; and
(5) Economic uncertainty for young couples has increased.

The Cabinet Office's analysis was rigorous and extensive, and the reasons they identified reasons were sound, but twenty years has passed since their analysis. Let us then re-visit the latest statistics to see if the conclusions in 2004 are still valid. Table 7 shows Japanese 18–34 year olds' marriage intentions from 1982 to 2019. The numbers show that the trend of marriage avoidance actually has accelerated in the last twenty years. Between 1982 and 2002, the share of males and females who intended not to marry increased by 2.7% and 0.9% respectively. Those shares jumped to as much as 12.3% and 9.6% respectively between 2002 and 2021.

Then what about the numbers of children young married couples wish to have? Table 8 shows that the number of children young married couples wish to have – an indicator of the value of children to them – declined by about the same magnitude in the later period of 2002 to 2021 compared to the previous period of 1982 to 2002. As a result, the number of children Japanese married couples plan to have are now less than 2, which is substantially lower than in 1982. We can conclude that the value of children for Japanese married couples has continued to decrease in the last forty years.

Revisiting the five reasons cited in 2004 as to why the actual number of children Japanese couples have is smaller than they would ideally like to have, let us look at Table 9, which shows the latest survey results of the same target couples. The table lists the three most cited reasons in 2021. The number one reason was 'too expensive to bear and raise children', which was the second most cited in 2004.

Table 7. Changing marriage intentions (%).

	Will marry		Won't marry	
Year (change)	male	female	male	female
1982	95.9	94.2	2.3	4.1
2002	87.0	88.3	5.0	5.0
2021	81.4	84.3	17.3	14.6
1982–2002 change	−8.9	−5.9	**2.7**	**0.9**
2002–2021 change	−5.6	−4.0	**12.3**	**9.6**

Samples are 18–34 year old single males and females.
Source: National Institute of Population and Social Security Research (2023). *Dai-16kai syussyō dōkō kihon chōsa hōkokusyo* (Report of the 16th National Fertility Survey). Figure 1-1-1.

Table 8. Number of children married couples wish to have.

	male	female
1982	2.33	2.28
2002	2.05	2.00
2021	1.82	1.79
2002–1982	**−0.28**	**−0.25**
2021–2002	**−0.23**	**−0.24**

Samples are 18–34 year old married couples
Source: National Institute of Population and Social Security Research (2023). *Dai-16kai syussyō dōkō kihon chōsa hōkokusyo* (Report of the 16th National Fertility Survey). Figure 3-3-1.

Table 9. Reasons for not having preferred number of children (mothers less than 35 years old, 2021).

Rank	Reasons	% of parents cited
1	Too expensive to bear and raise children	77.8
2	Too much physical and psychological burden	23.1
3	Raising children compromises my commitment to my work	21.4

Sources: National Institute of Population and Social Security Research. 2021. *Dai-16kai shusshō dōkō kihon chōsa hōkoku* (Report of The 16th National Fertility Survey). Figure 7-4-2. https://www.ipss.go.jp/ps-doukou/j/db_16/db_16HoukokuBaseData.html. Accessed 6 February 2024.

The second most cited reason in 2021, physical and psychological burden, was the most cited in 2004. And the third reason, 'raising children compromises my commitment to my work', was ranked third in 2021, which was rephrased from work-life balance in 2004. Thus the top three reasons for not having an ideal number of children in 2021 are the same, meaning the Cabinet Office (2004) analysis is still relevant now.

Quality side of human capital investment: college education

In the previous section we saw that a smaller share of the population in Japan goes to higher education than in other OECD countries, especially when it comes to higher degrees. Research on why people do or do not advance to higher education has accumulated in many countries, and Japan is no exception. It has shown that there are two deciding factors on college going, namely household income and college cost. (Fujimura 2009; Nakata and Mosk 1987; Shima 1999; Takaya 2022; Yano and Hamanaka 2006). Nakata and Mosk (1987) demonstrated the positive and negative impacts of family income and tuition on family demand for college education during Japan's rapid growth period. Yano and Hamanaka (2006) showed that even after Japan had become an affluent society, both family income and college tuition were still the two most important factors for college going decision by the Japanese families. Is this still the case, and is there any connection with low Japanese family investment in higher education? For the Japanese family income, two issues are relevant. One is Japan's sluggish labour productivity increase and the second is income distribution – more specifically, bipolarization – among Japanese families.

Let us start with Japan's labour productivity increase in recent years. Labour productivity is the economic value workers create in a unit of time such as one hour or one day,

Table 10. Labour productivity per hour for all engaged for work (US$ PPP, index = 100).

Year	Japan	UK	USA	Germany	France
2020	**49.5**	69.3	80.5	76.0	79.2
	100	140	163	154	160
2000	**29.0**	36.4	40.6	38.2	39.9
	100	126	140	132	138
2020/2000 ratio	**1.71**	1.90	1.98	1.99	1.98

Source: Japan Productivity Center (2021). *Rōdō seisansei no kokusai hikaku2021nen-ban* (International Comparison of Labor Productivity 2021 version).

and the workers are paid from this value they create. It sets the celling for the amount of economic value which can be distributed for workers. Given this relation between the labour productivity and worker remuneration, Table 10 shows us some alarming statistics. Even in 2000, Japan was the bottom among those five leading OECD countries in labour productivity. But the gap between Japan and the other four countries has widened in the last 20 years. Most other countries have increased their labour productivity almost two-fold, but Japan's labour productivity has increased 20 to 30% less than them. In other words, the economic pie Japanese workers create has increased, but much more slowly than others.

When it comes to the distribution of this slowly growing pie, from 2000 to 2020 the average total monthly salary decreased very slightly from ¥421,195 to ¥419,500.[1] Meantime, there occurred an important change in income distribution. Table 11 shows income share by quintile for the same 5 countries in the last 20 years. Two facts are immediately recognizable. One is that Japan is the only country whose lowest 20% income share dropped significantly in this period. Another is that Japan experienced the biggest jump for the share of the highest 20% among the five countries.

The pattern can also be observed when we compare the second quintile and the fourth quintile. This means there has been a huge income movement from lower income families to higher income families in Japan in the last 20 years. Synchronized with slower income growth, this income re-distribution has undermined Japan's low and middle class families' capability to pay their children's higher education.

Meantime the cost of college education has *increased* substantially relative to other education, as shown in Table 12. During the period between 2014 to 2021, average high school costs for families actually dropped by 16.9%, mostly due to increasing subsidies for private high school tuition by local and national governments. On the other hand, all

Table 11. Changing income shares by quintiles (%).

Quintiles	Year	Japan	UK	USA	Germany	France
Lowest 20%	2018	**5.4**	6.8	5.2	7.6	8.0
	(year)	**(2017)**	(2017)		(2016)	
	2000 or before	**10.6**	6.1	5.4	8.5	7.2
	(year)	**(1993)**	(1999)	(2000)	(2000)	(1995)
	change	**−5.2**	0.7	−0.2	−0.9	0.8
Highest 20%	2018	**43.3**	40.6	46.9	39.6	40.8
	(year)	**(2017)**	(2017)		(2016)	
	2000 or before	**35.7**	44.0	45.8	36.9	40.2
	(year)	**(1993)**	(1999)	(2000)	(2000)	(1995)
	change	**7.6**	−3.4	1.1	2.7	0.6

Source: JILPT (2022). *Databook of International Labour Statistics.* Tables 5–15, and 2010, *Databook of International Labour Statistics.* Table 5–16.

REMEDYING JAPAN'S DEFICIENT INVESTMENT IN PEOPLE

Table 12. Educational cost for family and its change by type of programme.

	High School	Technica school	Associate degree	BA, BS
2014	35.0	50.2	73.0	81.1
2021	29.1	58.8	76.8	102.2
% change	−16.9%	17.1%	5.2%	26.0%

Source: Japan Finance Corporation (2021, 2014). *Reiwa 3 nendo kyōikuhi futan no jittai chōsa kekka* (Survey Report of Educational Expenditure 2021), and *Heisei 26 nendo kyōikuhi futan no jittai chōsa kekka* (Survey Report of Educational Expenditure 2014).

tertiary education costs increased, but 4-year BA and BSc college costs increased most, by 26%. General consumer prices in Japan increased modestly, from 97.5 in 2014 to 99.8 in 2021 (Statistics Bureau of Japan 2020). Compared to this modest increase of 2.4%, a 26% increase in college costs is so large, which immediately created a strong negative impact on college going for low- and middle-class families. Given the above-mentioned two environmental changes surrounding Japanese middle-class families it is no wonder that the demand for higher education has stagnated in recent years.

Corporate sector

Our next analysis is about the corporate sector. Why do Japanese firms invest so little in their workers? Why is Japanese worker investment in learning so minimal? For the first question, we will examine the impact of changes in the management environment on corporate training and education. More specifically, we pick up the impacts of three management environment changes in Japan, namely: short-sightedness of recent Japanese financial markets; growing external labour markets; and digital transformation (DX).

Let us start with Japanese management's obsession with short term profits. Institutional investors' voices have increased over the last forty years. This shift has made the Japanese corporation sensitive to the market prices of their company stocks. These do not necessarily reflect the demand and supply situation of the stock market. As Ito (2014) pointed out in his well-known report, this voice was amplified by the incentive scheme for the Japanese stock traders as well as their career characteristics. Most Japanese traders are paid based on the commission fees they earn by the number of trades. A rational reaction to their incentives is to sell and buy more frequently with short intervals than if the incentive mechanism were based on other performance measures, such as return to investment. This short-term trade practice forces corporate managers to engage in either 'current' and/or 'short-term' profit maximization, instead of long-term profit maximization, to keep their corporate stock price high. To maximize short-term profits, the Japanese managers seem to have chosen to reduce all types of cost, particularly those easy to cut in the short term such as the training and education of employees.

The second important recent change in the management environment is the gradual but steady growth of the external labour market. As the external labour market grows, the Japanese firms turn to it more frequently than their internal labour markets or fresh school graduate market to fill internal vacancies. The more management uses the external labour market to fill an internal vacancy, the less they spend on training or reskilling their incumbent workers. Table 13 shows this labour market shift by company size from year 2000.

Table 13. Share of job changers among recruits by corporate size (employees).

Year	5–29	30–99	100–299	300–999	1000
2000	64.8	63.9	61.4	55.9	51.6
2005	63.6	63.9	65.2	67.6	55.0
2010	65.7	67.4	63.2	61.7	58.4
2015	68.7	65.1	69.0	65.3	59.9
2020	70.3	70.3	69.3	63.3	61.9
2020–2000 change	5.5	6.4	7.9	7.4	10.3

Source: Ministry of Internal Affairs and Communications, *Rōdōryoku chōsa (shōsai shūkei)* (Labor Force Survey: Detailed Report), respective years.

From 2000 to 2020, the share of job changers among those newly recruited increased steadily in all company sizes. The magnitude of this shift was larger among large corporations than small ones. In 2000, two thirds of new recruits in small firms were job changers, but for large firms it was only 50%. In 2020 for all sizes of corporations, more than 60% of new job needs was met by recruits from the external labour market. We can safely say that the Japanese labour market has transformed from internally-centred to more externally-centred market. This fundamental shift has reduced training and education expenditure.

The third management environment change during this period is the widespread adoption of digital transformation (DX) by Japanese corporations. Among the various responses by management to DX, those relating to corporations' human resource management seem most critical for successful implementation. Each function within a corporation has to reconsider task allocation between humans and non-humans, including AI. They also have to reconsider worker assignment to those re-defined tasks. When they assign workers to those tasks for humans, they have to decide if they should re-train the incumbent workers to perform the new tasks or recruit from the external labour market. One important consideration is the general nature of digital skills and knowledge. Most digital technology is not company specific; it is general. Once one masters a digital technology, she or he can use it in any place, at any company. This creates an incentive preference for management to use the external labour market to fill internal needs for workers with digital skills. They also fear possible loss of incumbent workers if they train them with DX skills, and with them the DX skills. This fear of management diverts training resources to other purposes. It explains the low level of Japanese corporate investment in workers as well as the decline from 2000 to 2020 as DX activities have spread among the Japanese corporations during this period.

Actually, the gap in total investment in workers between Japan and other countries may well be larger, as we can see from the next point, namely the impact of long working hours of Japanese workers on training and learning. Japanese workers work longer hours than their counterparts in other developed countries. But the impact of these long working hours on training and learning is not widely recognized. According to MHLW (2018), the most frequently cited obstacle for learning after work is the difficulty of securing learning time. MHLW also reports a negative correlation between weekly working hours and the time spent on learning after work. Nakata (2018) also reports that among software engineers in five countries surveyed, including Germany and France, Japanese engineers spent the least time on after-work learning. Based on those reports, we can conclude that it is not only Japanese firms who spend less on building human capital, but Japanese workers as well.

Public sector

Our third and last analysis of Japanese lack of investment in people concerns public spending on education. Why does the Japanese government spend so much less than other countries on education as we saw in Table 5? So far, the policy debates on public expenditure on education in Japan have mostly been about the impacts of the ageing population and shrinking youth population. But they are not necessarily the main causes for the limited public expenditure. To see why, let us first look at key relevant statistics in Table 14.

Table 14. Social welfare expenditure (total and for elders) and elderly population.

Year	Ⓐ Social welfare expenditure	Ⓑ Social welfare expenditure for elders	Ⓑ/Ⓐ	Social welfare expenditure per elder	Elderly share in population	Number of elderly (65 +)
	¥ billion in 2020	¥ billion in 2020	%	¥ in 2020	%	1,000
1975	2,226	730	32.8	82,290	7.9	8,869
1980	3,406	1,469	43.1	137,874	9.1	10,653
1985	4,259	2,247	52.8	180,153	1.3	12,472
1990	5,293	3,117	58.9	208,786	12.1	14,928
1995	6,777	4,245	62.6	232,267	14.6	18,277
2000	8,058	5,467	67.8	248,055	17.4	22,041
2005	9,333	6,509	69.7	252,679	2.2	25,761
2010	11,115	7,498	67.5	254,321	23.0	29,484
2015	11,896	7,917	66.6	233,759	26.7	33,868
2020	13,222	8,315	62.9	230,811	28.6	36,027
Growth rate % (45 yrs)	494	1039	92	180	261	306
Ratio (45 yrs)	5.9	11.4	1.9	2.8	3.6	4.1

Source: Cabinet Office (2023). *Annual Report on the Ageing Society*, Figure 1-1-13.

Table 15. Public expenditure on education.

	Ⓐ Educational & research expenditure	Ⓑ Educational expenditure	Ⓑ/Ⓐ	Educational expenditure per youth	Youth −19 ys (%)	Youth population (−19 ys)
	Real million yen	Real million yen	%	Real yen	(%)	1000 persons
1975	5,098,787	4,492,892	88.1%	127,693	31.4%	35,185
1980	6,292,153	5,816,497	92.4%	162,467	30.6%	35,801
1990	6,037,980	5,509,405	91.2%	169,109	26.4%	32,579
2000	7,062,374	5,844,117	82.8%	224,705	20.5%	26,008
2010	6,383,308	4,826,158	75.6%	210,455	17.9%	22,932
2020	9,194,205	4,499,184	48.9%	216,964	16.4%	20,737
% growth (45 ys)	80%	0%	−44%	70%	−48%	−41%
2020/1975	1.80	1.00	0.56	1.70	0.52	.59

Source: Ministry of Finance. *Zaimu tōkei* (State Budget Statistics), respective years.

Public expenditure on social welfare

From 1975 to 2020, the number of Japanese people aged 65 and above mushroomed by 4.1 times, and the proportion in the national population increased from 7.9% in 1975 to 28.6% in 2020, or 3.6-times (Table 14). This ageing 'big-bang' is the biggest in the world. Meanwhile, the public expenditure on social welfare increased even faster – 5.9 times in real terms, in those 45 years. Even more striking is public expenditure on the elderly, which increased with awesome speed by 11.4 times in the same period. When we adjust by population growth of the elderly, social expenditure per elder increased a modest 2.8 times from ¥82,290 in 1975 to ¥230,811 in 2020 after adjusting for price changes, but this is a significantly larger increase than that on education.

Table 15 shows educational expenditure on youth in the same 45 years. National public expenditure on education and research all together grew by 80% from 1975 to 2020 in real terms, which is less than one sixth of the 500% increase of social welfare. But when we look at only the education budget, the number is even smaller. In fact, it has stagnated over 45 years from 4493 billion yen in 1975 to 4499 billion yen in 2020, i.e. almost 0% growth in 45 years. This is a stark contrast to the 1000% growth of social welfare expenditure for elders. As a consequence, educational expenditure per youth has grown by 70%, which is significantly smaller than the 180% growth of social welfare expenditure per elder. This huge difference is a clear message that youth are secondary after the elderly for policy makers. Over 45 years until 2020, the youth population has shrunk by more than 40% when the elder population increased 500%. As a consequence, the share of educational expenditure in the national public expenditure shrank from 13% in 1975 to 5.5% in 2020.

Readers may wonder why young people have been treated so unfavourably in the state budget. We suspect the neo-liberalism of the Koizumi and subsequent governments are responsible. Two episodes seem to support this conjecture. First is the incorporation of national universities. This policy was proposed and approved by Koizumi Cabinet in 2004, which considered that national universities need incentives to rationalize their budgets and resources. So, since 2004 the national government budget for the national universities' core educational expenditure has been reduced every year. At the same time, the Ministry of Education, Culture, Sports, Science and Technology (MEXT) has increased what they call 'competitive research money', which is allocated based on merit of proposed research. This incorporation of national universities and subsequent change of budget allocation criteria has moved national universities' financial resources from education to research without increasing the total resources.

Second is the reduction of national government support for compulsory education since 2006. Since 1940 the national government paid a half of national compulsory education costs in order to guarantee the national minimum quality in compulsory education regardless of locality where youngsters live. But the Koizumi cabinet decided to reduce this support from one half to one third in 2006 in exchange for more discretion for local government, to raise local taxes for local policy needs, including local compulsory education. This reduction of the compulsory education budget by the national government was implemented under the wider political reform by the Koizumi cabinet, called the 'trinity reforms' (*sanmi-ittai kaikaku*). But local governments have never raised enough to fill the reduction by this policy change of national government, which consequently has contributed the decline of overall national public education expenditure.

Kishida policies on education

Kishida has been Prime Minister since 4 October 2021, and thus his term as prime minister is just over two years at the moment, which is a very short period to evaluate any policy effectiveness. But he has chosen 'investing in people' as one of his three key targets for his Grand Design and Action Plan for a New Form of Capitalism, so it is worth examining if his 'investing in people' policies may have the potential to change the state of insufficient human capital investment in Japan. Again, let us do this by sector.

Kishida's human capital investment policies for the household sector

Before Kishida, several policies existed to stimulate household investment in people, some of which were revised by Kishida. They can be grouped into two categories; the first group to improve the quality and the second to increase the quantity of human capital respectively. As for the first category, relevant policies are:

(a) Loans for high school and college students
(b) Scholarships for high school and college students

The Kishida did propose some amendments on these schemes, although some of them are not yet implemented. We can identify one common feature among his amendments, namely that his policy amendments are easing the conditions for applications. The above student supports have a common condition which applicants have to meet, namely family income ceiling. Children whose family income exceeds a certain threshold are not eligible for application. Kishida's proposals are to raise the income threshold so that more families can apply. Taking the national scholarship for example, the annual income threshold he proposed for a family with two children is 6 million yen, which is significantly lower than the average income of those working families with children (Ministry of Internal Affairs and Communication 2022). These common features indicate that those Kishida policies are in essence income redistribution policies. They are targeted at lower income families, not wider middle-class families. The policy target is limited and the policy purpose is not directly relevant to improve the quality of Japanese human capital.

Another important household sector human capital investment is those for babies. As we stated before, increasing new-born babies is the start for Japan to rebuild its human resources. Therefore, Kishida's policies on investment in people should include those for babies. Before Kishida, relevant policies were: (1) one-time payment for families with a newly born baby; (2) one-time income support for families with children during the Covid pandemic; (3) supplemental payment for daycare and pre-school teachers; and (4), two-year extension of reduction of inheritance tax for those who support their siblings' baby's birth and child raising. Kishida did add some new policies to these, but all are so far temporary, and not yet institutionalized into the Japanese social welfare system. They are either budgeted for one-year or for a fixed term. Another problem is the restrictions applied to those who are eligible for those supports. Some restrictions are not eased, but tightened, such as those for inheritance tax on income transferred to children for educational expenses. As a consequence, the number of those who applied for the inheritance tax reduction has declined substantially. In conclusion, policy effectiveness for increasing new-born babies is questionable.

Kishida's human capital investment policies for the corporate sector

The Kishida cabinet has proposed a wide menu of new human capital investment policies to the corporate sector for working adults, which it calls 'reskilling'. To name a few:

(1) Expansion of skill training menu of the benefit system for vocational and educational training (*kyōiku kunren kyūfu seido*), particularly in IT-related classes, with more emphasis on self-selection by individual workers for their career development;
(2) Raising the maximum support payment of study abroad for working adults;
(3) Installing new requirements of re-skilling of employees for those companies which apply for employment adjustment subsidies (*koyō chōsei josēkin*);
(4) Flexible use of income tax deduction for reskilling-related expenses of companies.

All these proposed policies were budgeted either by the 2022 Supplementary Budget or the 2023 State Budget. Proposed policies 1 and 3 are for firms and 2 and 4 are for workers. And policies 1 and 2 are an improvement of past policies and 3 and 4 are new policies. Overall, Kishida's policies on investment in people are targeted for the wider population.

Evaluation by budget size of education policies

We can make a birds-eye evaluation of Kishida's policies on investment in people by looking at changes in the state education budget before and after the Kishida cabinet, focusing on three budget items: national support for compulsory education; national support for secondary and tertiary education; and scholarship and tuition support. When we compare state government support on those three items between 2019, the benchmark year before the Covid pandemic, and 2022, the 2022-year budgets are 99%, 112% and 98% of those in 2019. Two of them actually decreased! As for the budget for child support policies, the 2022 budget is 137% of that of 2019, a substantial increase. So, Kishida's child policies are indeed improved, but important others are not.

Summary and policy implications

Japan's investment in people is small both in relative and absolute terms. We summarize the status-quo as follows:

(1) State support for education is small relative to other nations as well as relative to social welfare expenditure for the elderly, and it has declined over 45 years as the population has aged and the political ideology has changed.
(2) Corporate sector investment in employee training is small relative to other countries and it has declined over the last 20 years because of the changing business environment, such as DX and labour market externalization.

(3) Japanese workers do not learn much after work, the main reason being their long working hours.
(4) The primary reason for the decline of Japan's birth rate is the high cost of child raising, particularly educational costs and declining income of low- and middle-class families.
(5) Most of Kishida's policies on human investment are either one-off and/or short fixed term, which limit their policy effectiveness.

Given to these findings, we can draw a few implications for future policies, as follows:

(1) The Kishida cabinet should change its policy perspective from short to long-term. It should change one-off and fixed term policies related to human capital investment to institutionalized policy. Investment is not consumption. It does not give immediate satisfaction to people who invested; it provides future satisfaction. Unless people are assured of recouping their investment in the future, they do not invest. Policies to enhance human capital investment should be institutionalized in a stable long-term framework.
(2) The Kishida cabinet should coordinate their labour policies with human capital policies so that the two enhance the effectiveness of each other. There is a fundamental contradiction between Kishida's promotion of company-sponsored re-skilling of employees and the promotion of 'job-type employment'. The Kishida administration is rigorously promoting the latter to dispel the remaining internal labour market among medium-sized and large corporations so that the Japanese labour market is externalized (cf. Zou 2024 in this work). And as the type of skills and knowledge people acquire from the proposed company-sponsored 're-skilling' are general in nature, those who are re-skilled will be more prone to change job and employer. Therefore, those two policies look mutually enhancing. But given the risk that their re-skilled workers will leave, employers will be reluctant to adopt the re-skilling policies. 'Job-type employment' and company sponsored re-skilling are not compatible; support for re-skilling should go to workers.
(3) Kishida's re-skilling policies should be coordinated with work style reform policies, another important set of labour policies. Moving support from companies to workers is not sufficient for re-skilling workers. Japanese workers working long hours cannot find time for re-skilling after work. So far the work-style reforms have not produced significant results. Shorter working hours are a necessary condition for re-skilling by workers after work. The Kishida cabinet should not just support the work style reform policies but also take a stronger step forward.
(4) Further policy coordination is necessary between Kishida's policies of human investment and fiscal policy. Many of Kishida's human investment supports set rather strict eligibility conditions for applicants. Those restrictions are targeted mostly at 'well-off families and workers'. But in reality, the targets are neither high-income families nor high-paid employees. They are middle-class families and decently paid employees. Exclusion of those families and workers has two

problems. One is that it reduces the impact of those policies. The second is that it is not consistent with other important Kishida policies such as rebuilding a strong middle class in Japan as well as smooth transfer of idle financial resources of the elderly and corporations to investment in people.

(5) A more fundamental problem of Kishida's human investment policies is the lack of a clear philosophy. The above-mentioned problems reflect this. The policies are supposed to be for individual Japanese to grow, not for companies to compete. Equalizing opportunities for people from different economic and family backgrounds is an important policy philosophy. But an equally important policy philosophy is recognition of individual differences and provision of support tailored for individual differences. Regardless of the type and degree of talent individual possesses, we must find a way to help them shine.

Note

1. Ministry of Health, Labour and Welfare, *Maitsuki kinrō tōkei chōsa, heisei 12 nen (Monthly Labour Survey, 2000) and Reiwa 3 nen kakuhō (Final Report of 2020 Monthly Labour Survey)*. The figures are for *Ippan Rōdōsha* (full-time employees) of all industries.

Disclosure statement

No potential conflict of interest was reported by the author(s).

Funding

This work was supported by the JSPS [Kaken JP20KK0030].

References

Cabinet Office. 2004. *Heisei 16 nenban shōshika shakai taisaku hakusho* [Annual report on the declining birthrate 2000]. Tokyo: Cabinet Office.

Cabinet Office. 2022. *Shōshika shakai taisaku hakusho, Reiwa 4 nenban* [Annual Report on the Declining Birthrate 2022]. Tokyo: Cabinet Office.

Cabinet Office. 2023. *Reiwa 5 nen kōreika shakai hōkokushō* [Annual Report on the Ageing Society]. Tokyo: Cabinet Office.

Denki Rengō (Japanese Electrical Electronic & Information Union). 2015. *Kurashi to hatarakikata ni kansuru chōsa* [Survey on life and work]. Tokyo: Denki Rengo.

Fujimura, M. 2009. "Daigaku shingakuni okeru syotoku kakusa to kōtō kyōiku seisaku no kanōsei" [Economic disparities in access to universities and the potential of higher education policy]. *Kyōiku Shakaigaku Kenkyū* 85:27–48.

Japan Finance Corporation. 2014. *Kyōikuhi Futan no jittai chōsa kekka Heisei 26 nendo* [Survey Report of Educational Expenditure 2014]. Tokyo: Japan Finance Corporation.

Japan Finance Corporation. 2021. *Reiwa 3 nendo kyōikuhi futan no jittai chōsa kekka* [Survey Report of Educational Expenditure 2021]. Tokyo: Japan Finance Corporation.

Japan Productivity Center. 2021. *Rōdō seisansei no kokusai hikaku 2021 nen-ban* [International Comparison of Labor Productivity 2021 version]. Tokyo: Japan Productivity Centre.

JILPT. 2022. *Databook of International Labour Statistics*. Tokyo: JILPT.

JILPT. 2023. *Databook of International Labour Statistics*. Tokyo: JILPT.

MHLW (Ministry of Health, Labour and Welfare). 2018. *Heisei 30-nenban rōdō keizai no bunseki No Bunseki* [Analysis of the Labour Economy]. Tokyo: MIC (Ministry of Internal Affairs and Communication).

Ministry of Finance. Various years. *Zaimu tōkei: Yosan Kessan to Data (State Budget Statistics), Respective Years*. Tokyo.

Ministry of Health, Labour and Welfare. 2022. *Reiwa 4-nen jinkō dōtai tōkei (Kakuteisū) No Gaikyō* [Statistics on Population Dynamics, 2022]. Tokyo: MIC (Ministry of Internal Affairs and Communication).

Ministry of Internal Affairs and Communication. 2022. *Kakē chōsa* [Family Income and Expenditure Survey]. Tokyo.

Ministry of Internal Affairs and Communications. Various years. *Rōdōryoku chōsa: Shōsai shūkei (Labour Force Survey: Detailed Aggregation), Respective Years*. Tokyo.

Nakata, Y. 2018. "Nihon no sofutowea sangyō to gijyutusya no genjyō wo kokusaitekini hyōkasuru" [Comparative evaluation of Japanese software industry and its engineers]. *SEC Journal* 52:56–59.

Nakata, Y., and C. Mosk. 1987. "The Demand for College Education in Postwar Japan." *The Journal of Human Resources* 22 (3): 377–404. https://doi.org/10.2307/145745.

National Institute of Population and Social Security Research. 2023. *Dai-16 kai shusshō dōukō kihon chosa hōkokusō* [Report of the 16th National Fertility Survey]. Tokyo: National Institute of Population and Social Security Research.

OECD. 2023. *Education at a Glance 2023*. Paris: OECD.

Shima, K. 1999. "Daigaku shingaku kōdō no eizai bunseki" [Economic Analysis of Students' College Choice]. *Kyōiku Shakaigaku Kenkyū* 64:101–121.

Statistics Bureau of Japan. 2020. *Base Consumer Price Index, Respective Years*. Tokyo.

Takaya, T. 2022. "Chiiki betsu danjyo no daigaku shingaku yōin" [Factors of College Advancement by Sex and Region]. *Kenkyū innovation gakkai nenji gakujutsu taikai kōen yōshishū* 37:154–159.

Yano, M., and J. Hamanaka. 2006. "Naze daigaku ri shingaku shinainoka" [Why Don't High School Students Go to University?] *Kyōiku Syakaigaku Kenkyū* 79:85–104. https://doi.org/10.11151/eds1951.79.85.

Zou, F. 2024. "The 'New Trinity' Reform of Labour Markets in Japan." *Asia Pacific Business Review*. https://doi.org/10.1080/13602381.2024.2320550.

ₔ OPEN ACCESS

The 'new trinity' reform of labour markets in Japan

Fangmiao Zou

ABSTRACT
This paper discusses the 'new trinity' reform of labour markets proposed in 2023, which is an integral part of Japan's New Form of Capitalism. After providing an overview of the reform's three components – reskilling/upskilling, inter-company mobility, and job-based employment – it discusses how the reform may contribute to reduction of labour shortages, skill shortages, and inequality among workers. It then assesses challenges to this reform, ways to overcome these challenges, and how Japan may hold answers for other countries facing similar labour market problems.

Introduction: continuity and change of Japanese labour market policies

Japanese labour market policies have been incrementally shifting towards re-regulation and worker protection since around 2010. This was a backlash against the country's neoliberal labour market transition in the previous decades that led to rising inequality and precariousness, alongside economic stagnation. The initial stage of re-regulation was an attempt to increase the number of 'standard' employees by setting legal obligations for companies to convert their 'non-standard' workers to 'standard' workers under certain circumstances, in addition to explicitly banning exploitative practices that became ubiquitous during the early 2000s.[1] The next stage of re-regulation was an attempt to match the work conditions of 'non-standard' workers with those of 'standard' workers, signified by the 'work-style reforms' and associated 'equal pay for equal work' policies gradually being enacted since 2017. These re-regulation policies hint at a shift of government priorities from maintaining the integrity of 'standard' employment to protecting the rights of individual workers, regardless of their work status, and this approach has been strengthened even more with the recent New Form of Capitalism (referred to as 'new capitalism' in this paper) and Integrated Three-Pronged Labor Market Reform (*sanmi ittai no rōdōshijyō kaikaku*, referred to as the 'new trinity' reform in this paper) discussions.

Until the New Form of Capitalism Realization Council (NCRC) meetings, the assumptions behind individual-oriented labour market policy changes seemed to be that the achievement of worker protection and employment stability would depend on the expansion of 'standard' employment or equivalent practices. This was reasonable because dualism between 'standard' and 'non-standard' employment had undoubtedly

---

This is an Open Access article distributed under the terms of the Creative Commons Attribution-NonCommercial-NoDerivatives License (http://creativecommons.org/licenses/by-nc-nd/4.0/), which permits non-commercial re-use, distribution, and reproduction in any medium, provided the original work is properly cited, and is not altered, transformed, or built upon in any way. The terms on which this article has been published allow the posting of the Accepted Manuscript in a repository by the author(s) or with their consent.

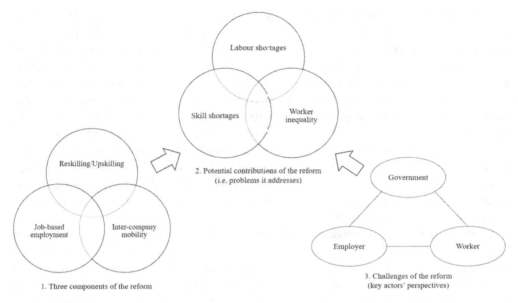

Figure 1. Outline of the paper: sections, topics, and their relations. Source: Author

exacerbated inequality and precariousness among workers. However, in the 'new capitalism' and 'new trinity' reform discussions, Japanese policymakers, and to some extent Japanese employers, began to view work-style diversity and flexible work arrangements as a possible and necessary means to achieve equality rather than a contributor to inequality.

This paper analyses the unfolding 'new trinity' reform of labour markets by reviewing NCRC meeting documents (Appendix A), 'new trinity' reform meeting documents (Appendix A), and recent labour market surveys conducted by various Japanese organizations, supplemented by interviews (Appendix B). Figure 1 presents a snapshot of the paper structure with associated section numbers. I will first provide an overview of the 'new trinity' reform, which consists of three intertwining components (1). Because these three components are designed to work simultaneously, their contributions have overlaps, but I will discuss each point separately for the sake of clarity (2). The reform's challenges will be discussed from different actors' perspectives, and I will also provide suggestions on how to address these challenges to optimize the reform's contributions (3). I will conclude with a brief discussion of potential implications for other countries facing similar challenges.

1. Three components of the 'new trinity' reform: an overview

The 'new trinity' reform is comprised of three main components, which are reskilling/upskilling, inter-company mobility, and job-based employment. As shown in Figure 1, enactment of one component will require the involvement of the other two, though some aspects of the reform have been more developed than others at this point. In this section, I will first briefly introduce each reform component's background, aims, and policy plans that have been under discussion.

Reskilling/upskilling may be the most straightforward concept of the three. The motivations behind this component are to provide workers with opportunities for gaining new skills (reskilling) or updating existing skills (upskilling). It aims to help workers to become more employable and competitive in the job market on the one hand, and help employers to acquire workers with desirable skills on the other. So far, the main reskilling/upskilling opportunities have been on-job training (OJT) or company-sponsored programmes in which employees attend training chosen by their employers. Reflecting on these practices, the 'new trinity' reform plans to shift government funding from the current 75% company-initiated training and 25% individual-based training, to over 50% individual-based training in the next five years, which will allow workers to choose training options on their own. Several NCRC members have also pointed out that this would give greater opportunities to unemployed workers searching for jobs by providing employable and transferable skills.

Government funding for reskilling/upskilling will be heavily concentrated in areas where employers are experiencing the most severe worker shortages. The 'new trinity' reform guidelines (*Sanmi-ittai no rōdō shijyō kaikaku no shishin*) published on 16 May 2023 identified job fields with 'high employability' as 'IT, data analytics, project management, technological research, sales and marketing, management and planning, tourism and transportation, etc'. In particular, Japan's projected IT worker shortages, especially of those with 'creative' skills rather than 'maintenance' skills, has been highlighted by various recent studies (for example, IPA 2022; JHR 2023; Mizuho 2019). In addition to increasing individual-based training, the reform also plans to design new certificate systems for various IT skills, incentivize workers to look for new jobs through reskilling/upskilling (e.g. abolishing unemployment benefit disadvantages for quitting a job after being recently trained), offer consultancy services to help workers with these transitions, promote side-jobs as an effective means to develop new skills, and collaborate with universities to increase students with specialized skills who can become 'immediate assets' (instead of long-term 'members') to the company.

The 'new trinity' reform objectives are to not only increase workers with 'highly employable' skills, but to 'smoothly transfer' them to industries and positions that are rapidly growing in demand, which is the second reform component: *inter-company mobility*. One of the plans under discussion is unemployment and retirement benefit reform. Policymakers have focused on relaxing conditions upon which workers receive unemployment pay, in particular, terminating the differentiation between workers who are laid off and workers who quit the job. (Under the current unemployment systems, while the former can receive unemployment benefits immediately, the latter need to wait for two or three months.) Another reform being discussed is the abolition of retirement tax systems favouring workers who have stayed with a company for 20 years or more, and to expand portable retirement (pension) plans, instead of company-specific plans.

So far, inter-company mobility has been most active among 'non-standard' workers and those who work at small businesses, or those with highly sought-after skills. By lowering incentives for workers to commit to an employer long-term, policymakers hope to stimulate greater mobility of 'standard' workers. However, as pointed out by various Japanese scholars, the disconnect between internal labour markets (concerning 'standard' employment) and external labour markets (concerning 'non-standard' employment), in addition to the stronger institutionalization of the former than the latter, have made it difficult for 'standard' workers to change employers without losing certain earnings or benefits (for example, Inoki and Higuchi 1995; Saguchi 2018; Sugeno 2004; Tsuru, Higuchi, and Mizumachi 2011). The Grand Design and Action Plan for a New Form of Capitalism (2023) points out that due to this disconnect, Japanese workers who change jobs mid-career tend to start with lower wages at their new jobs than their previous jobs, but the new policy will aim for more workers to secure immediate wage increases after a mid-career job change by attempting to 'seamlessly connect internal and external labour markets'.

The development of job intermediation services has become a key policy focus for labour market mobility. For example, the 'new trinity' reform suggests information-sharing among Hello Work (public employment security agencies), private employment agencies (such as Recruit, Persol, and Pasona), and certified career consultants regarding numbers of jobs posted, their projected wages, and required skills. So far, the operation of these organizations has been independent for the most part because they have been separately building databases that target different industries, worker groups, and locations. However, by curating employment information into one system, policymakers are hoping to achieve a government-led 'data-based' career consulting service modelled after Denmark's 'flexi-security' (Cabinet Secretariat 2022b). The reform also encourages side-jobs and associated job matching services. It cites overseas data (for example, Panos, Pouliakas, and Zangelidis 2014; Raffiee and Feng 2014) to show the benefits of holding side-jobs, including higher likelihood of starting up a business, lower likelihood of failing a start-up business, and lower likelihood of becoming unemployed, in addition to other more obvious benefits such as workers gaining higher income and new skills. Although all of these benefits align with the 'new capitalism' objectives, more conflicting motivations can be observed from employers' and workers' perspectives, which will be discussed later in this paper.

The third component, *job-based employment*, may seem simple but has been the least developed of all three policy components. It is a practice of hiring and paying workers based on the specific functions they are expected to perform, in contrast to so-called 'membership-based' employment relating to seniority-based wages. The 'new trinity' reform guidelines so far have merely presented case studies of various companies introducing job-based internal management (with Hitachi as the top example), which are to be referred to by individual companies for developing their own versions. Examples include drafting specific job descriptions, introducing skill-needs analysis and reskilling, developing certification systems, re-designing wage systems modelled after overseas job-based pay grade systems, creating an internal 'matchmaking' platform or agent through which workers can apply to other positions within the company, changing internal re-allocation patterns that focus on workers improving specialized skills instead of broadly experiencing all aspects of the company functions, and so on.

Although detailed plans are still at a rudimentary stage, the ultimate goal of this job-based employment reform has been consistent and clear in all policy documents, which is to achieve 'structural wage increases'. In fact, during the early NCRC meetings, 'structural wage increases' was mentioned as the third component of labour market reforms, but was later replaced by 'job-based employment'. For employers, a shift from 'membership-based' to 'job-based' employment will supposedly involve a comprehensive re-designing of existing internal labour market systems. Building institutions that connect these changes with reskilling/upskilling and inter-company mobility will be essential for the government – and other actors such as businesses, universities, labour unions, and employment agencies – to achieve the 'new capitalism' and 'new trinity' reform goals. I will further discuss the ideal outcomes of the reform in the next section.

2. Potential contributions of the 'new trinity' reform

If executed effectively, the 'new trinity' reform can potentially contribute to the reduction of Japan's labour shortages (i.e. overall workforce decline), skill shortages (i.e. lack of highly-skilled workers), and inequality (i.e. gaps between 'standard' and 'non-standard' workers). The reform's contribution to the first point, tackling labour shortages, may be the most indirect policy outcome of all, and in this section I will first point out how the reform can potentially expand worker supply and productivity in Japan. Then, I will briefly discuss ways the reform may contribute to the reduction of skill shortages and inequality.

2.1 Quantitatively expanding labour markets

Japan is trying to prevent workforce shrinkage by incorporating different worker demographics, one of which being foreign workers. The 2018 amendment of the Immigration Control and Refugee Recognition Act is viewed as the first step towards gradually opening a 'front door' to welcome foreign workers (Miyajima et al. 2019; Yamaguchi 2020), and this 'opening-up' attitude is reflected in the 'new capitalism' policies. For example, the revised Grand Design and Action Plan for a New Form of Capitalism (2023) stresses the importance of applying the 'equal pay for equal work' policies to foreign workers, attracting 'highly-skilled' foreign workers (especially in the field of digital and green transformation), increasing foreign students along with their employment opportunities after graduating, expanding visa support for foreign investors and entrepreneurs, nurturing and retaining foreign workers by revising the Technical Intern Training Programme,[2] and promoting cultural, educational, and business exchanges with foreign countries (detailed in MLIT 2023).

To this end, the 'new trinity' reform may help to attract more foreign workers by promoting job-based employment practices that better match the so-called 'global standard' (i.e. employment systems that are more clear and familiar to foreign workers), as adjustment difficulty to Japan's 'membership-based' practices has been one of the biggest obstacles to hiring and retaining 'standard' foreign workers (for example, Igarashi 2015; Oishi 2012; Watanabe 2013). In addition, Japanese companies may be losing their relative appeal compared to other rapidly growing economies, exemplified by the decrease of Chinese workers coming to Japan (interview I; see also Iguchi 2016). Achieving the reform's goal of 'structural wage increases', as well as encouraging the development of 'new and exciting' businesses, may make working in Japan more attractive to foreign workers overall (interviews I, K).

The second possibility of quantitatively expanding labour markets is to increase the participation of domestic workers, particularly elderly and female workers. The 2013 amendment of the Act on Stabilization of Employment of Elderly Persons required employers to continue employing workers until 65 years old,[3] and the 2021 'work-style reform' obligated employers to make efforts to extend this to 70 years old. However, various recent studies have indicated that although the employment of the elderly is increasing, many older workers are subject to inferior wages and welfare compared to their pre-retirement conditions (for example, Yamada 2009; Moriyama and Yamagishi 2020; MHLW 2022; interview C). The 'new trinity' reform may help bridge the wage gap between pre-retirement and re-employment by reinforcing 'equal pay for equal work' policies and promoting job-based employment relations that place less importance on seniority or 'standard' employment status.

In addition, because the gap between pre-retirement and re-employment conditions is attributed to the mismatch between the employees' willingness to continue working and employers' unwillingness to re-employ them (Yamada 2009; interviews F, H), the 'new trinity' reform's promotion of inter-company mobility may make it easier for retired workers to switch to an employer that is willing to offer better employment conditions. More specifically, the 'matchmaking' between retired workers and new employers may be promoted through the expansion of job intermediation services suggested by the reform. This trend can already be seen in private employment agency services. In fact, job intermediation services for 'high-income, mid-career' job changes have been one of the fastest growing business fields since 2010 for Recruit and many other private employment agencies, including services specifically designed for employers recruiting retired workers (Kurosawa 2022; interviews A, D).

Another domestic worker pool that has been expanding in Japan is female workers. On a macro level, there has been a greater number of 'non-standard' female workers than 'standard' female workers, but at the same time, overall female labour market participation has been increasing, and since around 2015, the increase in 'standard' employment has been more significant among females than males (*Labour Force Survey* 2009–22). On a micro level, according to the Ministry of Health, Labour and Welfare (MHLW 2023c), what it referred to as 'reluctant (*fuhon-i*) non-standard' employment (i.e. those who work 'non-standard' jobs because they could not find 'standard' positions) has decreased among female workers, from 14.7% in 2013 to 7.7% in 2022,[4] and the most common reasons for choosing 'non-standard' employment for female workers were personal reasons such as the need for flexible work time, specific work location, utilization of particular skills, and balancing with housekeeping duties. However, other studies have also revealed increased dissatisfaction among part-time female workers due to their lack of wage increase and promotion opportunities, despite the fact that part-time workers have been taking on more and more roles similar to 'standard' workers (Honda 2010; MHLW 2021).

The above trends suggest that it has become relatively easier for female workers to find 'standard' employment positions, and that many 'non-standard' female workers would want to become 'standard' workers if their personal or family situations allowed, but a major obstacle that keeps them from doing so is that the current 'standard' employment systems lack work time flexibility and job specificity. Ideally, the 'new trinity' reform will not only reduce the 'standard'-'non-standard' gap experienced by female workers, but also contribute to the increase of 'standard' female employment by promoting job-based employment and 'diversified (*tayō-na*) standard' employment[5] that offers work time flexibility and job specificity. In addition, 'structural wage increases' through the reform may provide justification for female workers who are currently making work adjustments to earn below so-called 'annual income walls' (*nenshū no kabe*)[6] to work past such limitations and increase their participation in the labour market (cf. Nagase 2024 in this collection).

Lastly, there are other ways the 'new trinity' reform attempts to address labour shortage problems. The reform documents cite studies on the correlation between income increase and higher likelihood of marriage and having children, supporting the government's intention to quantitatively expand labour markets in the long run by an increased birth rate achieved through 'structural wage increases'. It also hints at the idea of increasing per-worker workload as a solution to labour shortages, for example, by promoting side-jobs, increasing female work hours beyond 'annual income walls', and introducing job-based systems that can better adjust overall to companies' work load fluctuations and reduce workers' inactive periods. A worker's unemployment period is also viewed as 'wasteful' and hence a target of reduction (interview J). Prior to the reform, the government focused on training the unemployed to help them find their next job, but the 'new trinity' reform discusses the possibility of providing reskilling and upskilling for potential job changers during the employment period. It also suggests the abolition of unemployment benefit disadvantages for workers who voluntarily quit their job if they have participated in such training programmes in the past year. These discussions are closely related to Japan's second labour market challenge, skill shortages, which I will discuss next.

2.2 Adjusting to new skill demands

While the 'new trinity' reform's contributions to solving labour shortages may be indirect for the most part, the reform more directly addresses Japan's need for skill upgrading. The increased government support for reskilling/upskilling, reflecting the 'new capitalism' and 'new trinity' reform visions, can be seen in the various programmes and budgets announced by the Ministry of Health, Labour and Welfare (MHLW), Ministry of Education, Culture, Sports, Science and Technology (MEXT), and Ministry of Economy, Trade and Industry (METI) since 2022. In their 2023 budget reports, 'promotion of new trinity reforms' and 'realisation of structural wage increases' became one of the five major policy categories for MHLW (2023a) and MEXT (2023) respectively, and over a hundred billion JPY was allocated by METI (2023) for projects relating to 'human capital development'.

The resulting government-sponsored reskilling/upskilling programmes will all support the increase of individual-based training opportunities for workers to attain high-demand skills, and ideally for them to transfer out of declining industries into growing industries. Whether or not these budgets are enough or will be spent effectively remains to be seen (cf. Akai 2024 and Nakata 2024, in this volume). It is also questionable whether or not these government initiatives will motivate employers and workers to proactively participate, which will be discussed later in this paper.

According to the Japan Association of Human Resource Services Industry (JHR 2023), workers who experienced the highest wage increases after job changes were those who had 'proactive' career changes aimed at developing new skills and career paths. This study supports the possibility that the three components of the 'new trinity' reform can simultaneously increase wages for workers on one hand, and meet employer demands for skilled workers on the other. Although the third component, job-based employment, is discussed mostly at the individual company level so far, a successful enactment may incrementally lead towards a standardized job-based market across the industry, and ultimately an institutional merging of 'standard' and 'non-standard' employment relations that emphasize individual skills rather than company membership. The next sub-section will discuss possible ways the 'new trinity' reform may contribute to a reduction of the division between 'standard' and 'non-standard' employment, and between internal and external labour markets.

2.3 Filling gaps between 'standard' and 'non-standard' employment

There are three possible ways the 'new trinity' reform may achieve greater equality between 'standard' and 'non-standard' workers. The first is to match the work conditions of 'non-standard' employment to that of 'standard' employment, as is being encouraged by the current 'equal pay for equal work' policies. One of the biggest obstacles to this approach is the fact that under existing employment systems, it is difficult for employers to develop objective ways to compare the detailed job descriptions and skills of 'non-standard' workers with those of 'standard' workers, resulting in employers often opting for individual wage negotiation instead of wage-matching when hiring 'non-standard' workers (JILPT 2022).[7]

The 14th NCRC meeting document produced by the Cabinet Secretariat (2023a) cited MHLW studies and estimated that in 2021, the per-hour wage gap between 'standard' and 'non-standard' workers performing similar functions was 602 yen, and opined that it was unclear whether or not this gap is reasonable. On the one hand, 'standard' employment relations imply higher levels of responsibility, likelihood of working overtime, and commitment to the employer; on the other hand, as discussed earlier, dissatisfaction among 'non-standard' workers has increased because their roles have been expanding towards those of 'standard' workers, while the wage and welfare standards remain unchanged. Although raising the wage and welfare conditions of 'non-standard' workers to the comparable level of 'standard' workers may keep rising inequality at bay temporarily, more fundamental institutional changes may be required in the long run.

The second possible way to narrow the 'standard'-'non-standard' gap is by connecting internal and external labour markets through the introduction of universal job-based employment systems. This path seems to be what policymakers initially intended to achieve during the drafting period of the 'new trinity' reform guidelines. However, as policymakers collected data on individual companies' human resource management practices, it became clear that a complete abolition of 'standard' employment systems is not feasible anytime soon because every company has established internal employment systems unique to its vision, industry, required skills, and so on, which cannot be easily matched with other company practices.

Reflecting this reality, more recent reform discussions have gradually shifted towards 'strengthening and expanding internal labour markets', which is the third way of potentially shrinking job-type-based inequality. Although this policy idea is still at a rudimentary stage, existing studies of company groups and networks in Japan, such as 'intermediary labour markets' (Hirano and Enatsu 2018; Itami 1987) or 'quasi-internal labour markets' (Inagami and Whittaker 2005), may be useful for conceptualizing this transition. The first step would be to gradually introduce internal job-based employment by establishing job descriptions, wage grades, training programmes, certification systems, and internal hiring departments in charge of 'matchmaking' workers and open positions to promote within-company mobility. The next step would be to expand this system to group companies, subsidiaries, overseas offices, and other affiliated organizations. The 'new trinity' reform documents frequently refer to Hitachi's example, which is currently at this second step, pointing out that incrementally expanding company participation in these practices may eventually lead to an entire labour market shift towards job-based employment. However, almost all the other company examples mentioned during reform meetings are still at the first stage, and most smaller companies have made no move towards job-based employment because they have no clear guidelines or incentives. This leads to the next point of discussion, on the 'new trinity' reform's challenges and its need to incorporate employers' and workers' perspectives.

3. Challenges of the 'new trinity' reform

Having discussed the potential outcomes of the 'new trinity' reform, this section turns to the reform's obstacles, and how Japan may overcome them and realize the 'new capitalism' goal of a 'virtuous cycle of growth and distribution'. The central discussion of the reform seems to be focused on creating labour markets in which workers have equal access to career advancement and skill development opportunities, and, as discussed earlier, this emphasis on individual workers can be seen as a push back against Japan's earlier neoliberal policies. However, although protecting individual workers' rights is certainly important, the reform plans so far seem to lack realistic input from employers, as well as from workers to some extent, in addition to clear timelines for achieving various levels of reform goals.

To list some questions that the policymakers have not yet fully addressed, *Why should employers allow side-jobs and individual training that encourage leaving, and abolish retirement plans that favour long-term, loyal employees? How do employers assess equality between 'standard' and 'non-standard' workers when they have different responsibilities and expectations? How do employees decide what skills to develop without guidance from employers? What are the milestones and end goals of the 'new trinity' reform?* To address these questions, I will focus on three challenges in this section: understanding employers' perspectives, understanding workers' mindsets, and lack of clarity between short-term and long-term goals.

3.1 Considerations from employers' perspectives

An example of a disconnect between government and employer viewpoints can be found in the discussion of side-jobs. In 2021, over 40% of large employers explicitly prohibited side-jobs, and had no intention of accepting any side-job workers in the near future, even though the MHLW had been clearly encouraging them since 2018 by incorporating them into the MHLW 'model' office guidance (Cabinet Secretariat 2022a; Persol 2021). The ratio of side-job prohibition was generally lower among small and medium-sized enterprises (SMEs), but this is likely for non-proactive reasons such as the result of SMEs having more difficulties recruiting and retaining workers, rather than SMEs more actively promoting them for employees' skill and career development.

Similar concerns can be noted regarding the reform's planned changes to training, unemployment, and retirement policies discussed above, which all add monetary and administrative burdens to employers directly and indirectly, but provide few clear incentives for them to make such changes. The reform papers so far suggest population ageing, worker shortages, and skill shortages as universal justifications for all policy changes. However, for many employers, especially large employers that can still attract enough workers at least in the short term, these reasons are probably insufficient to actively support the reforms right away.

In contrast, pressure to attract workers is growing, especially among SMEs and in industries that require engineers and so-called 'essential workers'.[8] Various studies have indicated SMEs' preference for hiring 'standard' employees, their difficulties in attracting new graduates, and their reluctant reliance on the higher ratio of mid-career hires and 'non-standard' workers (for example, MHLW 2019; Recruit Works Institute 2015–23; *Survey on Employment Trends* 2012–23; interviews B, C, D). The ratio of 'standard' workers hired mid-career, as well as 'non-standard' workers, is also high for 'essential workers' because of the industries' relatively inferior work conditions compared to white-collar jobs (ILO 2023), but the 'new trinity' reform does not seem to pay enough attention to them despite their crucial socioeconomic roles.

The challenges for recruiting engineers are not only a matter of labour shortages but skill shortages as well. The 'new trinity' reform seems to more directly tackle this issue by promoting reskilling/upskilling. An engineer dispatching agency manager informed me that they had no choice but to provide comprehensive training programmes for their employees, because that was the only way they could attract and maintain enough skilled workers, and even though many workers leave the company after gaining competitive skills, all they could do was strive to be an attractive employer (interview B). Not limited to engineering companies, this may become the case for all employers after the full realization of the 'new trinity' reform.

As discussed above, of the three reform components, policymakers have been especially struggling to crystallize the concept of 'job-based' employment, which directly challenges persisting 'membership-based' institutions. With the exception of those with overseas backgrounds, managers in Japan have little to no experience with job-based employment systems, nor clear ideas about how to design them. A policymaker who has been involved in the 'new trinity' reform informed me that because most reform committee members have extensive overseas experience, they have no trouble imagining a shift towards job-based labour market systems, but the initial policy announcements caused great confusion among Japanese managers because they interpreted 'job-based' employment in many different ways (interview J). Efforts to adjust to this reality can be seen in policy document wording changes throughout 2022 and 2023, from pursuing 'structural wage increases' to general 'job-based employment' to 'introducing job-based wages according to individual company situations'. They also changed the Japanese language for 'job-based', from a relatively new term *jobu-gata* back to an older term more familiar to Japanese managers: *shokumu-kyū* (wage systems according to a worker's duties).

The abovementioned policymaker also said that the government is currently collecting company case studies to be reflected in updated draft policies regarding unemployment (and possibly retirement) reforms, which will be soon published. In addition, the documents prepared for the 22nd NCRC meeting (held on

27 September 2023) mentioned that the government would come up with a conclusion regarding reskilling/upskilling support and unemployment reforms (that favour those who recently underwent training) by the end of 2023. However, it is likely that updates on retirement reforms will take longer, as no documents have mentioned specific dates, and job-based employment reform will take even longer, as policy-makers need to continue studying employers' specific cases.

3.2 Considerations from the worker perspective

The main 'new trinity' reform policy goals seem to be built upon an assumption that workers are motivated for career development and will actively seek reskilling/upskilling and job change opportunities. In reality, however, few workers place heavy importance on career planning when choosing jobs. Various studies have shown that wage, welfare, co-worker relations, work hours, and work type ('standard' or 'non-standard') take priority over career paths for most workers; they are not motivated or clear about career paths at all, let alone do they actively seek training opportunities (for example, Cabinet Office 2023; ManpowerGroup 2023). According to a policymaker I interviewed (J), the reform committee members were all 'special' in the sense that they have proactively pursued their career and skill development, and may not realize that most Japanese workers do not possess such clear career visions and high levels of motivation.

This disconnect from workers' reality might be partly due to the lack of labour union influence during the reform discussions. Throughout NCRC and 'new trinity' meetings (Appendix A), labour union representatives seemed agreeable to the overall reform plans. Although they have expressed concerns about labour mobility threatening job security, they did not change policy outcomes. Concerns of a possible lack of worker motivation to reskill/upskill were only brought up at the 'new trinity' reform subcommittee meeting after the reform plans had already been announced.

In order to fully reach the 'new trinity' reform goals, it is necessary to better understand workers' attitudes towards work, and provide guidance according to their diverse motivations. In addition to labour unions, increased school participation is also crucial. During the 'new trinity' reform meetings, several policymakers brought up the need for education reform that would help develop career-oriented ways of thinking at a young age, but these views have not yet been reflected in policy outputs. Of all the reform meeting attendees so far, the push for incorporating 'career education' at schools has been the strongest from employment agencies, in particular Recruit and Parsol, which have already been providing 'career education' products and services on a small scale. Meeting attendees representing large employers seem to be more keen on shifting workers' mindsets while at the workplace from membership-based to job-based, although as above studies suggest, this may not be early enough.

Nurturing a career mindset that is suitable for flexible labour markets and job-based employment practices will require long-term planning and coordination among a broad range of stakeholders. In the meantime, workers would benefit from the 'new trinity' reform's suggested plans to develop personalized 'career consulting' services that inform workers of current and future labour market needs, and offer realistic training options to achieve wage increases. In 2022, there were about 64,000 certified career consultants, with the largest number working at corporations (Cabinet Secretariat 2023a), but career consultants at public and private employment agencies, as well as universities, are more likely to support unemployed individuals and promote inter-company mobility.

3.3 Organising short-, mid-, and long-term objectives

As mentioned throughout this paper, some reform plans seem attainable within the next year, while others will require long-term institutional change over the course of decades. The 'new trinity' reform documents are unclear about these timelines, but organizing Japan's short-, mid-, and long-term labour market problems and potential ways to address them may help future development of detailed reform policies and desirable labour market outcomes. Table 1 is a suggestion for how a timeline could be organized, which I hope will trigger further discussion about Japan's future labour markets and economy. As shown in the table, most of the imminent problems may be addressed by enhancing existing policies such as 'work-style reform', immigration policies, and retirement policies. In terms of labour market change, the strength of the 'new trinity' reform may be in mid-term plans, and the 'new capitalism' reform in long-term plans.

Conclusion and further discussion: does Japan hold answers?

Optimistically speaking, the three intertwining components of the reform (reskilling/upskilling, inter-company mobility, and job-based employment) can contribute to the reduction of Japan's labour shortages, skill shortages, and inequality between 'standard' and 'non-standard' workers, although considerations from employers' and workers' perspectives, as well as clearer reform timelines, are much needed. As concluding remarks, I will briefly discuss how Japan's reform plans may provide implications for other countries, which is a consideration of this volume.

The most direct lessons the 'new trinity' reform can provide are its approaches to addressing labour shortages and skill shortages. Regarding labour shortages, although Japan has been gradually expanding its foreign workforce, its immigration policies are stricter than many countries that are also facing population ageing and labour shortages. Japan's attempts to quantitatively expand labour markets by increasing domestic worker pools while reducing their unproductive time, either on the job or due to unemployment, may provide implications for other countries facing similar demographic challenges, especially those facing a 'backlash' against globalization and ever-rising immigration (Leonhardt 2023). Even for countries not facing imminent labour shortages, many are, or will, face skill shortages along with industrial and technological development. Japan's new reform plans most directly tackle this problem, and will likely provide implications for both policies and practices regarding reskilling/upskilling and worker mobility towards new and growing industries.

I would like to point out a specific labour market actor that may be a key player in upcoming labour market changes, which is employment agencies (or the human resource service industry). As discussed in this paper, some of the biggest challenges to the reform are the disconnects between internal and external labour markets, and among government, employers, and workers. Employment agencies have traditionally served as the connector between workers and employers through job advertising and intermediation,

Table 1. Suggestions for how to organize reform timelines.

	Problems	Potential solutions	Examples of detailed plans discussed in this paper
Imminent	Labour shortages, particularly of 'essential workers'.	Quantitatively expanding labour markets.	Deregulating restrictions on foreign workers; Extending the retirement age.
		Increasing workload and productivity per-worker.	Permitting side-jobs; Increasing job-based assignments to reduce worker down time; Increasing part-timers' work hours by abolishing 'annual income walls'; Enhancing 'equal pay for equal work' to improve the conditions of 'non-standard' workers.
Mid-term	Skill shortages.	Promoting reskilling/upskilling.	Shifting from employer-oriented training to individual-oriented training; Creating certification systems for desirable skills; Supporting consultation services for skill development analysis.
		Encouraging worker mobility from declining to growing industries.	Enacting unemployment and retirement reforms that remove disadvantages for workers changing jobs; Developing job intermediation services.
Long-term	Greater worker shortages induced by population ageing and decline.	Improving birth rates to increase young population.	Realising 'structural wage increases'.
	Widening inequality.	Merging 'standard' and 'non-standard' employment.	Gradually changing employment practices, possibly through the expansion of internal and 'middle'/'quasi-internal' labour markets.
	Low labour productivity.	Virtuous cycle of growth and distribution.	Achieving 'new capitalism' reforms; Achieving education reforms to nurture career-oriented mindsets; Continuing 'structural wage increases'.

Source: Author.

and in recent years, have been expanding their services for government-sponsored re-employment programmes, consultancy for human resource management strategies, and training and seminar programmes (Zou 2023). All these roles of employment agencies will contribute to the implementation of the 'new trinity' reform by providing an alternative but realistic option to better connect government, employers, and workers, while bridging internal and external labour markets.

One of the most unique characteristics of employment agencies in Japan compared to other countries is attentiveness to individual workers, jokingly referred to by some agency managers as being 'nosey' (*osekkai*) (interviews A, E, K). Unlike employment agencies in other countries, which tend to focus on serving client companies, Japanese employment agencies have a stronger tendency to help individual workers with finding jobs. For example, they personally meet all individuals registered with job intermediary services and help them with CVs and job interviews. These existing practices can be expanded to formal 'career consulting' services, which help individual workers make career and skill development plans, while making use of database-sharing suggested by the reform to analyse broader market needs and trends. According to a manager at Recruit who had been involved in starting up various major projects, this is exactly the direction she hopes Japanese employment agencies are heading towards (interview K). This means that they will not only continue to enhance the flexibilization of labour markets, but may also serve as guardians and mentors for workers. Such practices may provide practical implications for human resource service industries in other countries.

The 'new capitalism' goals align with the global trends of 'care economy', 'green enterprises', and 'just transition' (which combines sustainable development with human rights), in the sense that they all stress the simultaneous achievement of sustainability and equality in economic development. The 'new trinity' reform may be able to add a third dimension to this development goal, which is flexibility. Postwar labour market evolution has shown that the 'flexibilization' of labour markets, in association with the rise of 'non-standard' employment, led to greater inequality and precariousness among workers. However, the 'new trinity' reform is designed to achieve these traditionally conflicting labour market outcomes (employment stability, flexibility, and equality) at the same time. As shown in this paper, although there are certainly challenges and the details of this reform are not yet crystallized, realization of the 'new trinity' reform may improve Japan's economy and quality of life, and possibly provide other countries with a positive example of how the coexistence of sustainability, flexibility, and equality may be attained.

Notes

1. For example, the 2012 Labour Contract Law and the 2015 amendment of Labour Dispatching Law specified conditions in which employers were obligated to convert fixed-term workers and dispatched workers to full-time workers respectively. Also, various rampant 'grey zone' labour dispatching and subcontracting practices during the early 2000s, in addition to a large number of 'non-standard' worker dismissals after the 2008 global financial crisis, resulted in prohibition of these exploitative practices.
2. A full draft of revised policy was published on 18 October 2023. See ISA (2023).

3. It gave employers options to (1) continue the 'regular' employment relations until 65 years old, (2) keep the retirement age of 60 years old, but re-employ retired workers until 65 years old, or (3) abolish retirement age altogether.
4. The ratio of 'reluctant non-standard' male workers has been higher but is also decreasing, from 31.1% in 2013 to 16.8% in 2022.
5. 'Diversified standard' employment systems allow one or more of the following for 'standard' workers: shorter work hours, specific work location, and specific job function.
6. Many female workers in Japan adjust their workload to be under certain annual income caps for tax exemption, spousal deduction, or healthcare enrolment. On 27 September 2023, the Ministry of Health, Labour and Welfare published tentative plans to address 'annual income walls' (MHLW 2023b; Nagase 2024 in this collection).
7. 'Equal pay for equal work' regulations require employers to match 'non-regular' workers' wages with those of 'regular' workers based on job content, or alternatively, to allow the option of reaching wage agreements by negotiating with individual workers.
8. They are also referred to as 'key workers'/'critical workers', and their importance was realized during COVID-19 (ILO 2023).

Disclosure statement

No potential conflict of interest was reported by the author.

References

"Atarashī shihon shugi no gurando dezain oyobi jikkou keikaku [Grand Design and Action Plan for New Form of Capitalism]." June 16, 2023. https://www.cas.go.jp/jp/seisaku/atarashii_sihonsyugi/pdf/ap2023.pdf.

Akai, N. 2024. "Evidence-Based Policy Making in Japan's Public Expenditure: Compatibility of Fiscal Health and Investing for the Future." *Asia Pacific Business Review*. https://doi.org/10.1080/13602381.2024.2320543.

Cabinet Office. 2023. "Shingata korona uirusu kansenshou no eikyouka ni okeru seikatsu ishiki, koudou no henka ni kansuru chōsa [Survey on Lifestyle Changes Under COVID-19]." October 30. https://www5.cao.go.jp/keizai2/wellbeing/covid/pdf/result6_covid.pdf.

Cabinet Secretariat. 2022a. *Kiso shiryō* [Basic Data Prepared for the Seventh New Capitalism Meeting], May 20. https://www.cas.go.jp/jp/seisaku/atarashii_sihonsyugi/kaigi/dai7/shiryou1.pdf.

Cabinet Secretariat. 2022b. *Kigyōkan no rōdō idō no enkatsuka, sukiringu, kōzōteki chingin hikiage ni kansuru kiso shiryō* [Basic Data on Smooth Inter-Company Labour Mobility, Skilling, and Structural Wage Increases], November 10. https://www.cas.go.jp/jp/seisaku/atarashii_sihonsyugi/kaigi/dai12/shiryou1.pdf.

Cabinet Secretariat. 2023a. *Kiso shiryō* [Basic Data Prepared for the 14th New Capitalism Meeting], February 15. https://www.cas.go.jp/jp/seisaku/atarashii_sihonsyugi/kaigi/dai14/shiryou1.pdf.

Cabinet Secretariat. 2023b. *Atarashii shihonshugi no suishin ni tsuite no jyūyou Jikō* [Important Points Regarding New Capitalism Promotion], September 27. https://www.cas.go.jp/jp/seisaku/atarashii_sihonsyugi/kaigi/dai22/juutenjikou_set.pdf.

Hirano, M., and I. Enatsu. 2018. *Jinji kanri: Hito to kigyō, tomoni ikiru tameni* [Human Resource Management]. Tokyo: Yuhikaku.

Honda, K. 2010. *Shufu pāto: Saidai no hiseiki koyō* [Housewives Working Part-Time: The Largest Non-Standard Employment]. Tokyo: Shueisha.

Igarashi, Y. 2015. "Gurōbaru-ka no saizensen ga toikakeru shatei [Range of Questions Raised by the Frontline of Globalisation]." In *Gurōbaru jinzai wo meguru seisaku to genjitsu* [Policies and Realities Surrounding Global Human Capital], edited by Y. Igarashi, J. Akashi, and H. Komai, 9–20. Tokyo: Akashi Shoten.

Iguchi, Y. 2016. "Gaikokujin rōdōsha mondai to shakai seisaku: Genjyō hyōka to aratana jidaino tenbō [Foreign Worker Problems and Social Policy: Evaluation of Current Situations and Considerations for New Era]." *Social Policy and Labor Studies* 8 (1): 8–28.

ILO (International Labour Organization). 2023. *The Value of Essential Work*. Geneva: International Labour Office.

Inagami, T., and D. H. Whittaker. 2005. *The New Community Firm: Employment, Governance and Management Reform in Japan*. Cambridge: Cambridge University Press.

Inoki, T., and Y. Higuchi. 1995. *Nihon no koyō shisutemu to rōdō shijō* [Japanese Employment Systems and Labour Markets]. Tokyo: Nikkei Business Publications.

IPA (Information-technology Promotion Agency, Japan). 2022. *Dejitaru jidaino sukiru henkaku tōni kansuru chōsa* [Survey on Skill Changes Etc. in Digital Age], April 14. https://www.ipa.go.jp/jinzai/chousa/qv6pgp000000bv6s-att/000097873.pdf.

ISA (Immigration Services Agency). 2023. *Ginō jisshū seido oyobi tokutei ginō seido no arikata ni kansuru yūshikisha kaigi, dai 12 kai* [The 12th Expert Meeting on Technical Intern Training and Specified Skilled Worker Programs], October 18. https://www.moj.go.jp/isa/policies/policies/03_00001.html.

Itami, H. 1987. *Jinpon shugi kigyō* [Network-Based Corporations]. Tokyo: Chikuma Shobō.

JHR (Japan Association of Human Resource Services Industry). 2023. *Jobu chenji tenshoku/saiyō jittai chōsa* [Suevey on Mid-Career Job Change and Recruitment], March 6. https://j-hr.or.jp/wp/wp-content/uploads/2a4e37cbe90d8e5d5d05c811aa885588.pdf.

JILPT (The Japan Institute for Labour Policy and Training). 2022. "Haken rōdōsha no dōitsu rōdō dōitsu chingin rūru shikō jōkyō to koronaka ni okeru shūgyō jōkyō ni kansuru chōsa [Survey on the Enactment of Equal Pay for Equal Work Rules for dispatched Workers and Employment Conditions During COVID-19]." *JILPT Survey Series* (219).

Kurosawa, T. 2022. "Tenshoku to chūto saiyō ni tsuite kangaeru: kyaria saiyō no torikumi wo chūshin ni [Considering Job Change and Mid-Career Recruitment: Centring on Career-Track Recruitment Practices]." *JILPT Labour Policy Forum* (1).

Labour Force Survey. 2009–22. "Statistics Bureau of Japan E-Stat Code: 00200531."

Leonhardt, D. 2023. "The Global Immigration Backlash." *The New York Times*, July 11.

ManpowerGroup. 2023. "Shūkatsu-ji ni dou kangaete ita? [What Were You Thinking During Job Hunting?]" October 11. https://www.manpowergroup.jp/client/jinji/231011.html.

METI (Ministry of Economy, Trade and Industry). 2023. *Yosan no pointo* [Budget Highlights]). Accessed February 2, 2024. https://www.meti.go.jp/main/yosan/yosan_fy2023/pdf/01.pdf.

MEXT (Ministry of Education, Culture, Sports, Science and Technology). 2023. *Hosei yosan jigyō betsu shiryō shū* [List of Projects Under Revised Budget]. Accessed February 2, 2024. https://www.mext.go.jp/content/20231129-ope_dev03-2.pdf.

MHLW (Ministry of Health, Labour and Welfare). 2019. *Chūto saiyō ni kakaru genjyō ni tsuite* [Current Mid-Career Recruitment Situations], September 27. https://www.mhlw.go.jp/content/12602000/000557900.pdf.

MHLW (Ministry of Health, Labour and Welfare). 2021. *Pāto taimu, yūki koyō rōdōsha sōgō jittai tyōsa* [Survey on Part-Time and Fixed-Term Employment]. Accessed October 24, 2023. https://www.mhlw.go.jp/toukei/list/170-1/2021/dl/2_04.pdf.

MHLW (Ministry of Health, Labour and Welfare). 2022. *Kōnenrēsha koyō jyōkyō tōno hōkoku* [Press Release on Employment Situations of the Elderly], December 16. https://www.mhlw.go.jp/content/11703000/000955633.pdf.

MHLW (Ministry of Health, Labour and Welfare). 2023a. *Hosei yosan an no shuyō shisaku shū* [Major Policies Under Revised Budget Plan]. Accessed February 2, 2024. https://www.mhlw.go.jp/wp/yosan/yosan/23hosei/dl/23hosei_20231110_01.pdf.

MHLW (Ministry of Health, Labour and Welfare). 2023b. *'Nenshū no kabe' heno tōmen no taiō saku* [Tentative Plans to Address 'Annual Income Walls'], September 27. https://www.mhlw.go.jp/content/12500000/001150703.pdf.

MHLW (Ministry of Health, Labour and Welfare). 2023c. *Rōdō keizai no bunseki: Jizoku tekina chin-age ni mukete* [Labour Economic Analysis: Toward Continuous Wage Increases]. Accessed October 24, 2023. https://www.mhlw.go.jp/wp/hakusyo/roudou/23/dl/23-1.pdf.

Miyajima, T., H. Fujimaki, S. Ishihara, and E. Suzuki. 2019. *Hirakareta imin shakai he* [Toward an Open Immigration Society]. Tokyo: Fujiwara-Shoten.

Mizuho Information and Research Institute. 2019. *IT jinzai jyukyū ni kansuru chōsa* [Survey on Supply-Demand of IT Workers]. Accessed October 24, 2023. https://www.meti.go.jp/policy/it_policy/jinzai/houkokusyo.pdf.

MLIT (Ministry of Land, Infrastructure, Transport and Tourism). 2023. *Shinjidai no inbaundo kakudai akushon puran* [Action Plan for Inbound Expansion in New Era], May 30. https://www.mlit.go.jp/kankocho/content/001612100.pdf.

Moriyama, T., and M. Yamagishi. 2020. "Kōrēsha no koyō ni kansuru chōsa [Survey on Employment of Older Persons]." *The Japan Institute for Labour Policy and Training (JILPT) Survey Series* (198).

Nagase, N. 2024. "Much to Be Done in Japan's Family and Gender Equality Policies." *Asia Pacific Business Review*. https://doi.org/10.1080/13602381.2024.2320546

Nakata, Y. 2024. "Remedying Japan's Deficient Investment in People." *Asia Pacific Business Review*. https://doi.org/10.1080/13602381.2024.2320549

Oishi, N. 2012. "The Limits of Immigration Policies: The Challenges of Highly Skilled Migration in Japan." *The American Behavioral Scientist* 56 (8): 1080–1100. https://doi.org/10.1177/0002764212441787.

Panos, G. A., K. Pouliakas, and A. Zangelidis. 2014. "Multiple Job Holding, Skill Diversification, and Mobility." *Industrial Relations* 53 (2): 223–272. https://doi.org/10.1111/irel.12055.

Persol Research and Consulting. 2021. *Fuku gyō ni kansuru chōsa* [Survey on Side-Jobs], August 11. https://rc.persol-group.co.jp/news/202108111000.html.

Raffiee, J., and J. Feng. 2014. "Should I Quit My Day Job?: A Hybrid Path to Entrepreneurship." *Academy of Management Journal* 57 (4): 936–963. https://doi.org/10.5465/amj.2012.0522.

Recruit Works Institute. 2015–23. *Chūto saiyō jittai chōsa* [Survey on Mid-Career Recruitment]. Accessed October 24, 2023. https://www.works-i.com/surveys/adoption/mid-career.html.

Saguchi, K. 2018. *Employment System in Japan: Theory, Institutions, and History*. Tokyo: Yuhikaku.

Sanmi-ittai no rōdō shijyō kaikaku no shishin [Guidelines for Trinity Labour Market Reforms], May 16, 2023. https://www.cas.go.jp/jp/seisaku/atarashii_sihonsyugi/pdf/roudousijou.pdf.

Sugeno, K. 2004. *Shin koyō shakai no hō* [New Laws on Employment Society]. Tokyo: Yuhikaku.

Survey on Employment Trends. 2012–23. "Statistics Bureau of Japan e-stat code: 00450073."

Tsuru, K., Y. Higuchi, and Y. Mizumachi. 2011. *Hiseiki koyō kaikaku* [Non-Standard Employment Reform]. Tokyo: Nippon Hyoron sha.

Watanabe, H. 2013. "Kigyō ni okeru kōdo gaikoku jinzai no ukeire to katsuyō ni kansuru chōsa [Survey on Companies' Recruitment and Utilisation of Highly-skilled Foreign Workers]." *The Japan Institute for Labour Policy and Training (JILPT) Survey Series* (110).

Yamada, A. 2009. "Kōreisha shūgyō ritsu no kitei yōin: teinen seido, chingin purofairu, rōdō kumiai no kouka [Regulatory Factors of the Elderly Employment Rate: Effects of Retirement Systems, Wage Profiles, and Labour Unions]." *The Japanese Journal of Labour Studies* (589): 4–19. August. Accessed February 17, 2024. https://www.jil.go.jp/institute/zassi/backnumber/2009/08/pdf/004-019.pdf.

Yamaguchi, Y. 2020. "Nihon no gaikokujin ukeire seisaku no hensen to kadai [The Transition and Challenges of Immigration Policy in Japan]." *Journal of the Faculty of Humanities, the University of Kitakyushu* (90): 87–108. Accessed February 17, 2024. https://ndlsearch.ndl.go.jp/books/R000000004-I030409060.

Zou, F. 2023. "An Emerging Labour Market Player: The Evolving Role of Employment Agencies in Japan and China." DPhil diss., University of Oxford.

Appendices

Appendix A. List of New Form of Capitalism Realization Council meeting topics

The following lists the New Form of Capitalism Realization Council (NCRC) meeting dates and topics. Topics particularly relevant to this paper are highlighted in **bold**. The NCRC meeting documents are available at the Cabinet Secretariat website: https://www.cas.go.jp/jp/seisaku/atarashii_sihonsyugi/index.html (accessed 21 January 2024). Documents from the 'new trinity' reform subcommittee meetings (also highlighted in **bold**) are also available at the Cabinet Secretariat website: https://www.cas.go.jp/jp/seisaku/atarashii_sihonsyugi/bunkakai/index.html (accessed 21 January 2024).

	Date	Topic(s)
1	26/10/2021	Japan's New form of Capitalism visions and its realizations
2	8/11/2021	Urgent Proposal: Pioneering the future with 'new capitalism' (draft)
3	26/11/2021	**Wage and human capital**
4	8/3/2022	Science and technology
5	12/4/2022	1. Rebuilding post-pandemic economic systems 2. Visualising non-financial information towards 'new capitalism'
6	28/4/2022	1. Multipolarization of economy and society 2. Public roles of private businesses
7	20/5/2022	**1. Human capital investment (wages, training, side-jobs, gender inequality, etc.)** 2. Fair exchanges, advocacy by Fair Trade Commission
8	31/5/2022	Grand Design and Action Plan for a New Form of Capitalism (draft)
9	7/6/2022	1. Grand Design and Action Plan for a New Form of Capitalism (draft) 2. Basic Policy on Economic and Fiscal Management and Reform 2022 (draft)
10	4/10/2022	1. Important economic measures for enacting Grand Design and Action Plan for a New Form of Capitalism (draft) **2. Strengthening support for SMEs along with general and minimum wage increases**
11	26/10/2022	Presentation and discussion by Rebecca Henderson: Reimagining Capitalism
12	10/11/2022	**Smooth inter-company labour mobility, re-skilling, structural wage increases**
13	28/11/2022	Startup Development Five-year Plan, Doubling Asset-based Income Plan
14	15/2/2023	**Re-skilling, labour mobility, structural wage increases**
15	29/3/2023	Follow-up: Grand Design and Action Plan for a New Form of Capitalism
16	12/4/2023	**Integrated Three-Pronged Labor Market Reforms** (*This is the government's provisional translation of what is referred to in this paper as 'new trinity' reforms)
17	25/4/2023	1. Additional considerations for science, technology, and innovation 2. Smooth company entry/exit for GX and DX
	26/4/2023	**First 'new trinity' reform subcommittee meeting (drafting guidelines)**
18	16/5/2023	**Guidelines for Integrated Three-Pronged Labor Market Reforms (draft)**
19	6/6/2023	Revisions for Grand Design and Action Plan for a New Form of Capitalism
20	16/6/2023	1. Grand Design and Action Plan for a New Form of Capitalism (2023 revision draft) 2. Basic Policy on Economic and Fiscal Management and Reform 2023 (draft)
21	31/8/2023	**Ways to move towards a virtuous cycle of growth and distribution, including wage and investment**
22	27/9/2023	Promotion of New form of Capitalism (draft)
23	25/10/2023	**1. Strengthening the supply side (labour reduction investment, employment of the elderly, re-skilling, etc.)** 2. Promoting 'content' industry (anime, games, manga, movies, music, broadcasting, etc.)
	16/11/2023	**Second 'new trinity' reform subcommittee meeting (case study)**
	14/12/2023	**Third 'new trinity' reform subcommittee meeting (case study)**
	18/12/2023	**Fourth 'new trinity' reform subcommittee meeting (case study)**
	15/1/2024	**Fifth 'new trinity' reform subcommittee meeting (case study)**

Appendix B. List of interviews

The following lists the interviews mentioned in this paper. They were all semi-structured 'elite' interviews that lasted between one and two hours. Interviews with employment agencies were centred around their business development, and interviews with other companies were centred around changes in their human resource strategies and practices. Interviews in 2019 were conducted in-person in Japan as part of my DPhil fieldwork research. Interviews in 2023 were conducted remotely and specifically for the purpose of this paper.

	Date(s)	Industry/company	Interviewee's title
A	5/4/2019, 28/5/2019	Employment agency	Business development manager
B	18/4/2019	Engineer dispatching agency	HR manager
C	22/4/2019, 29/5/2019	Employment agency	Consultant
D	24/4/2019	Consulting company	HR manager
E	9/5/2019, 13/6/2019	Employment agency	Chief editor of job magazines
F	15/5/2019	Insurance company	HR manager
G	22/5/2019	Engineering company	HR manager
H	27/5/2019	Advertising company	HR manager
I	31/5/2019	Employment agency	Consultant
J	2/10/2023	Member of the 'new trinity' reform subcommittee	
K	3/10/2023	Employment agency	Head of research centre

Japan's 'consensual' variety of digital capitalism and its global relevance

Harald Kümmerle ⓘ and Franz Waldenberger

ABSTRACT

Data regulation has been framed as a global battle between the market-driven US, the state-driven Chinese, and the rights-driven EU models. We argue that Japan is pursuing a distinct fourth, consensus-driven approach. It is based on soft regulation and aims at striking a balance between privacy concerns and commercial and public interests in the usage of data. The concept of consensus is deeply rooted in Japan's legal tradition. Its application to data regulation is apparent in the domestic certification scheme for information banks and the international initiative 'Data Free Flow with Trust'. We also show that Japan's COVID-19 counter-measures relied on data strategies fully compatible with its consensual regulatory model. By combining rights-driven and market-driven aspects, Japan can potentially mediate between the EU and the US regimes. Japan's approach also offers an attractive alternative for countries that do not want to pick a side in the Sino-American competition.

1. Introduction

It has been forecasted and increasingly becomes clear that the Fourth Industrial Revolution, driven by the widespread introduction of data technology, is not only impacting many parts of the economic system (Schwab 2016), but that the digital transformation, as it has been more generally termed, also changes how we as humans define ourselves and our relation to society. All this bears enormous opportunities as well as fundamental risks (Harari 2017). Like previous technological revolutions, digital transformation has not been unfolding in a uniform way, and much of its future course remains speculation. For example, geopolitical analyst Bremmer (2021) has considered digital transformation as leading to a 'technopolar' world order. As most of the dominant platform companies are based in the US and China, this order would be mostly bipolar. Even academic studies from Europe that comprehensively build on platform theory arrive at such a conclusion (Seemann 2021). The Russian war of aggression against Ukraine seems to confirm this view, as the provision of critical infrastructures in this conflict depends on decisions made by private US-based technology companies like SpaceX.

There are nevertheless good reasons to challenge the proposition of a bipolar digital order. It not only leaves out the regulatory power of the EU epitomized by the 'Brussels Effect' (Bradford 2020), but also the momentum regulatory schemes promoted by the Japanese government have been showing. For Bremmer (2023), Japan is still one of the five major economic powers besides the US, China, the EU and India, and has been instrumental for maintaining a unipolar military order, importantly by promoting the geopolitical concept of the Indo-Pacific. However, in the digital sphere, he ignores Japan's similarly important international initiative Data Free Flow with Trust (DFFT), which has been developing into a framework for the flow of data between countries (Arasasingham and Goodman 2023). Domestically, Japan's certification scheme for information banks offers new business models concerning data usage within a regulatory framework, which partially converges with the concept of data intermediaries promoted by the Data Governance Act of the EU (Kümmerle 2023a).

Our paper makes two arguments. Firstly, we outline how these two regulatory schemes promote a consensual variety of digital capitalism that deserves more attention, especially from Western scholars. The term consensual is borrowed from comparative law scholar John O. Haley, who characterized Japan's domestic governance as consensual (1991, 166–168) and positioned it as an 'antidote' to Western approaches that tend 'to equate effective enforcement of contractual undertakings and protection of private property with legal regimes and state power' (1991, 15). Secondly, we show that Japan has managed to elevate its consensus-driven approach to the international level in recent years. In times of systemic competition and momentous shifts in the international order, stakeholders especially in democratic states must take this into account. Japan's response to the COVID-19 pandemic provides evidence of the particular nature and workings of Japan's approach. In all countries, national responses depended on the collection and processing of data. Despite some shortcomings, Japan's consensus-driven regime was more successful than that of most other countries. China's drastic measures proved at first to be promising even in Western countries, but failed catastrophically in the end. The data dimension of the pandemic shows that the digital order in Asia cannot be reduced to a Chinese pole and that Japan's trajectory not only deserves attention, but also bears global relevance.

By discerning and interpreting developments inside of Japan and emerging from Japan, we apply the 'diffractive genealogy' approach from Science and Technology Studies (Barad 2007; Mauthner 2016). In this way, we can trace the emergence of ideas, concepts and narratives while paying attention to entanglements between different analytical levels. Our approach is attentive to local developments that have not been reflected in the Western-language literature and contributes to critical international relations scholarship (Zanotti 2021).

We proceed as follows. Section 2 outlines two important perspectives on capitalism in the digital age; that of 'surveillance capitalism' by economist Zuboff (2015, 2019) and that of 'regulatory models' by legal scholar Bradford (2023). Both perspectives are valuable for analytical purposes, and they also capture key categories and discourses that experts from various fields were in fact relying on while drafting regulations. In section 3, we trace the regulatory trajectories of information banks and Data Free Flow with Trust, assess their impact and discuss their relevance. We also show that, during the pandemic, data was used in a way that aligns with these regulatory schemes. Section 4 concludes the paper.

2. Perspectives

2.1. Surveillance capitalism

The origins of Shoshana Zuboff's concept of surveillance go back to work in her early career. In *In the Age of the Smart Machine: The Future of Work and Power* (1988), she showed how in digital settings, automating a process is intimately linked with gaining information about the process that can then be used for other purposes (see also Zuboff 1985). At that time, her case studies concerned single companies. However, surveillance capitalism extends to the digital economy in general, and was first described in detail in a paper from 2015 (Zuboff 2015). At its core, she develops what she later calls the 'behavioral surplus', which involves learning increasingly more about individuals' actions so as to be able to predict and potentially control future behaviour. In this way, companies configure environments and situations in which action becomes more predictable, while, at the same time, generating as many data points as possible in order to better such predictions (Curran 2023, 4).

Zuboff historically locates the birth of surveillance capitalism at Google following the burst of the Dotcom bubble and the terror attacks on 11 September 2001. As a consequence of the former, executives were incentivized to use data in ways they would have considered unethical before, and as a consequence of the latter, the US political establishment dropped earlier moves towards a strengthening of privacy. Instead, companies were allowed to gain deep insights into their user's lives on condition that they provided access to such data to national security organizations. Zuboff also highlights the promise of modelling human behaviour ever more closely as 'Social Physics' (Pentland 2014), an idea which can be traced back to 19th century France and has been criticized by sociologists of knowledge as being flawed (Adolf and Stehr 2018). However, the natural science approach to modelling behaviour has high currency among surveillance capitalists. Its instrumentalist logic is fundamentally indifferent to the freedom of individuals, a freedom Zuboff considers to be vital to democracy (Zuboff 2019). It is worth noting that Zuboff's reasoning gives a convincing explanation as to why the i-mode 'feature phone' ecosystem, which pioneered the mobile internet in the early 2000s (Steinberg 2019), was outcompeted: Unlike Google with its Android ecosystem, its operator NTT Docomo could not capitalize on the behavioural surplus at sufficient scale (Kümmerle 2022, 140).

To understand its influence, it is necessary to take into account the context in which surveillance capitalism was conceived. Parts of Zuboff's arguments were developed in an influential public debate that took place in the German newspaper *Frankfurter Allgemeine Zeitung* (FAZ) between 2013 and 2014, following the leaks of Edward Snowden and leading up to the election of the European Parliament.[1] The debate was initiated by Social Democrat politicians in Germany and strongly focused on the regulation of US tech giants,[2] but paid no attention to parallel developments in China. In Zuboff's (2019) book, the activities of Chinese surveillance capitalists are confined to the Chinese market, while US tech giants are seen to dominate the rest of the world. Zuboff strongly criticizes 'neoliberalism' as an ideology of unregulated markets that allowed surveillance capitalists to gain and maintain their dominance (Zuboff 2019). However, 'neoliberalist interests' may also prompt regulatory interventions against dominant platforms. For example, at the height of the migrant crisis in 2015, Facebook had to respond to a sudden request by the German government for hate speech moderation to contain social unrest (York 2021, 19–20). One driving force for this intervention at the time were business interests, which were delighted about the prospects of migrant labour supply (Süddeutsche Zeitung 2015).

2.2. Regulatory models

Even before the FAZ debate, Anu Bradford had in 2012 presented a justification as to why the EU could indeed decisively engage in regulating technology corporations: With the term 'Brussels effect', she pointed to 'the unprecedented and deeply underestimated global power that the European Union is exercising through its legal institutions and standards, and how it successfully exports that influence to the rest of the world' (Bradford 2012, 1). Covering many different topics, but also regulation of digital technology, her 2020 book on the topic bore the tongue-in-cheek subtitle *How the European Union Rules the World*. This was not without basis given that GDPR started to be applied two years earlier and had, in fact, already influenced many legislatures abroad. Still, she had to admit that while then-recent laws on privacy protection in China closely resembled the European model de jure, the de facto impact was markedly different due to drastically different political environments. In her 2023 book *Digital Empires: The Global Battle to Regulate Technology*, Bradford took into account such complexities, and also divergences that had happened in the meantime like the Schrems II judgement in 2020, which declared the EU-US Privacy Shield invalid, restricting the flow of personal data between the EU and the US and thereby confirming the non-adequacy of the underlying data protection regimes (Bradford 2023). The book identifies 'three leading regulatory models [that] could be thought of as representing three "varieties of digital capitalism" – drawing on different theories about the relationship between markets, the state, and individual and collective rights. As described throughout this book, the US has pioneered a largely *market-driven* model, China a *state-driven* model, and the EU a *rights-driven* model' (2023, 6–7). She detects a convergence between the EU and the US models, and clarifies that 'the direction of that convergence comes from the US adjusting towards the EU model' (2023, 369). As a likely outcome, 'the US and the EU would jointly lead the coalition of techno-democracies to challenge digital authoritarian norms and values embraced by China and its ideological allies' (2023, 387).

While Bradford's perspective provides an important starting point, it also has some shortcomings. As mentioned above, while the EU regulatory power aims at protecting both 'individual and collective rights' (2023, 25), the legal tools can and have been appropriated by autocracies. The German NetzDG (*Netzwerkdurchsetzungsgesetz*) of 2017, which introduced compliance rules for internet content providers regarding the quick handling of complaints concerning unlawful content, was soon copied almost exactly by Russia and Turkey (York 2021, 45), and as Bradford notes (2023, 141), the new European Digital Services Act (DSA) may unleash a similar dynamic. While Germany's – then ad-hoc – pressure during the migrant crisis in 2015 on Facebook can be justified on the grounds of hate speech moderation, the same legal basis has been used for building a 'sovereign internet' in authoritarian countries (Thumfart 2022). The argument has also been made in the other direction. Maximilian Mayer, an international relations scholar focusing on science and technology policy, has pointed out that authoritarian practices using digital technology are proliferating not only in China, but also in the US and the EU. He argues that if Westerners associate the spread of these practices particularly with China, they risk falling prey to 'digital orientalism', mirroring 'Western discourses [that] portray other cultures and societies as different and problematic' (Mayer 2020, 177). While Mayer correctly points out a dynamic that runs counter to Bradford's hope of techno-democracies confronting techno-autocracies, he too discounts the possibility that Japan is on a trajectory that justifies particular attention.

3. Creating consensual surveillance

3.1. Information banks

In Japan, information banks (*jōhō ginkō*)[3] a low individuals to 'deposit' personal data, which the banks then 'lend', in aggregated form, to third parties, where the data can generate 'value'. Although the term bank is used, the intermediation is not limited to commercial applications. Compared to the market-driven approach, information banks provide more transparency, both with regard to data usage and the mutual benefit to be gained from the cooperation. As a result, individuals can exercise more control over how their data is used and may expect a fairer share in the value added. Together with other types of data collecting and processing systems, information banks are supposed to become part of a market-driven Japanese data space. In order to standardize such spaces internationally, Japanese engineers are developing the standard IEEE P3800 (Mano 2021). The functionality can also be integrated into the business of a traditional bank (Hatakeyama 2022). To help information banks gain trust from individuals, a certification scheme has been devised using a multi-stakeholder approach. However, the operation of information banks does not require official certification.

The information bank concept can be considered Japanese in origin. While the first official certification scheme for information banks had been put in place in 2018, its origins can be traced back to the 2000s. In 2008, the year when the iPhone was introduced in Japan and when most cell phones in the domestic market were feature phones running on platforms like NTT Docomo's i-mode, the information bank had already acquired the nature of a larger project. Emerging from research at the University of Tokyo, an 'information bank task force' included members from companies like NTT, Yahoo and Panasonic and served as part of the *Working Group for the Maintenance of the Value Chain of the Near Future* that had been set up by the Next Generation Electronic Commerce Promotion Council of Japan (ECOM), an industry alliance. In addition to personal information like recorded activities, specifically concerning shopping and medicine, information banks in this conceptualization could also use a variety of sensor data. They were designed for the age of ubiquitous computing, the goal being to show 'the information necessary to myself at one glance' (Kin-mirai Baryūchēn Seibi Gurūpu 2009, 3, 14).

Much conceptual work was carried out in the following years. The emerging designs required information bank operators to obtain explicit consent from individuals for using their data. The yearly MyData conferences provided important input on how to concretize information banks in concordance with international trends in data protection. At the first such conference in 2016, which took place in Finland and became a formative step for activists in the MyData community, two leaders of the Japanese project introduced the idea of information banks in great generality under the title 'Risk or Asset? How to change people's recognition of personal information: Social-design approach using a metaphor of "bank"' (Shibasaki and Sunahara 2016). Japanese members have since regularly introduced their system at the yearly conferences. As far as is reflected in the sparse literature on the topic, this open attitude towards making use of personal information did not resonate overly well. A Japanese participant had the impression that many thought the system was estranged from the spirit of the movement. Reportedly, the certification scheme gained in acceptance in the movement after the requirements for user assent were made more strict (Sasaki, Haruyama, and Shida 2020, 167). Although the GDPR had not been in effect yet, this outcome can be considered a manifestation of an anticipated de facto Brussels effect (Kümmerle 2023a, 199).

By 2018, detailed regulations for information banks had been drafted by a public–private initiative between the Ministry of Internal Affairs and Communications (MIC) and the Ministry of Economy, Trade and Industry (METI) on the one side, and the Information Technology Federation of Japan (IT Renmei) on the other side. While devising these regulations, fundamental questions concerning trust and economic institutions had to be sorted out in detail (Sakashita 2022, 248–251). The resulting version 1.0 of the MIC's Guidebook did not allow for the handling of health information; it was nevertheless adopted as a basis for the certification scheme even though right from the beginning this limitation was considered to considerably constrain the scope of business applications. Despite all the efforts put in by the public–private partnership, almost 80% of people, according to a government poll in 2019, answered they 'did not want to use' information banks unless they were provided with concrete examples (Nikkei 2019). Privacy law specialists pointed out that the data protection regime in Japan was still not as strict as in the EU, specifically that fines in the case of data leaks were much lower.

Can information banks be expected to prosper? Information banks represent a kind of synthesis between the EU rights-driven and the US market-driven approach. The rights-driven element, however, introduces extra setup costs. Consensus requires much more ex-ante communication and persuasion than implicit arrangements for data usage in exchange for convenience and often free of charge services. Informed consent presupposes that potential customers are not only willing to afford the time, but also have the cognitive abilities to understand the technical and legal details. They are forced to reflect on whether they are willing to trust the intermediary they are dealing with. In Zuboff's perspective, surveillance capitalists have succeeded in undermining the concept of informed consent (2019). The same fundamental critique can be applied to data intermediaries defined by EU regulations.

Being a domestic scheme, the success of information banks also depends on how concerned Japanese people are about their privacy. The difficulties of the Japanese government with the introduction of the MyNumber card following the implementation of the MyNumber ID system in 2016 indicate that Japanese citizens have a strong preference for privacy and little trust in the government's intentions or capabilities to duly serve their concerns (Nemoto 2018). The still widespread use of cash payments might be interpreted in the same way. On the other hand, Japanese consumers are very fond of using loyalty point systems (Okina 2022), which allow companies to record their shopping history. E-commerce and social media have been equally well accepted in Japan. Recent steps by Softbank aimed at integrating existing domestic data platforms could make the company a surveillance capitalist (Kümmerle 2022, 146–147). Privacy concerns of Japanese citizens are clearly not strong enough to contain such development.

By June 2022, seven companies had obtained a TPDMS ('Trusted Personal Data Management Service') certification from the Information Technology Federation of Japan, which meant that they complied with MIC's version 1.0 guidebook for information banks. Acquiring the certification is often considered a pragmatic choice for companies who aim at developing more comprehensive business models (Kümmerle 2023a, 200–201). One noteworthy example is a regional information bank operated by Chubu Electric Power in the city of Toyota, seat of the automotive company Toyota and one of the most advanced smart cities in Japan; the following refers to the situation in early 2020. When starting the app called MINLY, a virtual avatar with a chatbot function provided a detailed explanation about the service and what the information would be used for. Chubu Electric Power considered it important that users were aware of how the app worked, including its inevitable risks. Knowing that this would stop many from even finishing with the registration, it nevertheless ensured that user consent was in fact informed and thus meaningful. Users had to enter manually their place of living, the composition of their family, their hobbies and their interests, information on when and how long they usually went out during a week, and the like. Apart from this manually entered information, they would also provide information through sharing their search history on events, their history of purchases, and confirmations that they read or liked incoming offers and notifications. With growing engagement, it was expected that the information users received from companies would steadily better match what they were most interested in. According to the lead developer, expanding cooperation with other municipalities and combining traffic data from Mobility as a Service (MaaS) could create additional value streams (Morita 2020, 182–189).

In connection with the use case of this application, researchers have pointed out that the benefit provided to customers for their information can also be non-monetary, and that this would be one of the most beneficial scenarios. Thus, especially for regional information banks, users are likely to see value in engaging with the community beyond their own financial gain (Kümmerle 2023a, 202–203). Based on the experience gained during the COVID-19 pandemic, among other reasons, the MIC's guidebook was revised so as to allow the usage of certain types of health information. Creating information banks that handle this type of information is now in fact part of the policy for regional development (Kanzaki 2022). That regional projects with a strong public policy character can win wide support among citizens, especially in the field of healthcare, is exemplified by the Iwaki Health Promotion Project initiated in 2005 by the city of Hirosaki in Aomori Prefecture and Hirosaki University. The project 'has been producing the world's largest number of health data with more than 3000 items recorded per person per year' (Nakaji et al. 2021, 6). Numerous research institutions and companies are now collaborating with the project, allowing them to use the data for scientific and business purposes.

One important element in Japan's approach is the fact that not all of the companies that operate information bank-like services as part of their business are required to be officially certified. This is of course in line with the consensus principle, as nobody is obliged to accept the certification model. Non-certified information banks are likely to benefit from the general awareness created by the promotion of the government scheme.

Dai-Nippon Insatsu has set up information banks for third parties including providers of fitness-related apps. A certification was only obtained in March 2023 following the MIC's version 2.2 guidebook that allowed for using less sensitive health information (Nihon IT Dantai Renmei 2023). Even if strict government criteria are not applied, the basic idea of information banks is still preserved. By avoiding some of the setup costs implied by certification, non-certified information banks can strike a better balance between the value and the cost of providing transparency and obtaining consent.

3.2. Data Free Flow with Trust

Unlike information banks, which represent an intermediation scheme for personal data within Japan, Data Free Flow with Trust (DFFT) is primarily concerned with the cross-border flow of non-personal data. The term 'flow' is very general and does not presuppose any specific mode of exchange. DFFT, too, can be traced back to at least the 2000s. The First National Strategy on Information Security framed Japan as 'a nation which should be revitalized by the value of trustworthiness' and stipulated that its 'efforts in information security would be applied on a global scale as the "Japan Model"' (Information Security Policy Council 2006, 5). This sounded ambitious, because, in international comparisons, Japanese users seemed to have relatively little trust in exchanges on the internet at that time (Kimura 2010).

It was at the World Economic Forum in Davos in January 2019 that Prime Minister Abe introduced DFFT in a speech entitled 'Toward a New Era of "Hope-driven Economy"' (Abe 2019). The vision, while not concrete at this stage, was consistent with already existing Japanese regulation, as metaphors of data flowing smoothly, though not freely, had already been well established in Japan: Five of the six times the word 'flow' (*ryūtsū*) appeared in the text of the Basic Act on the Advancement of Public and Private Sector Data Utilization that was passed in December 2016, it appeared as 'smooth flow' (*enkatsu na ryūtsū*) (Digital Agency 2023a). It was compatible internationally, as the EU had officially signalled support for the 'free flow of non-personal data' (European Commission 2017) a few years earlier, at least in as far as it was confined to the European market. Using the – in the strict sense, false, but productive – binary opposition of personal and non-personal data, Abe declared much more radically: 'We must, on one hand, be able to put our personal data and data embodying intellectual property, national security intelligence, and so on, under careful protection, while on the other hand, we must enable the free flow of medical, industrial, traffic and other most useful, non-personal, anonymous data to see no borders, repeat, no borders' (Abe 2019). This bore universalist undertones. It also aimed to bridge political systems: In a speech in October 2020 before the Japanese National Diet, Abe emphasized that he had gained support from both President Donald Trump and Chairman Xi Jinping for DFFT and that the 'Osaka Track' was progressing under the auspices of the WTO, where Japan was a co-convenor of the Joint Statement Initiative on E-Commerce. Abe went on to recall that Japan had, 100 years ago, proposed the principle of the equality of races at the Peace Conference of Versailles (Shushō Kantei 2019). However, just as the proposal for the equality of races was not adopted in Versailles, the 'Osaka Track' promoting DFFT had already encountered opposition at the G20 meeting in Osaka earlier that year, when India, Indonesia and South Africa decided to opt out (Goodman 2021). China and Russia had signed it even though their own national regulatory trajectories appeared incompatible. That the initiative continued under the auspices of the WTO was a very meagre outcome given the WTO's de-facto dysfunctionality in face of rising rivalry between the US and China and consequent protectionist policies.

It was only in 2021, that DFFT regained momentum following a clear change in public perception concerning the importance of trust for data flows. A scandal involving the messaging app LINE revealed that Chinese subcontractors of Japanese companies had to provide access to personal information of LINE users in accordance with the Chinese National Intelligence Law. This new sense of danger was increased when the US, the UK, Canada and the EU imposed sanctions on several officials involved in the oppression of the Uighur Muslim population in the Chinese province of Xinjiang, and China reacted with counter-sanctions. This allowed proponents of economic security in Japan to significantly gather momentum for their agenda (Kümmerle 2022, 148–151), and contributed to a notable shift away from the former 'Osaka Track'. The National Data Strategy from June 2021 emphasized that DFFT should be promoted with 'like-minded countries' (National Strategy Office of IT, Cabinet Secretariat 2021, 22), and the focus shifted to the G7.

At the G7 meetings in 2021 (UK) and 2022 (Germany), the DFFT concept was further developed and concretized, and at the G7 meetings in 2023 in Japan, the decision was made to establish a permanent institution coordinating DFFT, the so-called Institutional Arrangement for Partnership (IAP) that will be hosted in the framework of the OECD. While the IAP's structure still leaves much room for priority-setting, an excerpt of the final agreement on its establishment reflects both pragmatism and an acknowledgement of new geopolitical realities: 'The COVID-19 crisis and current global situation has demonstrated the value and need for like-minded partners to find consensus on approaches to data sharing in priority sectors [...]' (G7 Digital and Tech Track 2023). While these developments occurred in the context of the G7, the influence of DFFT is supposed to go far beyond it. In schemes of the Japanese Ministry of Economy, Trade and Industry (METI), DFFT is portrayed as defining the rules for data flows between data spaces, for example those of EU's GAIA-X, those of Japan's Ouranos, and equivalent systems in the US and in ASEAN countries (METI 2023).

While Japan has been able to strongly leverage its position as a G7 member, its promotion of DFFT also happened as a form of 'neo-middle-power diplomacy'.[4] At the meeting of the G7 Digital Ministers in Takasaki in April 2023, the Japanese Digital Minister emphasized the attendance of India and Indonesia as two representatives of the Global South who rapidly drive innovation (Dejitaru Chō 2023). While this made sense given that India was presiding over the G20 and Indonesia was presiding over ASEAN that year, it is also notable given their opposition to DFFT at the Osaka Track in 2019. India was represented at the Stakeholders' Conference on Digital Technologies for Trust that took place in March 2023, in the leadup to the official G7 meetings (Digital Agency 2023b); the working groups and stakeholders cooperating at the IAP will doubtless take developments in India and ASEAN countries into account while concretizing DFFT.

Japan's recent demonstration of leadership in such areas as infrastructure, trade and economic security provide good reasons why the country may also create a momentum for trust-enhancing policies in the area of cross-border data flows. Japan's infrastructural investments abroad, especially in Asia, are wielding considerable influence. Although they are receiving far less attention internationally than China's Belt and Road Initiative (BRI), Japanese infrastructure investments are of similar magnitude in South and Southeast Asia. Confronting China's Belt and Road Initiative, Japan's Partnership of Quality Infrastructure launched in 2015 and was supposed to give Japanese companies an advantage. The Japanese 'quality principle' has consequently been adapted by the G7, the G20 and the OECD. Indeed, the G7 integrated 'quality' in the 2021 'Build Back Better' framework of the Biden administration and the 2022 Partnership for Global Infrastructure and Investment. Moreover, Japan was instrumental in bringing the TPP – renamed as CPTPP – to a conclusion after the US had pulled out, while also playing an important role in the less ambitious RCEP in which China is the biggest economy (Pascha 2022, 56–59). As a geo-economic actor, Japan's 'mobilisation of smaller countries to create coalitions of the "like-minded" has been able to maintain and promote a liberal international order, offering such countries an alternative to having to choose between supporting either China or the US' (Koshino and Ward 2022, 130).

3.3. Response during the COVID-19 pandemic

Characteristics of Japan's consensual variety of digital capitalism became manifest during the COVID-19 pandemic. The country devised a response that was unique in its focus on infection clusters. While many countries engaged in large-scale data collection and processing as they pursued the basic tasks of systematically carrying out PCR testing, isolating infected persons and tracing contacts, Japan's approach showed some specific characteristics, which were closely related to the country's National Data Strategy.

The dense network of public health centres at the municipal level provided the basis for the Japanese response. When a person tested positive, personnel at these centres aimed to create a detailed contact log in order to get a clear picture on the infection path both in its spatial and temporal dimensions. Based on early data in this form, Japanese health experts decided to focus on infection clusters, which, according to their calculations, would reduce the spread of the virus without aiming for elimination. Information on these clusters was categorized and circulated in anonymized and simplified form. In this sense, the health centres served as data intermediaries similar to information banks, and the 'free flow' and the 'open data' governance paradigm fostered a transparent communication of cluster data. On this basis, decisions for or against restrictions were made and justified (Kümmerle 2023b, 61–62).

There were other factors that contributed to the early decision to focus on clusters, particularly the very limited availability of PCR tests. The national strategy devised in late March 2020 did not opt for strict lockdowns, but instead called on citizens to engage in 'self-restraint' (*jishuku*) – particularly by not going out – depending on the number of infections in the specific region. The possibility that health centres could not reliably trace infections due to overload was explicitly accounted for: In that case, the 'core' (*shutai*) of cluster countermeasures would shift towards the health and care facilities (Oshitani 2020a, 29). Although the PCR testing capacity was increased, this happened much more slowly than in other developed economies. However, this does not explain why Japan was not following comprehensive testing strategies implemented elsewhere. Lead virologist Hitoshi Oshitani justified the decision to limit access to PCR testing throughout the

JAPAN'S 'CONSENSUAL' VARIETY OF DIGITAL CAPITALISM

pandemic on the basis that the virus also spread among people with only light or no symptoms (Oshitani 2020b, 2022, 8).

Japan's government earned much criticism from the public for its deviation from the WHO's explicit recommendation to carry out widespread testing. Municipalities that, contrary to the national strategy, allowed easy access to PCR testing reportedly fared better both in terms of containing infections and in terms of public approval (NIRA Sōgō Kenkyū Kaihatsu Kikan 2020, 12–13). Still, it was essential that the public largely followed the non-binding self-restraint requests of the national and local governments, in line with Haley's model of consensual governance (Kodama 2023, 2). On a darker note, but also consistent with the model, there were citizens who openly enacted 'self-restraint policing', enforcing the government's requests through publicly shaming those who did not comply. A legal basis for sanctioning persons and venues for non-compliance with pandemic rules was introduced on the national level in February 2021, but even then, strict lockdown measures were not implemented.

Since the contact tracing in health centres was mostly carried out by telephone and most of the data was entered manually, it may appear as if Japan's pandemic response can hardly be connected to digitalization. However, this is far from true. Japan's official tracing app used the iOS and Android framework, both of which applied privacy norms. This meant that Japan was the only country in East Asia to implement a privacy-first instead of a data-first solution (Fahey and Hino 2020, 3). The analysis of early tracing data concluded that most clusters occurred in closed and crowded spaces and close-contact settings. The rule to avoid the '3Cs' (crowded places, confined spaces and close-contact settings), which was widely communicated to the public already in March 2020, constituted a core element in Japan's strategy. Depending on the evolution of the infection rate, public venues were supposed to reduce capacity and allow for adequate distancing. The most advanced aspect in the usage of data technology was the simulations on the spread of the virus through aerosol and droplet simulations with Fugaku, the then fastest supercomputer in the world. The results of these simulations, particularly on how to adjust environments and behaviour in high-risk settings, were communicated to the institutions involved and to the broader public through mass media. This approach of optimizing environments and social behaviour based on data modelling applied the concept of 'data assimilation' as envisioned in the digital strategy documents of Society 5.0 (Kümmerle 2023b, 61). While it required intensive private-public sector cooperation, the data gathered through health surveillance and later used in aggregated form could not be connected to any specific person or group. Again, the implementation of the simulation results had to rely on consensus and social self-monitoring.

Although these measures cannot fully explain the positive outcomes like the very low per-capita mortality in Japan, they certainly contributed to informed decisions on how to operate public facilities and control the risk of infection without overly strong restrictions. This was especially marked in late 2020 to early 2021, when vaccines were not yet widely available and many countries declared a lockdown. In Germany, for example, all schools closed in December 2020 and remained so well into 2021. In hindsight, German health officials stated that the closing had been unnecessary, but that the decision had been made based on the scientific knowledge available at the time (Das Erste 2023). Japan, on the other hand, avoided such extreme measures. Many schools that could switch to online classes did so, while municipalities made their decisions based on the information available to them, including the results of the aerosol and droplet simulations (Kümmerle 2023b, 62). The well-founded assumption that teachers and students would be engaging in self-restraint, for example with regard to mask-wearing and distancing, represented another important element in the effectiveness of Japan's consensual variety of digital capitalism during the COVID-19 pandemic.

4. Conclusion and wider implications

In this paper, we set out to show that Japan pursues a distinct regulatory approach to digital transformation. At the domestic level, this approach can be seen in the regulatory scheme of information banks. At the international level, it shows in Japan's initiative for DFFT. Defining features of Japan's approach are soft regulations, multi-stakeholder involvement and a consensus orientation. The aim is to strike a balance between privacy concerns and commercial and public interests in the usage of data. Borrowing from Bradford's terminology, we characterize Japan's approach as a consensual variety of digital capitalism and show that surveillance operates differently from Zuboff's characterization in the US case. We further argue that the Japanese consensus-driven regulatory model constitutes an important alternative to the US market-driven, the Chinese state-driven and the EU rights-driven regulatory models.

While in August 2020 Japan's later Minister of Digital Affairs declared that the country had suffered 'digital defeat' in its pandemic response (Hirai 2020), we see Japan's counter-measures as evidence that the consensual nature of Japan's digital capitalism had been effective. The future success of information banks will largely depend on whether the higher set-up costs implied by their consensual nature will be outweighed by the value generated by the usage of data, including the portion which can be appropriated by those who provide their personal data. As examples show, value need not to be confined to pecuniary benefits, but may include more general rewards such as the personal satisfaction of contributing to the achievement of social policy goals at local or regional levels. DFFT has already established itself as a promising framework within the OECD as shown by the recent decision to establish the IAP for coordinating DFFT. Japan's 'neo-middle-power' diplomacy in the Indo-Pacific will be essential for winning support among 'like-minded' developing countries.

Political scientist Herfried Münkler conceptualized digital transformation as a spatial revolution that would make the empires of the present more akin to sea empires than to land empires. For the former, a major source of power is the establishment of rules concerning flows, including those of data (Münkler 2017, 324–325). Since Japan has taken a leading role in the rulemaking process of DFFT, it can be expected to substantially profit from shaping the norms of 'trust' and 'free flow' of data streams. As a digital empire, Japan can mediate between the EU and the US and at the same time use neo-middle-power diplomacy by engaging countries that do not want to pick a side in the Sino-American competition.

Many scholars in the field of international relations and science and technology studies tend to analyse the digital future within a two or three-polar world, where Japan's trajectory is either ignored (Mayer 2020) or seen to be confined by the insularity of its ecosystem (Bratton 2015, 60). We hope to have shown that this is mistaken. Japan's consensus-driven regulatory regime represents a distinct and important alternative to the widely discussed US, Chinese and EU regimes. More analyses of Japan's approach need to be undertaken. They should not just be done in isolation as studies on Japan, but should be positioned as contributions to global discourses on digital futures.

Notes

1. The debate was later published in book form (Schirrmacher 2015) and Zuboff references several articles from it in (Zuboff 2015).
2. Not coincidentally, Zuboff's book (Zuboff 2019) shows optimism towards European regulation like the General Data Protection Regulation (GDPR) (Lucas 2020).
3. The Japanese Act on the Protection of Personal Information (APPI), which corresponds to the European General Data Protection Regulation (GDPR), uses the term *kojin jōhō*, despite the fact that there would have been a literal translation of personal data (*kojin dēta*). Generally, legal texts do not offer a clear distinction between data and information (Bygrave 2015).
4. '[M]iddle powers in the Indo-Pacific are engaging in a new type of diplomacy, one that includes lobbying, insulating, and rulemaking in the realms of security, trade, and international law, to protect their national interests from Sino-U.S. strategic competition' (Nagy 2022, 162).

Disclosure statement

No potential conflict of interest was reported by the author(s).

ORCID

Harald Kümmerle (iD) http://orcid.org/0000-0001-8804-5278

References

Abe, S. 2019. "Speech by Prime Minister Abe at the World Economic Forum Annual Meeting." *Ministry of Foreign Affairs of Japan*. Accessed December 9, 2021. https://www.mofa.go.jp/ecm/ec/page4e_000973.html.

Adolf, M. T., and N. Stehr. 2018. "Information, Knowledge, and the Return of Social Physics." *Administration & Society* 50 (9): 1238–1258. https://doi.org/10.1177/0095399718760585.

Arasasingham, A., and M. P. Goodman. 2023. "Operationalizing Data Free Flow with Trust (DFFT)." *CSIS Briefs* 2023 (4). CSIS: Center for Strategic and International Studies, Washington, DC.

Barad, K. 2007. *Meeting the Universe Halfway: Quantum Physics and the Entanglement of Matter and Meaning*. Durham: Duke University Press.

Bradford, A. 2012. "The Brussels Effect." *Northwestern University Law Review* 107:1–68.

Bradford, A. 2020. *The Brussels Effect: How the European Union Rules the World*. New York: Oxford University Press.

Bradford, A. 2023. *Digital Empires: The Global Battle to Regulate Technology*. New York: Oxford University Press.

Bratton, B. H. 2015. *The Stack: On Software and Sovereignty*. Cambridge, Massachusetts: The MIT Press.

Bremmer, I. 2021. "The Technopolar Moment." *Foreign Affairs* 100 (6).

Bremmer, I. 2023. "The Next Global Superpower Isn't Who You Think." *Foreign Policy*. Accessed June 9, 2023. https://foreignpolicy.com/2023/06/17/china-russia-us-multipolar-world-technology/.

Bygrave, L. A. 2015. "Information Concepts in Law: Generic Dreams and Definitional Daylight." *Oxford Journal of Legal Studies* 35 (1): 91–120. https://doi.org/10.1093/ojls/gqu011.

Curran, D. 2023. "Surveillance Capitalism and Systemic Digital Risk: The Imperative to Collect and Connect and the Risks of Interconnectedness." *Big Data & Society* 10 (1): 20539517231177620. https://doi.org/10.1177/20539517231177621.

Das Erste. 2023. "Lauterbach: Lange Schulschließungen rückblickend unnötig." *Das Erste*. Accessed February 13, 2023. https://www.daserste.de/information/politik-weltgeschehen/morgenmaga zin/politik/Bundesgesundheitsminister-Karl-Lauterbach-lange-Schulschliessungen-rueckblickend-unnoetig-100.html.

Dejitaru Chō. 2023. "Kōno-daijin kisha kaiken G7 gichō koku kisha kaiken, Reiwa 4 gatsu 30 nichi [Minister Kōno at the press conference of the G7 presidency, 30 April 2023]." *Dejitaru Chō*. Accessed October 25, 2023. https://www.digital.go.jp/speech/minister-230430-01.

Digital Agency. 2023a. "Kanmin dēta katsuyō suishin kihon hō" [Basic law for the promotion public-private data usage]. *e-GOV hōrei kensaku*. Accessed October 31. https://elaws.e-gov.go.jp/docu ment?lawid=428AC1000000103.

Digital Agency. 2023b. "Stakeholders' Conference on Digital Technologies for Trust Was Held." *Digital Agency*. Accessed October 31, 2023. https://www.digital.go.jp/en/ab120c32-4495-4372-b10b-ae5f635b280f-en.

European Commission. 2017. "State of the Union 2017: A Framework for the Free Flow of Non-Personal Data in the EU." *European Commission*. Accessed May 12, 2023. https://ec.europa.eu/commission/presscorner/detail/en/IP_17_3190.

Fahey, R. A., and A. Hino. 2020. "COVID-19, Digital Privacy, and the Social Limits on Data-Focused Public Health Responses." *International Journal of Information Management* 55:102181. https://doi.org/10.1016/j.ijinfomgt.2020.102181.

G7 Digital and Tech Track. 2023. "G7 Digital and Tech Track - Annex 1: Annex on G7 Vision for Operationalising DFFT and Its Priorities." *G7 Japan 2023*. Accessed October 29, 2023. https://www.meti.go.jp/press/2023/04/20230430001/20230430001-ANNEX1.pdf.

Goodman, M. P. 2021. "Advancing Data Governance in the G7." *CSIS: Center for Strategic and International Studies*. Accessed August 15, 2021. https://www.csis.org/analysis/advancing-data-governance-g7.

Haley, J. O. 1991. *Authority without Power: Law and the Japanese Paradox*. New York: Oxford University Press.

Harari, Y. N. 2017. *Homo Deus: A Brief History of Tomorrow*. New York: Harper.

Hatakeyama, H. 2022. "Jōhō ginkō No ginkō hō Oyobi kin'yū shōhin Torihiki hō Nado No Toriatsukai Ni Tsuite - gyōmu han'i No Kaisei: Reiji Fuzui gyōmu No Tsuika" [On the Application of the Banking Act and the Financial Instruments and Exchange Act in Relation to Information Banks – Revision of the Scope of Duties: Addition of the Duty to Provide Examples]. In *Dejitaru-Ka Shakai Ni Okeru Atarashii Zaisanteki Kachi to Shintaku [Trust and New Asset Values in a Society Undergoing Digital transformation]*, edited by I. Gotō, 302–316. Tōkyō: Shōji Hōmu.

Hirai, T. 2020. "Dejitaru gyōsei - Jimin, Dejitaru Shakai Suishin Tokubetsu iinchō Hirai Takuya-Shi, shireitō Soshiki de Yosan haibun" [Digital Administration – Hirai Takuya, Head of the LDP's Digital Society Promotion Committee, Budget Allocation Using a Control Tower Like Organization]. *Nihon Keizai Shinbun*, August 28, 2020. (morning edition): 4.

Information Security Policy Council. 2006. The First National Strategy on Information Security - "Toward the Realization of a Trustworthy society". Accessed October 12, 2022. https://www.nisc.go.jp/eng/pdf/national_strategy_001_eng.pdf.

Kanzaki, T. 2022. "dejitaru den'en kenkō Tokku, Kibi Chūō Chō Nado 3 shichō shitei" [Specially Designated Digital Garden Health Districts, the Three Cities and Towns Kibi, Chūō and Chō Designated]. *Asahi Shinbun Digital.* March 21, 2022. Accessed March 22, 2022. https://www.asahi.com/articles/ASQ3N6RHSQ3CPPZB00N.html.

Kimura, T., 2010. "The digital divide as cultural practice: A cognitive anthropological exploration of Japan as an 'information society'." Ph.D. Thesis, New York: State University of New York at Buffalo.

Kin-mirai Baryūchēn Seibi Gurūpu. 2009. *Kin-Mirai baryūchēn Kiban Seibi gurūpu WG katsudō hōkoku Sho 2009* [*2009 Activities Report by the Working Group for the Maintenance of the Value Chain of the Near Future*]. Tokyo: Ji-sedai Denshi Shō Torihiki Suishin Kyōgikai.

Kodama, S. 2023. "Ethical Challenges of the COVID-19 Pandemic: A Japanese Perspective." *Journal of Medical Internet Research* 25:e44820. https://doi.org/10.2196/44820.

Koshino, Y., and R. Ward. 2022. *Japan's Effectiveness as a Geo-Economic Actor: Navigating Great-Power Competition.* Abingdon, Oxon: Routledge.

Kümmerle, H. 2022. "Japanese Data Strategies, Global Surveillance Capitalism, and the "LINE Problem"." *Matter: Journal of New Materialist Research* 3 (1): 134–159. https://doi.org/10.1344/jnmr.v3i1.38966.

Kümmerle, H. 2023a. "More Than a Certification Scheme: Information Banks in Japan Under Changing Norms of Data Usage." In *Adopting and Adapting Innovation in Japan's Digital Transformation*, edited by A. Khare and W. W. Baber, 193–211. Singapore: Springer. https://doi.org/10.1007/978-981-99-0321-4_12.

Kümmerle, H. 2023b. "On the Relation Between Japan's COVID-19 Response and the National Data Strategy." In *The SSI 2023 Annual Conference Proceedings*, 60–64. Tōkyō: The Society of Socio-Informatics.

Lucas, R. 2020. "The Surveillance Business." *New Left Review* 121:132–141.

Mano, H. 2021. "Nihon ga torikumubeki dēta ryūtsū no seidoka to hyōjunka: Dēta ryūtsū o torimaku jōhō gijutsu to seido" [Standardization and institutionalization for data circulation Japan needs to address: Systems and technologies for surrounding data circulation]." *ISOS* 26:12–19.

Mauthner, N. S. 2016. "Un/re-Making Method: Knowing/Enacting Posthumanist Performative Social Research Methods Through 'Diffractive Genealogies' and 'Metaphysical Practices." In *Mattering: Feminism, Science, and Materialism*, edited by V. Pitts-Taylor, 258–283. New York: New York University Press.

Mayer, M. 2020. "China's Authoritarian Internet and Digital Orientalism." In *Redesigning Organisations: Concepts for a Connected Society*, edited by D. Feldner, 177–192. Cham: Springer. https://doi.org/10.1007/978-3-030-27957-8_13.

METI (Ministry of Economy, Trade and Industry). 2023. "Regulations, Data and the Agile Governance." Presented at the workshop Discursive and Material Dimensions of the Digital Transformation: Perspectives from and on Japan. Tōkyō: German Institute for Japanese Studies.

Morita, H. 2020. *Jōhō ginkō Bijinesu sannyū Gaido: Rikatsuyō Bijinesu Kara jigyō sannyū Made* [*Guide for Entering Information Bank Business: From Business Applications to Market Entry*]. Tōkyō: Shōeisha.

Münkler, H. 2017. "«Raum» im 21. Jahrhundert. Über geopolitische Umbrüche und Verwerfungen." In *Kriegssplitter: Die Evolution der Gewalt im 20. und 21. Jahrhundert*, 301–330. Reinbek: Rowohlt Taschenbuch Verlag.

Nagy, S. R. 2022. "Middle-Power Alignment in the Free and Open Indo-Pacific: Securing Agency Through Neo-Middle-Power Diplomacy." *Asia Policy* 29 (3): 161–179. https://doi.org/10.1353/asp.2022.0039.

Nakaji, S., K. Ihara, K. Sawada, S. Parodi, T. Umeda, I. Takahashi, K. Murashita, S. Kurauchi, and I. Tokuda. 2021. "Social Innovation for Life Expectancy Extension Utilizing a Platform-Centered System Used in the Iwaki Health Promotion Project: A Protocol Paper." *SAGE Open Medicine* 9:20503121211002610. https://doi.org/10.1177/20503121211002606.

National Strategy Office of IT, Cabinet Secretariat. 2021. "National Data Strategy." *Digital Agency.* Accessed August 8, 2022. https://www.digital.go.jp/assets/contents/node/basic_page/field_ref_resources/0f321c23-517f-439e-9076-5804f0a24b59/20210901_en_05.pdf.

Nemoto, R. 2018. "Kiro ni tatsu mainanbā, katsuyō saku ga kagi ni" [MyNumber at the crossroads, application policies hold the key]. *Nihon Keizai Shinbun*, January 26, 2018. (evening edition): 2.

Nihon IT Dantai Renmei. 2023. "Nihon IT Dantai Renmei, 'Jōhō ginkō' Nintei (Dai 7 Dan Nintei) O kettei" [Information Technology Federation of Japan Decides on the 7th Round of "Information bank" Designations]. *Nihon IT Dantai Renmei.* Accessed November 6, 2023. https://itrenmei.jp/topics/2023/3736/.

Nihon Keizai Shinbunsha (Nikkei). 2019. "'Jōhō ginkō' dēta shiyō tōitsu, Baibai Rieki Nado Taika Barai katsuyō, Seifu, Nendo-Nai Ni Gutaian, Enkotsu Na ryūtsū atooshi" [Integrating the Data Usage of 'Information banks', Gains from Transactions Through Compensation Payments, Concrete Plan by the Government within the Current Fiscal Year, Pushing for a Smooth Circulation]. *Nihon Keizai Shinbun*, May 28, 2019. (morning edition): 5.

NIRA Sōgō Kenkyū Kaihatsu Kikan. 2020. *Michi No kansenshō Ni Idomu Jichitai Toppu No Kakugo [Readiness of Heads of Local Government Bodies to Challenge the Unknown Infectious Disease].* Tokyo: NIRA Sōgō Kenkyū Kaihatsu Kikan.

Okina, Y. 2022. "Digitalization of Payment Instruments: Cashless Payments and Loyalty Points Systems." In *The Future of Financial Systems in the Digital Age*, edited by M. Heckel and F. Waldenberger, 117–131. Singapore: Springer. https://doi.org/10.1007/978-981-16-7830-1_7.

Oshitani, H. 2020a. "COVID-19 E No Taisaku No gainen" [Outline of Measures Against COVID-19]. *Japanese Society for Public Health.* Accessed March 24, 2022. https://www.jsph.jp/covid/files/gainen.pdf.

Oshitani, H. 2020b. "Kansenshō Taisaku "Mori O miru" shikō O – Nani Ga Nihon to Ōbei O Waketa No Ka" [Infectious Disease Response: To See the Forest, Not Just the Trees — What Differentiated Japan from the Western Countries?] *Gaikō (Diplomacy)* 61:6–11.

Oshitani, H. 2022. "COVID Lessons from Japan: The Right Messaging Empowers Citizens." *Nature* 605 (7911): 589. https://doi.org/10.1038/d41586-022-01385-9.

Pascha, W. 2022. "Vorbereitung auf eine neue Weltordnung: Das Vermächtnis Shinzō Abes in der Außenwirtschaft." In *Japan 2022: Politik, Wirtschaft und Gesellschaft*, edited by D. Chiavacci and I. Wieczorek, 54–63. München: Iudicium.

Pentland, A. 2014. *Social Physics: How Good Ideas Spread — the Lessons from a New Science.* Melbourne: Scribe Publications.

Sakashita, T. 2022. "Shinrai Ni Motozuku dēta ryūtsū No Kiban Ni Kansuru kōsatsu - jōhō ginkō Nado No Torikumi O Daizai Ni Shite" [Thoughts About a Platform for Data Circulation Based on Trust – Taking Information Bank Initiatives as Example]. In *Dejitaru-Ka Shakai Ni Okeru Atarashii Zaisanteki Kachi to Shintaku [Trust and New Asset Values in a Society Undergoing Digital transformation]*, edited by I. Gotō, 236–260. Tokyo: Shōji Hōmu.

Sasaki, T., Y. Haruyama, and D. Shida. 2020. *MyData ekonomī: Pāsonaraizu to jōhō ginkō [MyData Economy: Information Banks and Personalization].* Tokyo: Nikkei BP.

Schirrmacher, F., ed. 2015. *Technologischer Totalitarismus: Eine Debatte.* Berlin: Suhrkamp.

Schwab, K. 2016. *The Fourth Industrial Revolution.* Geneva: World Economic Forum.

Seemann, M. 2021. *Die Macht der Plattformen: Politik in Zeiten der Internetgiganten.* Berlin: Ch. Links Verlag.

Shibasaki, R., and H. Sunahara. 2016. "Risk or Asset? How to Change people's Recognition of Personal Information; Social-Design Approach Using a Metaphor of 'Bank.'" Presented at the Conference MyData 2016, Helsinki. Accessed August 31, 2022. http://mydata2016.org/wordpress/wp-content/uploads/gravity_forms/11-2433af647b81b22175aebfabe50c0572/2016/09/Ryosuke_Shibasaki_Risk-or-Asset.pdf.

Shushō Kantei. 2019. "Reiwa gannen jūgatsu yokka: Dainihyakukai kokkai ni okeru Abe naikaku sōri daijin shoshin hyōmei enzetsu" [4 October 2019: General policy speech by Prime Minister Abe at the 200th parliamentary session]. *Prime Minister's Office of Japan*. Accessed August 14, 2022. https://www.kantei.go.jp/jp/98_abe/statement/2019/1004shoshinhyomei.html.

Steinberg, M. 2019. *The Platform Economy: How Japan Transformed the Consumer Internet*. Minneapolis: University of Minnesota Press.

Süddeutsche Zeitung. 2015. "Was Wirtschaftsbosse zur Flüchtlingskrise sagen." *Süddeutsche.de*. September 16, 2015. Accessed December 27, 2021. https://www.sueddeutsche.de/wirtschaft/unternehmen-was-wirtschaftsbosse-zur-fluechtlingskrise-sagen-1.2649991.

Thumfart, J. 2022. "The Norm Development of Digital Sovereignty Between China, Russia, the EU and the US: From the Late 1990s to the COVID Crisis 2020/21 as Catalytic Event." In *Data Protection and Privacy: Enforcing Rights in a Changing World*, edited by D. Hallinan, R. Leenes, and P. de Hert, 1–44. Oxford: Hart Publishing.

York, J. C. 2021. *Silicon Values: The Future of Free Speech Under Surveillance Capitalism*. London: Verso.

Zanotti, L. 2021. "De-colonizing the Political Ontology of Kantian Ethics: A Quantum Perspective." *Journal of International Political Theory* 17 (3): 448–467. https://doi.org/10.1177/1755088220946777.

Zuboff, S. 1985. "Automate/Informate: The Two Faces of Intelligent Technology." *Organizational Dynamics* 14 (2): 5–18. https://doi.org/10.1016/0090-2616(85)90033-6.

Zuboff, S. 1988. *In the Age of the Smart Machine. The Future of Work and Power*. New York: Basic Books.

Zuboff, S. 2015. "Big Other: Surveillance Capitalism and the Prospects of an Information Civilization." *Journal of Information Technology* 30 (1): 75–89. https://doi.org/10.1057/jit.2015.5.

Zuboff, S. 2019. *The Age of Surveillance Capitalism: The Fight for a Human Future at the New Frontier of Power*. New York: Public Affairs.

Index

Note: Figures are indicated by *italics*; Tables are indicated by **bold**; Endnotes are indicated by the page number followed by 'n' and the endnote number e.g., 20n1 refers to endnote 1 on page 20.

agile governance 9
Akai, N. 6, 94
Amable, B. 48
annual income walls 161
Arimoto, T. 5

BigTech 2
biotech 51
Boyer, R. 60
Brussels effect 176
Buchanan, J. 3, 13, 34

care-led innovation model 59, 62
ChatGPT 135
Cheryan, S. 130
community firms 25
comply or explain approach 3, 21
corporate governance: agency theory 13; community firms 25; comply-or-explain approach 21; FSA 15, 16, 27; hard law 24; investors 13; METIs 20; political support, reform initiative 14–15; principles-based approach 13; radical innovation 22; reform success 18–19; shareholder activist 27; shareholder protection norms 26; shareholders rights 23; soft law 24; subsequent developments 17–18; TSE 15, 16
Council for science, technology and innovation (CSTI) 125
COVID-19 pandemic 9, 176, 184, 186

data free flow with trust (DFFT) 176, 182
data–basedinformation and communication technologies (ICT) 51
Deakin, S. 3, 13, 34
digital capitalism: bipolar digital order 175; consensus-driven regulatory regime 186; COVID-19 pandemic 184–6; DFTT 182–4, 186; digital capitalism 176; information banks 179–82; neo-middle-power diplomacy 186;

regulatory models 178–9; surveillance capitalism 177–8
digital transformation (DX) 94

Eiichi, S. 54
environmental policy 82; carbon neutrality 83–4; environment, economy and society *83*; environment/economy/society 90–1; GX policies, Kishida administration 87–8; Kishida administration, policy progress 84–6; local circular and ecological sphere 89–90; maintain/restore/enrich natural capital 91–2; MoE 82; transitions, society 88–9, *89*
environment, social, governance (ESG) 83
essential workers 165
evidence-based policy making (EBPM) 6

family/gender equality policies: annual income distribution/domestic work hours 111–13, *112*; equal pay for equal work' principle 120; gender-role division, labour 119–20; labour practices, employment 113–15; membership employment 120; policies for childrens 109; proposed changes, family policy 110–11; social insurance regulation 115–18; TFR 108; type of expenditure, benefits *110*; unlimited contract employment 120; wage gap policies 109; weekly work/domestic work hour **113**; younger generation 118–19
Fangmiao Zou 156
foreign direct investment (FDI) 3

green growth strategy (GGS) 40
green transformation (GX), sustainability: climate change 80–1; economic and social challenges 88; economy 79; transitions, redesign society *89*

Hamaguchi, K. 39, 113
Hamanaka, J. 145
Hara, J. 35

INDEX

I mode feature phone capitalism 177
Ikkatai, Y. 123
increase-the-pie-first strategy 42
Inoue, A. 123
international corporate governance network (ICGN) 20
interviews 174
investments, people: corporate sector investment 141–2, 147–9, 153; household investment 139–40, 143–5; human capital investment 145–7; human investment policies 154; kishida policies, education 151–2; public expenditure 142–3, 149–51; public sector 149; scepticism 139; territory education **141**
Ito, K. 50

Japan corporate governance forum (JCGF) 17
Japan economic revival headquarters (JERH) 14
Japanese capitalism: digital/green transformations 2; domestic information banks 9; EBPM 6; economic model 1, 2; economic model 10; environmental policy 5; GX 6; innovation system 5, 10; job-based employment 8; lost decades 4; new trinity 8; new/sustainable capitalism 3; non-regular employment 7; post-war model 1; STEM 7
Japan's political economy: business federation 31; distribution policies 32; employee-favouring firm 35–7; finance and corporate governance 34–5; finance/innovation 32–4; GDP 41; people-centred 32; post-war model 32; shareholders/executives 42; society5.0 37; state-business relations 40–1
job-type employment 153

Kano, K. 123
Kim, Y. G. 33
Kishida shock 1
Kümmerle, H. 8, 175

labour market policies *see* new trinity reforms
Laugier, S. 60
Lazonick, W. 35
Lechevalier, S. 4, 47, 49, 50
liberal democratic party (LDP) 14, 82, 109

McKay, E. 123
membership-based employment 159
Minamizaki, A. 123
Ministry of economy, trade, and industry (METI) 15, 74
Ministry of the environment (MoE) 82
mission-oriented industrial and innovation policy 43
mission-oriented innovation policy (MOIP) 5, 65, 71, 72
Miyajima, H. 35
Monfort, B. 49

Mosk, C. 145
Murakami fund 25

Nagase, N.6, 108, 113, 118
Nakai, T. 79
Nakata, Y. 1, 7, 42n12, 139, 145, 148
nationally determined contributions (NDCs) 82
neo-middle-power diplomacy 9
new capitalism policies 160
new form of capitalism realization council (NCRC) meeting 173
new trinity reforms: challenges 164–7; employment agencies 169; flexibilization 169; inter-company mobility 158, 159, 167; job-based employment 159; labour markets 157; new skill demands 162–3; quantitatively expanding labour markets 160–2; reskilling/upskilling 158; standard employees 156; standard/non-standard employment 163–4, 167; work style reforms 156
Nippon individual savings account (NISA) 34
non-profit organizations (NPOs) 74

Ochiai, E. 116
Ogawa, R. 35
on-job training (OJT) 142

Palombarini, S. 48
Paperman, P. 60
program for international student assessment (PISA) 125
public-private ITS (intelligent transportation system) roadmap 72

Quinn, D. M. 125

regular employees 114
régulation theory 47; growth regimes 48; innovation crisis, Japan 51–3; Japanese capitalism 49–51

Sato, H. 114, 120
science and technology agency (STA) 5
science, technology and innovation (STI) policy:basic law system **69**; economic value/competitiveness 65; Horizon Europe 70; innovation policy **68**; modern science and technology 66–7; MOIP 65, 74; S&T legal framework 67–70; SIP programme 71–4, *73*; STI 66, 74–6
science, technology, engineering and mathematics (STEM) 6
STEM gender inequality: academic field key words/gender image 127–8; accelerated gender affirmative action 132–5; brilliance 126–7; equality 131; gender in Japan 131–2; general science, women 128; government policy 123; higher education 129–30; low proportion of women 125–6; nursing girls 127; physics over biology, male

students 130; research environment/climate change 124–5; social climate 130–1
shareholder-favouring firm 37
Silicon Valley model 48, 52
society 5.02, 42n 10; CSTI 37; institutional and public policy 48; intellectual and political dynamism 47; Japanese-style employment 39–40; post-industrial economies 48; reforming capitalism 38–9; régulation theory 48; sustainable capitalism 48; technology/society 53; capitalism 54–5; complementarities 55–6, 62; sources of dissonance 56–8; care-led innovation model 59–60; anthropogenic mode of development 60–2
Spencer, S. J. 125
Steele, C. M. 125
Strategic innovation programme (SIP) 5, 65, 70
surveillance capitalism 176

task force on climate-related financial disclosures (TCFD) 83
total fertility rate (TFR) 108
trinity reforms 150

United nations sustainable development goals (SDGs) 70

Waldenberger, F. 8, 175
wedding cake model 83
what works network (WWN) 101
Whittaker, D. H. 1, 3, 4, 31, 47, 54, 56
Womenomics policy 111

Yano, M. 145
Yokoyama, H. M. 7, 123

Zou, F. 8